Edinburgh Critical Guides to Literature
Series Editors: Martin Halliwell, University of Leicester and
Andy Mousley, De Montfort University

Published Titles:
Gothic Literature, Andrew Smith
Canadian Literature, Faye Hammill
Women's Poetry, Jo Gill
Contemporary American Drama, Annette J. Saddik
Shakespeare, Gabriel Egan
Asian American Literature, Bella Adams
Children's Literature, M. O. Grenby

Forthcoming Titles in the Series:
Eighteenth-Century Literature, Hamish Mathison
Contemporary British Fiction, Nick Bentley
Contemporary American Fiction, David Brauner
Victorian Literature, David Amigoni
Crime Fiction, Stacy Gillis
Renaissance Literature, Siobhan Keenan
Modern American Literature, Catherine Morley
Scottish Literature, Gerard Carruthers
Romantic Literature, Richard Marggraf Turley
Modernist Literature, Rachel Potter
Medieval Literature, Pamela King
Women's Fiction, Sarah Sceats
African American Literature, Jennifer Terry

Children's Literature

M. O. Grenby

Edinburgh University Press

© Matthew Grenby, 2008

Edinburgh University Press Ltd
22 George Square, Edinburgh

Typeset in Ehrhardt
by Servis Filmsetting Ltd, Manchester, and
printed and bound in Great Britain by
Antony Rowe Ltd, Chippenham, Wilts

A CIP record for this book is available from the British Library

ISBN   978 0 7486 2273 3 (hardback)
ISBN   978 0 7486 2274 0 (paperback)

The right of Matthew Grenby
to be identified as author of this work
has been asserted in accordance with
the Copyright, Designs and Patents Act 1988.

Contents

Series Preface

The study of English literature in the early twenty-first century is host to an exhilarating range of critical approaches, theories and historical perspectives. 'English' ranges from traditional modes of study such as Shakespeare and Romanticism to popular interest in national and area literatures such as the United States, Ireland and the Caribbean. The subject also spans a diverse array of genres from tragedy to cyberpunk, incorporates such hybrid fields of study as Asian American literature, Black British literature, creative writing and literary adaptations, and remains eclectic in its methodology.

Such diversity is cause for both celebration and consternation. English is varied enough to promise enrichment and enjoyment for all kinds of readers and to challenge preconceptions about what the study of literature might involve. But how are readers to navigate their way through such literary and cultural diversity? And how are students to make sense of the various literary categories and periodisations, such as modernism and the Renaissance, or the proliferating theories of literature, from feminism and Marxism to queer theory and eco-criticism? The Edinburgh Critical Guides to Literature series reflects the challenges and pluralities of English today, but at the same time it offers readers clear and accessible routes through the texts, contexts, genres, historical periods and debates within the subject.

Martin Halliwell and Andy Mousley

Acknowledgements

An introduction to children's literature might be written in many different ways. The particular approach I have adopted here derives from my experiences teaching in the School of English at Newcastle University. I am very grateful therefore to all the students who have taken my 'Beyond Wonderland' undergraduate module since it first began. Their responses to the course, and their comments about how difficult it can be for those new to the subject to find their bearings, have shaped my thinking about what a new introduction might try to do. But I am equally grateful to the community of postgraduate students in the Children's Literature Unit at Newcastle. Their suggestions and criticisms, given as a group and individually, in person and by correspondence, have helped this book very much, and I have greatly enjoyed the challenge of responding to their forthright assessments. More than this, their own master's and doctoral projects have prompted me to think in different ways about children's literature. Above all, the enthusiasm and commitment of all the students in the Children's Literature Unit has been an inspiration.

My colleague Professor Kim Reynolds has read some sections of this book and, as ever, her advice has been constructive, astute and erudite. Dr Jenny Litster has taken the time to talk with me about my plans, and has generously shared her bright ideas and detailed knowledge. The anonymous reviewers of the proposal made many useful comments. All of the errors that remain are entirely my own.

I must also thank Dr Andy Mousley for suggesting that I should write this book, and, with Dr Martin Halliwell, for commissioning me to do so. Jackie Jones and James Dale, at Edinburgh University Press, have been sympathetic editors. I am very grateful for the patience and forbearance of them all.

Finally, and above all, thank-you to Mary.

Chronology

The timeline lists only those children's books mentioned in this *Edinburgh Critical Guide*. The chapters in which the texts are discussed are given in brackets. Where the year of first publication is uncertain, an approximate date has been given.

1617   Evaldus Gallus, *Pueriles Confabulatiunculae: or Children's Dialogues* (School)

1672   James Janeway, *A Token for Children* (Introduction; Moral Tales; Family)

1673   Benjamin Keach, *War with the Devil* (Introduction)

1686   John Bunyan, *Divine Emblems*, also known as *A Book for Boys and Girls* or *Country Rhimes for Children* (Introduction; Poetry)

1692   Roger L'Estrange, *Fables of Æsop* (Fables)

1693   Cotton Mather, *The Wonders of the Invisible World* (Fantasy)

1700   Anon., *The Friar and the Boy*, a new version (Poetry)

1708   Joseph Jackson, *A New Translation of Æsop's Fables* (Fables)

1712	Thomas Gills, *Useful and Delightful Instructions* (Poetry)
1715	Isaac Watts, *Divine Songs Attempted in Easy Language for the Use of Children* (Poetry)
1719	Daniel Defoe, *Robinson Crusoe* (Adventure)
1722	James Greenwood, *The Virgin Muse* (Poetry); Samuel Croxall, *Fables of Aesop and Others* (Fables)
1726	Jonathan Swift, *Gulliver's Travels* (Adventure)
1727	John Wright, *Spiritual Songs for Children* (Poetry)
1734	Mary Barber, *Poems on Several Occasions* (Poetry)
1740–50	Jane Johnson, home-made verses and stories (Poetry)
1743	John Vowler, 'The Young Student's Scheme' (Poetry)
1744	Mary Cooper, *Tommy Thumb's Pretty Song Book* (Poetry)
1749	Sarah Fielding, *The Governess; or, Little Female Academy* (School)
1751	John Marchant, *Puerilia: Amusements for the Young* (Fables; Poetry)
1758–63	Christopher Smart, *Jubilate Agno* (Poetry)
1760	Anon., *The Top Book of All, for Little Masters and Misses* (Poetry)
1765	Anon., *The History of Goody Two-Shoes* (School; Adventure); Anon., *Mother Goose's Melody, or Sonnets from the Cradle* (Poetry)
1770	Anon., *The Prettiest Book for Children* (Fantasy); Christopher smart, *Hymns for the Amusement of Children* (poetry)
1774	Anon., *The Lilliputian Magazine; or, Children's Repository* (Moral Tales)

1812	Barbara Hofland, *The Son of a Genius* (Moral Tales)
1813	Barbara Hofland, *The Panorama of Europe* (Family)
1814	Johann David Wyss, *The Swiss Family Robinson* (Family; Adventure)
1818	Mary Belson Elliott, *The Adventures of Thomas Two-Shoes* (Adventure) Mary Martha Sherwood, *The Little Woodman, and his Dog Cæsar* (Moral Tales); William Francis Sullivan, *Pleasant Stories* (Adventure)
1818–42	Mary Martha Sherwood, *The Fairchild Family* (Moral Tales)
1821	Isaac Taylor, *Scenes in Africa* (Adventure)
1822	Barbara Hofland, *Adelaide; or, the Intrepid Daughter* (Adventure)
1823	Barbara Hofland, *The Daughter of a Genius* (Moral Tales)
1823–41	James Fenimore Cooper, *Leather-Stocking Tales* (Adventure)
1825	Charlotte Finch, *The Gamut and Time-Table in Verse* (Poetry)
1830	Barbara Hofland, *The Stolen Boy* (Adventure)
1833	H. G. Keene, *Persian Fables* (Fables)
1839	Catherine Sinclair, *Holiday House* (Moral Tales; Fantasy)
1841	Harriet Martineau, *The Crofton Boys* (School)
1841–42	Frederick Marryat, *Masterman Ready* (Adventure)
1842	Robert Browning, 'The Pied Piper of Hamelin' (Poetry)
1846	Edward Lear, *A Book of Nonsense* (Poetry)

1847   Frederick Marryat, *Children of the New Forest*
        (Family; Adventure)

1848   Cecil Frances Alexander, *Hymns for Little Children*
        (Poetry); Heinrich Hoffmann, *Shock-Headed Peter*
        (Introduction; Poetry)

1850   Elizabeth Wetherell, *The Wide, Wide World*
        (Family)

1853   Lewis Carroll, 'Solitude' (Poetry)

1854   Henry Wadsworth Longfellow, *The Song of
        Hiawatha* (Poetry); Louisa Charlesworth, *Ministering
        Angels* (Moral Tales); W. M. Thackeray, *The Rose
        and the Ring* (Fantasy)

1856   Charlotte Yonge, *The Daisy Chain* (Moral Tales;
        Family)

1857   Thomas Hughes, *Tom Brown's Schooldays* (School)

1858   F. W. Farrar, *Eric, or Little by Little, a Tale of Roslyn
        School* (School); R. M. Ballantyne, *The Coral Island*
        (Adventure)

1861   R. M. Ballantyne, *The Gorilla Hunters* (Adventure)

1862   Coventry Patmore, *The Children's Garland* (Poetry)

1863   Charles Kingsley, *The Water-Babies* (Fantasy);
        Henry Wadsworth Longfellow, 'Paul Revere's Ride'
        (Poetry)

1864   Jules Verne, *Journey to the Centre of the Earth*
        (Fantasy; Adventure)

1865   Lewis Carroll, *Alice's Adventures in Wonderland*
        (Introduction; Poetry; Fantasy)

1867   Hesba Stretton, *Jessica's First Prayer* (Moral Tales);
        Horatio Alger, *Ragged Dick; or, Street Life in New
        York* (Moral Tales)

1868   Louisa May Alcott, *Little Women* (Family)

1869   Louisa May Alcott, *Little Women Part Two*, known as *Good Wives* in the UK (Family)

1870   Edward Lear, *Nonsense Songs, Stories, Botany, and Alphabets* (Poetry; Fantasy)

1871   George MacDonald, *At the Back of the North Wind* (Fantasy); Lewis Carroll, *Through the Looking Glass* (Fantasy; Poetry); Louisa May Alcott, *Little Men* (School)

1872   Christina Rossetti, *Sing-Song: A Nursery Rhyme Book* (Poetry); Susan Coolidge, *What Katy Did* (Family)

1873   Charlotte Yonge, *The Pillars of the House* (Family); Jules Verne, *From Earth to the Moon Direct* (Fantasy); Jules Verne, *Twenty Thousand Leagues Under the Sea* (Fantasy; Adventure); Susan Coolidge, *What Katy Did At School* (School)

1875   O. F. Walton, *Christie's Old Organ, or Home Sweet Home* (Moral Tales)

1876   Edward Lear, *Laughable Lyrics* (Poetry); Lewis Carroll, 'The Hunting of the Snark' (Poetry); Mrs Molesworth, *Carrots: Just a Little Boy* (Moral Tales; Family)

1877   Anna Sewell, *Black Beauty* (Fables)

1879   Frances Hodgson Burnett, *Haworth's* (Moral Tales)

1880   Joel Harris Chandler, *Uncle Remus: His Songs and His Sayings* (Fables); G. A. Henty, *The Young Buglers: a Tale of the Peninsular War* (Adventure)

1881–82   Talbot Baines Reed, *The Fifth Form at St. Dominic's* (School)

1882   F. Anstey, *Vice Versa; or, A Lesson to Fathers* (Fantasy); Mark Twain, *The Prince and the Pauper* (Adventure)

1882–83   Elizabeth Whittaker, 'Robina Crusoe, and her Lonely Island Home', in *The Girl's Own Paper* (Adventure)

1883	Robert Louis Stevenson, *Treasure Island* (Adventure)
1884	G.A. Henty, *By Sheer Pluck* (Adventure); Mark Twain, *The Adventures of Huckleberry Finn* (Adventure)
1885	Henry Rider Haggard, *King Solomon's Mines* (Adventure); Robert Louis Stevenson, *A Child's Garden of Verses* (Poetry); Robert Louis Stevenson, *Kidnapped* (Adventure)
1886	Frances Hodgson Burnett, *Little Lord Fauntleroy* (Moral Tales); L. T. Meade, *A World of Girls* (School)
1887	Walter Crane, *The Baby's Own Aesop* (Fables)
1892	G. A. Henty, *Those Other Animals* (Fables); L. T. Meade, *Four on an Island* (Adventure)
1893	G. A. Henty, *Beric the Briton: a Story of the Roman Invasion* (Adventure)
1895	Kenneth Grahame, *The Golden Age* (Family); Mrs Molesworth, *Sheila's Mystery* (Family)
1896	Eugene Field, *Love Songs of Childhood* (Poetry)
1898	Mrs. George Corbett, *Little Miss Robinson Crusoe* (Adventure)
1899	E. Nesbit, *The Treasure Seekers* (Family); Rudyard Kipling, *Stalky & Co.* (School)
1900	L. Frank Baum, *The Wonderful Wizard of Oz* (Fantasy)
1901	Bessie Marchant, *Three Girls on a Ranch: A Tale of New Mexico* (Adventure); E. Nesbit, *The Wouldbegoods* (Moral Tales; Family; Adventure); Rudyard Kipling, *Kim* (Adventure)
1902	John Masefield, 'Sea Fever' (Poetry); Rudyard Kipling, *Just So Stories* (Fables); Walter De la Mare, *Songs of Childhood* (Poetry)

1903   G. A. Henty, *With Kitchener in the Soudan* (Adventure); Kate Douglas Wiggin, *Rebecca of Sunnybrook Farm* (Family)

1904   First performance of J. M. Barrie, *Peter Pan, or The Boy Who Wouldn't Grow Up* (Family)

1905   Frances Hodgson Burnett, *A Little Princess*, originally published as *Sara Crewe* in 1887 (Moral Tales; School)

1906   Angela Brazil, *The Fortunes of Philippa* (School); E. Nesbit, *The Railway Children* (Family)

1907   Hilaire Belloc, *Cautionary Tales for Children* (Introduction; Poetry)

1908   First of Frank Richards, *Greyfriars* stories in *The Magnet* (School); Kenneth Grahame, *The Wind in the Willows* (Fables; Fantasy); L. M. Montgomery, *Anne of Green Gables* (Family); L. T. Mcadc, *The School Favourite* (School)

1909   L. M. Montgomery, *Anne of Avonlea* (School)

1911   J. M. Barrie, *Peter and Wendy* (School; Family; Fantasy)

1913   Alfred Noyes, 'The Highwayman' (Poetry); Eleanor Hodgman Porter, *Pollyanna* (Family); Walter De la Mare, *Peacock Pie* (Poetry)

1915   'Charlie Chaplin's Schooldays' in *Boy's Realm* magazine (School); Bessie Marchant, *Molly Angel's Adventures* (Adventure)

1916   Alec Waugh, *The Loom of Youth* (School)

1916–17   Eleanor Farjeon, *Nursery Rhymes of London Town* (Poetry)

1918   Angela Brazil, *For the School Colours* (School)

1920   Dorita Fairlie Bruce, *Dimsie Goes to School* (School)

1924	A. A. Milne, *When We Were Very Young* (Poetry)
1927	A. A. Milne, *Now We Are Six* (Poetry)
1929	Erich Kästner, *Emil and the Detectives* (Adventure)
1930	Arthur Ransome, *Swallows and Amazons* (Adventure); Hergé, *Tintin au pays des Soviets* (Adventure)
1931	J. B. Morton, 'Now We Are Sick' (Poetry)
1932	Laura Ingalls Wilder, *Little House in the Big Woods* (Family)
1933	Elinor Brent-Dyer, *Exploits of the Chalet Girls* (School)
1934	Elinor Brent-Dyer, *The Chalet School and the Lintons* (School); Geoffrey Trease, *Bows Against the Barons* (Adventure); P. L. Travers, *Mary Poppins* (Fantasy)
1935	John Masefield, *The Box of Delights* (Fantasy); Laura Ingalls Wilder, *The Little House on the Prairie* (Family; Adventure)
1937	Eve Garnett, *The Family From One-End Street* (Family); J. R. R. Tolkien, *The Hobbit* (Fantasy; Adventure); Release of Walt Disney's first animated feature film, *Snow White and the Seven Dwarfs* (Fantasy)
1939	DuBose Hayward, *The Country Bunny and the Little Gold Shoes* (Fables)
1940	James Thurber, *Fables for Our Time* (Fables)
1941	Enid Blyton, *The Twins at St. Clare's* (School); W. E. Johns, *Worrals of the W.A.A.F.* (Adventure)
1942	Enid Blyton, *Five on a Treasure Island* (Adventure); Laura Ingalls Wilder, *The Long Winter* (Family)
1945	E. B. White, *Stuart Little* (Fantasy); George Orwell, *Animal Farm* (Fables)

1946	Enid Blyton, *First Term at Malory Towers* (School)
1947	Laurence Maynell, *The Old Gang* (School)
1949	C. Day Lewis, *The Otterbury Incident* (Adventure); Geoffrey Trease, *No Boats on Bannermere* (School)
1950	Anne Barrett, *Caterpillar Hall* (Fantasy); Anthony Buckeridge, *Jennings Goes to School* (School); C. S. Lewis, *The Lion, the Witch and the Wardrobe* (Family; Fantasy; Adventure)
1951	J. D. Salinger, *The Catcher in the Rye* (Moral Tales)
1952	Mabel Esther Allan, *The School on Cloud-Ridge* (School); E. B. White, *Charlotte's Web* (Fables)
1954	Lucy Boston, *The Children of Green Knowe* (Fantasy)
1954–55	J. R. R. Tolkien, *The Lord of the Rings* (Fantasy)
1955	C. S. Lewis, *The Magician's Nephew* (Fantasy); Rosemary Sutcliff, *Outcast* (Adventure); William Mayne, *A Swarm in May* (School)
1956	Ian Serraillier, *The Silver Sword* (Adventure)
1957	Eleanor Farjeon, *The Children's Bells* (Poetry)
1958	Catherine Storr, *Marianne Dreams* (Fantasy); E. W. Hildick, *Jim Starling* (School); Philippa Pearce, *Tom's Midnight Garden* (Fantasy)
1959	Cynthia Harnett, *The Load of Unicorn* (Adventure)
1960	John Knowles, *A Separate Peace* (School)
1961	John Rowe Townsend, *Gumble's Yard* (Family)
1963	Ann Holm, *I Am David* (Adventure); Maurice Sendak, *Where the Wild Things Are* (Fantasy); Ted Hughes, *How the Whale Became* (Fables)
1964	Leon Garfield, *Jack Holborn* (Adventure); Louise Fitzhugh, *Harriet the Spy* (School); Nina Bawden,

On the Run (Adventure); Roald Dahl, *Charlie and the Chocolate Factory* (Poetry)

1965   Alan Garner, *Elidor* (Fantasy); Susan Cooper, *Over Sea, Under Stone* (Adventure)

1966   William Mayne, *Earthfasts* (Fantasy)

1967   Henry Treece, *The Dream-Time* (Adventure); Ursula Le Guin, *The Wizard of Earthsea* (Fantasy)

1969   Penelope Farmer, *Charlotte Sometimes* (Fantasy); Russell Hoban, *The Mouse and His Child* (Fantasy)

1970   Betsy Byars, *The Summer of the Swans* (Moral Tales); Charles Causley, *Figgie Hobbin* (Poetry); E. B. White, *The Trumpet of the Swan* (Fantasy); Judy Blume, *Are You There God? It's Me, Margaret* (Moral Tales); Roald Dahl, *Fantastic Mr Fox* (Fables)

1971   Robert O'Brien, *Mrs Frisby and the Rats of* NIMH (Fables)

1972   Helen Cresswell, *Lizzie Dripping* (Fantasy); Mary Rogers, *Freaky Friday* (Fantasy); Richard Adams, *Watership Down* (Fantasy); Richard Peck, *Don't Look and It Won't Hurt* (Moral Tales)

1973   Penelope Lively, *The Ghost of Thomas Kempe* (Fantasy); Susan Cooper, *The Dark is Rising* (Adventure)

1974   Bernard Ashley, *The Trouble with Donovan Croft* (Moral Tales); Jill Murphy, *The Worst Witch* (Fantasy); Louise Fitzhugh, *Nobody's Family is Going to Change* (Family); Michael Rosen, *Mind Your Own Business* (Poetry); Robert Cormier, *The Chocolate War* (School)

1975   Judy Bloom, *Forever* (Moral Tales); Roald Dahl, *Danny the Champion of the World* (School); Robert O'Brien, *Z for Zachariah* (Fantasy)

1976   Richard Peck, *Are You in the House Alone?* (Moral
            Tales); Roger McGough, 'First Day at School'
            (Poetry)

1976–78   Alan Garner, *The Stone Book Quartet* (Family)

1977   Betsy Byars, *The Pinballs* (Family); Gene Kemp,
            Cricklepit Combined School (School); Gene Kemp,
            The Turbulent Term of Tyke Tiler (School)

1978   Aidan Chambers, *Breaktime* (School); Anne
            Digby, *First Term at Trebizon* (School); First episode
            of Phil Redmond's television series, *Grange Hill*
            (School); Jan Needle, *My Mate Shofiq* (Moral tales);
            Louis Sachar, *Sideways Stories from Wayside School*
            (School)

1979   Deborah Hautzig, *Hey, Dollface* (School); Katherine
            Paterson, *The Great Gilly Hopkins* (Moral Tales;
            Family); Ogden Nash, *Custard and Company*
            (Introduction); Robert Cormier, *After the First Death*
            (Adventure)

1980   Anne Digby, *Boy Trouble at Trebizon* (School);
            Arnold Lebel, *Fables* (Fables); Gene Kemp, *Dog
            Days and Cat Naps* (School); Robert Leeson, *Grange
            Hill Rules OK?* (School)

1981   Cynthia Voigt, *Homecoming* (Family); Peter
            Dickinson, *The Seventh Raven* (Adventure); Shel
            Silverstein, *A Light in the Attic* (Poetry)

1982   Gillian Cross, *The Demon Headmaster* (School);
            Roald Dahl, *Revolting Rhymes* (Introduction; Poetry)

1983   Aidan Chambers, *The Present Takers* (School);
            Susanne Bösche, *Jenny lives with Eric and Martin*
            (Family)

1984   Francine Pascal, *Sweet Valley High* (School); Ted
            Hughes, *What is the Truth? A Farmyard Fable for the
            Young* (Fables; Poetry)

1985	Beverley Naidoo, *Journey to Jo'burg* (Adventure); David Macaulay, *Baaa* (Fables)
1986	Diana Wynne Jones, *Howl's Moving Castle* (Fantasy); Jack Prelutsky, *The New Kid on the Block* (Poetry)
1987	Anne Fine, *Madame Doubtfire*, known as *Alias Madame Doubtfire* in the USA (Family); Jenny Pausacker, *What Are Ya?* (School); John Mole, *Boo to a Goose* (Poetry); Louis Sachar, *There's a Boy in the Girls' Bathroom* (School)
1988	Janet and Allan Ahlberg, *Starting School* (School)
1989	Allan Ahlberg and Fritz Wegner, *Heard it in the Playground* (Poetry); Anne Fine, *Goggle-Eyes* (Family); Bruce Coville, *My Teacher is an Alien* (School); Jean Ure, *Plague 99* (Fantasy); Leslea Newman, *Heather Has Two Mommies* (Family); Morris Gleitzman, *Two Weeks With the Queen* (Family)
1990	Jamie Rix, *Grizzly Tales: Cautionary Tales for Lovers of Squeam!* (Introduction); Ursula Le Guin, *Tehanu* (Fantasy)
1990–92	Adèle Geras, *Egerton Hall Trilogy* (School)
1991	Berlie Doherty, *Dear Nobody* (Moral tales); Jacqueline Wilson, *The Story of Tracy Beaker* (Family)
1992	Jackie Kay, *Two's Company* (Poetry); Mick Gowar, 'Rat Trap' (Poetry)
1993	Robert Westall, *Falling into Glory* (School); Alida E. Young, *Losing David* (Introduction)
1994	Benjamin Zephaniah, 'According to My Mood' (Poetry)
1995	Gary Kilworth, *The Brontë Girls* (Family); William Mayne, *Cradlefasts* (Fantasy)
1995–2000	Philip Pullman, *His Dark Materials* (Introduction; Family; Fantasy; Adventure)

Introduction

The aim of this *Critical Guide* is to deepen understanding of individual children's books, and of children's literature as a whole, by examining the history of the form and, especially, the generic traditions that have emerged over the course of the last three hundred years. The idea is not that a great deal of detailed information about particular books or authors will be found here. Specific texts will certainly be discussed, often in some depth. But this short survey is primarily intended as an introduction to the subject, providing a sound foundation for further study. This is a book that explores how particular texts and authors fit into the wider pattern.

Each of the main chapters examines one of the major genres of children's literature. These genres have existed since children's literature was first established as a separate part of print culture in the seventeenth and eighteenth centuries, and sometimes even before that. What a short study like this cannot do is to provide a complete account of children's literature. After all, it is a vast subject: texts have been read by children from the very earliest periods of recorded history to today, across all continents and there are important genres besides those covered here. To attempt to consider all this would be preposterous – as preposterous as trying to cover all of 'adult literature' in a few dozen pages. Some limits, then, have been necessary. First, in general it is only the children's books of Britain and North America that will be considered here. Occasionally, some authors from outside these geographical limits have been discussed – Jules

Verne from France and Erich Kästner from Germany, and Beverley Naidoo from South Africa, not to mention Aesop – but these are usually authors who have become implanted in the Anglo-American tradition. Comparing Anglo-American texts with work from the wider world – from European or Asian literature, from colonial and post-colonial traditions – is fascinating, and criticism is beginning to explore these connections, but it would not have been possible in such a short book as this.

The second limit is generic. Children have consumed, and still consume, a huge variety of material – from fiction to textbooks, from Shakespeare to the scriptures, from verse to adverts, from picturebooks to computer games. Taken in its widest sense, the term 'children's literature' covers all these forms, and many others. Some are so expansive, and have generated so much critical discussion, that they demand a whole book to themselves – fairy stories and folk tales, for example – and so they do not feature here. Others are only partially represented by this book's seven chapters: for instance war stories and historical novels are subsumed into the chapter on adventure stories. Still others do not feature at all: comics, plays and films for example. Important as the range of material is, and absorbing as it may be to trace the adaptation of texts from one medium to another, this study will concentrate only on those texts which appear in book form, those which have been intended primarily for children, those which have been intended to entertain children at least as much as to instruct them, and those which have a high textual, as opposed to graphic, content. Thus comics, films and games are excluded under the first clause; some adults books which have been widely read by children are excluded under the second; school-books and ABCs are omitted under the third; and picturebooks and pop-up books are left out under the fourth. There are a few exceptions to these general rules. Some picturebooks and television programmes are discussed, but only when they fall squarely within one of the main genres under discussion, and have made an important contribution to their development.

The third limit is chronological. Texts have been produced for children since Roman times, and very probably before. Children in medieval and Renaissance Britain were certainly provided with a wide range of reading material, books produced primarily for older readers that they were permitted or encouraged to read, as well as texts designed especially for them.[1] But should we consider this children's literature? The critic Peter Hunt certainly thought not, arguing vociferously that children's literature is properly comprised only of texts that were 'written expressly for children who are recognizably children, with a childhood recognizable today'. Books of 'no interest to the *current* librarian or child', he insisted, even if they were actually written for children once, are not rightly part of our subject, and ought to be the preserve of historians and bibliographers.[2] There is an undeniable logic to this argument, although a number of critics responded to Hunt with indignation and incredulity.[3]

More questionable is Hunt's attack on what he thinks an erroneous assumption, that there is a 'flow, a stream of history, that connects all books written for children, and that we in the present can learn from the past about books for children'.[4] Hunt may well have been correct that because notions of childhood have altered over time, so the purposes and practice of children's literature will have changed, meaning that children's books do not now do the same things that they once did and that we should not, therefore, try to place them in a continuum. But generic continuities certainly do exist in the minds of authors and illustrators, and publishers anxious to contract only books that will sell. A school story published today will be written for a wholly different kind of child than a school story written in the sixteenth century, but the producers of the twenty-first century text will nevertheless be inheriting traditions, expectations and perhaps limits from a long succession of previous practitioners. J. K. Rowling's *Harry Potter* novels, for example, are evidently part of the long history of evolution of the school story, with literary genes having been passed on by, amongst many other ancestors, the television programme *Grange Hill*, the school stories of Enid Blyton, Frank Richards, Angela Brazil, L. T. Meade, Thomas Hughes, Maria Edgeworth and Sarah Fielding, whose *The Governess* (1749) is often cited as the first school story. But even Fielding did not magic her formula out of nothing, for she too drew on a tradition of children's books set in schools that dated back to the Renaissance or even before. What is true of school stories is true of the other genres in this book too, although sometimes in less obvious ways. The continuities between Judy Blume writing in

America in the 1970s, and Maria Edgeworth, say, writing in Britain almost two centuries before, may not be immediately apparent, but both were writing moral tales of a sort, and the generic continuities outweigh the differences of style and subject. In each intervening generation the formula has been modified in many new ways, so much so that today's children might find little to interest them in the moral tales or school stories of the eighteenth, or even the nineteenth, century. But this does not undermine the unavoidable importance of past children's books in the formation of today's children's literature, nor, therefore, the relevance of tracing these generic genetics.

There is still, though, a need to delimit the chronological range of children's literature, and the survey offered in this book begins only in the late seventeenth century. The decision for this starting point is not based on any claim about relevance to today's children, but on the notion that children's literature began to be presented and recognised as a distinct part of print culture in Britain and America only in the decade or so on either side of 1700. This is not to say that texts written earlier were not enjoyed by children, nor that there are not clear stylistic and thematic links between what classical, medieval and Renaissance children were reading and what would follow. But it is to say that children's literature began to be widely understood as a separate product only in the half-century or so following 1660, when Puritan authors realised how effective it could be in furthering their campaign to reform the personal piety of all individuals, adults and children alike.

James Janeway's *A Token for Children* (1672) is perhaps the classic example of a Puritan children's book. His morbid, not to say traumatic, account of the 'Joyful Deaths of Several Young Children' (as part of the full title puts it) is, in terms of tone and subject, very far from today's children's literature (although a 1990s series taking a similar subject, *Sweet Goodbyes*, can seem eerily equivalent).[5] But his insistence that a work of imaginative literature can be as important to a child's future as any exclusively didactic or devotional text was an important foundation for modern children's literature. After all, the same principle could very easily be applied to secular concerns. That children's literature developed when, where and how it did was due not so much to the daring of pioneering publishers or the genius of avant-garde authors but to the emergence of a new market: affluent parents who were willing to invest in their children. Above all, eighteenth-century children's books, however pious and conservative they also were, were fundamentally designed to enlist fiction and verse to expedite the secular, socio-economic advancement of their readers.

Puritan writers like Janeway were also modern in their conviction that their writing would be most effective if children enjoyed reading it. We might like to think that children would not have taken pleasure from rigid piety and accounts of childhood deaths, but the evidence we have suggests otherwise. Autobiographies can speak of 'delight in reading, especially of Mr. Janeway's *Token for Children*', and when one young reader, as late as 1821, described *A Token for Children* as 'the most entertaining book that can be', it was surely not (or not only) because he had enjoyed reading about pious prigs expiring in agonies.[6] Indeed, if we can get past the religiosity, it is not so difficult to see why some Puritan texts would have been attractive to child readers. John Bunyan's *A Book for Boys and Girls* (also called *Country Rimes for Children* or *Divine Emblems*, 1686) contained poems which, though remorselessly devout, were light in tone and cleverly constructed to draw in the reader. 'The Boy and Watch-Maker' tells of a golden watch given to a boy by his father, but which does not work. It is an alluring subject, and frustratingly familiar. Only the third stanza, the 'Comparison', explains the poem's meaning: the boy is a Christian soul and the watch is divine grace within his heart. The watch does not tell the time because it has not been well-cared for. The analogy is spelled out in language that is kindly and approachable (and, incidentally, reminds the modern reader of Philip Pullman's *His Dark Materials*, 1995–2000, with its golden compass rather than watch):

> Do not lay ope' thy heart to Worldly Dust,
> Nor let they Graces over grow with Rust.
> Be oft renew'd in th' Spirit of thy mind,
> Or else uncertain thou thy Watch wilt find.[7]

The verses function as a sort of riddle, evidently designed to entertain as well as reform. The same might even be said of Benjamin

Keach's *War With the Devil* (1673), a dialogue in verse between a 'Youth' and his 'Conscience'. The text is as undeviating as any hell-fire sermon, but it still contains almost comic elements as the two characters berate one another. Youth treats Conscience as if he was an annoying, old-fashioned friend: 'I'd have you know,' says Youth, 'that I | A Person am of some Authority; | Are you so saucy as to curb and chide | Such a brave Spark, who can't your Ways abide?'[8] Even *A Token for Children* has its attractions. The language could be powerful and moving, Janeway being surprisingly tender with his death-scenes. The child-centric nature of these texts was deliberately designed to be attractive to children too. Each narrative revolves around a single child, the adults playing only minor roles. In this sense, Janeway's characters were not so different from Lewis Carroll's Alice or Pullman's Lyra. Janeway's children are wiser and nobler than any adult, and frequently admonish them. This appealed, no doubt, to children's fantasies of empowerment. They were heroic too, battling valiantly against sin in a way neatly demonstrated by an illustration to Keach's *War With the Devil* in which the 'youth in his converted state' single-handedly stands up to the armed assault of a band of sinners and the Devil himself. One might even speculate that the protagonists' deaths in Janeway dramatised another common children's fantasy: the desire to be lost from parents so that the adults realise how much they miss their children when they are gone.

In numerous ways, then, the origins of modern children's literature can be seen in the books produced by the Puritans for children, however unpalatable we might think them today. Any attempt to trace continuities in children's literature, though, is open to criticism. It might seem too teleological, as if all the literature of the past is to be understood and appraised only as it has contributed to form the literature of the present. And it might seem to be canon-building. This would be particularly regrettable since children's literature (largely because its study began in earnest only at a time when canons were becoming unfashionable) has remained comparatively free of the sort of 'Great Tradition', or division into 'important' and 'marginal' books, that has afflicted adult literature. The best antidote to teleology is the appreciation of all texts on their own merits, and in their own contexts, without defining them in terms of their difference from, let alone inferiority to, what was to come. This is the approach taken in this book. If Maria Edgeworth can be understood as the ancestor of Judy Blume, this is not to say that any relative value is embedded in the comparison, nor that the connections between them should be read in only one direction. Reading Edgeworth in the light of Blume can be just as enlightening as reading Blume in the light of Edgeworth. This explains why some of the chapters in this study take a broadly chronological approach while others dart backwards and forwards through the history of a genre.

Similarly, a strong preventative against the stealthy materialisation of a children's literature canon is the inclusion of an extensive array of material from the most neglected corners of the field. While it is true that by looking at fiction and poetry, rather than work appearing in more undervalued and ephemeral media (comics, or textbooks), this book concentrates mostly on the sort of texts that are likely to feature on university children's literature courses, it is also a survey that features a great many non-canonical works. Alongside the sorts of authors who feature in most histories of children's books other much less well-known works are discussed, from early eighteenth-century collections of children's verse to largely forgotten 'problem novels' published in 1970s America, and from Victorian monthly magazines stories to picturebooks from the Harlem Renaissance. The inclusion of such a wide range of texts has not been prompted by any particular ideological agenda or canonic iconoclasm. Rather it reflects a conviction that the history of children's literature is by no means described only by those books that are still well-known today. As with literature for adults, the history of children's literature is littered with books, and whole sub-genres, that were once hugely popular but are now neither read nor widely known. Yet in many cases, these obscure works were extremely important in constructing generic traditions that shape children's books today. A good example are the cautionary tales popular in the eighteenth and early nineteenth centuries: long-forgotten stories and poems warning about the horrible fates befalling naughty children. These texts were no longer in fashion even when they were parodied by Heinrich Hoffmann's *Shock-Headed Peter* (1848), Lewis Carroll's *Alice's Adventures in Wonderland* (1865) and Hilaire Belloc's *Cautionary Tales for*

Children (1907). But somehow they have remained ingrained in the fabric of children's culture. Authors like Ogden Nash, Roald Dahl and Jamie Rix were still riffing on them at the end of the twentieth century (*Custard and Company*, 1979; *Revolting Rhymes*, 1982; *Grizzly Tales: Cautionary Tales for Lovers of Squeam!*, 1990).

One further dilemma that must confront anyone now attempting to write a concise account of children's literature is how best to do justice to the increasing amount, and sophistication, of the scholarship devoted to it. Much innovative and searching criticism of children's literature has now accumulated. It has been possible to mention only a small fraction of it in the footnotes and the Guide to Further Reading. Some of the best criticism presents careful new readings of particular texts. Some concentrates on authors, or publishers, or readers. Some is concerned more with how children's books can be positioned in larger contexts: social or political history say, or discourses of gender, race or child development. Some critics have taken a more abstract approach, seeking to pose, or solve, theoretical problems about the very nature of children's literature. How, for instance, is childhood to be defined, and how has this changed over time? Is there such a thing as children's literature in any case? Might it be more accurate to speak of a boys' literature and a girls' literature? Can children's literature exist for an audience that ranges from infants to pre-teens to young adults and beyond? And is it perhaps really produced for the adults who commission, write and buy it, rather than any actual children?

The current status of children's literature studies, and some possible future directions, are briefly considered in the conclusion to this book, but by and large, this study is not designed to provide a survey of current methodologies, nor is it overly concerned with problematising the concept of children's literature. No one particular kind of analysis is favoured, but rather different critical approaches are taken when they seem to offer important insight into how each major genre has developed. The fundamental argument presented here is simply that a book written for children should be treated no differently than a book for adults. Both can make equally serious artistic statements. Both have a place in particular literary traditions. And both may be analysed without theorising about how the intended audience, rather than the text itself, determines meaning. The challenges of children's literature are many, and they are complex and fascinating. But the greatest challenge, which all of the best children's literature criticism meets, is to give children's books the kind of careful, nuanced and disinterested critical attention that for many years was reserved only for books written for adults.

NOTES

1. See Gillian Adams, 'Medieval Children's Literature: Its Possibility and Actuality', *Children's Literature*, 26 (1998), 1–24.
2. Peter Hunt, *Criticism, Theory and Children's Literature* (Oxford: Blackwell, 1991), pp. 67 and 61. Emphasis added.
3. For instance, Perry Nodelman, 'The Second Kind of Criticism', *Children's Literature Association Quarterly*, 17 (1992), 37–9; Richard Flynn, 'The Intersection of Children's Literature and Childhood Studies', *Children's Literature Association Quarterly*, 22 (1997), 143–5; Susan R. Gannon, 'Report from Limbo: Reading Historical Children's Literature Today', *Signal. Approaches to Children's Books*, 85 (1998), 63–72.
4. Peter Hunt, 'Passing on the Past: The Problem of Books That Are for Children and That Were for Children', *Children's Literature in Education*, 21 (1996–97), 200–2 (p. 200).
5. For instance Alida E. Young, *Losing David* (London: Lions, 1993), about an HIV-positive girl and a boy with leukaemia.
6. *An Account of the Life of the Late Reverend Mr David Brainerd* (Edinburgh: William Gray, 1765), p. 3: Brainerd was born in Connecticut in 1718; *The Sunday Scholars' Magazine*, quoted in Gillian Avery, 'The Puritans and Their Heirs' in *Children and Their Books: A Celebration of the Work of Iona and Peter Opie*, ed. Gillian Avery and Julia Briggs (Oxford: Oxford University Press, 1989), pp. 95–118 (p. 113).
7. John Bunyan, *A Book for Boys and Girls* (London: printed for N.P., 1686), pp. 54–5.
8. Benjamin Keach, *War With the Devil, or, The Young Man's Conflict with the Powers of Darkness in a Dialogue* (London: Benjamin Harris, [1673] 1676), p. 15.

CHAPTER I

Fables

The classic fable is a short, fictional tale which has a specific moral or behavioural lesson to teach. This lesson is often explained at the end of the tale in an epigram or 'moral'. Some are about humans: 'The Boy Who Cried Wolf' for instance. But most feature animals as their main characters, representing human beings, or perhaps particular types of people or kinds of behaviour. In these 'beast fables' the animals are generally fairly lifelike – except that they can often talk – and they do not usually encounter humans. This distinguishes them from animals in fairy tales, often enchanted in one way or another, who interact with humans and live what are essentially human lives. Like fairy tales, fables probably had their origins in an oral folk tale tradition and were not originally intended only for children. Also like fairy tales, fables subsequently came to be associated primarily with the young. Fables are still being written, mainly for children, but sometimes with the hope of appealing to a mixed-age audience. These modern fables can be much grander affairs that the short, allegorical animal stories that first defined the genre. They are often novel-length, with many characters and intricate plots, like Robert O'Brien's *Mrs Frisby and the Rats of* NIMH (1971). They can have complicated themes and enigmatic meanings, like E. B. White's *Charlotte's Web* (1952). Sometimes they seek to give much more scientifically accurate representations of animal life, as in Richard Adams' *Watership Down* (1972). They have sometimes taken their lessons from a much wider range of animals than generally feature in Aesop, as in *Those Other Animals* (1892) by G. A. Henty, who preferred to draw lessons from animals 'whose good points have been hitherto ignored' – like the bacillus – and 'to take down others from the pedestal upon which they have been placed'.[1] And often they are very political, as with George Orwell's *Animal Farm* (1945). But what is more remarkable than the developments within the fable tradition are the continuities. However sophisticated the fable has become it remains fundamentally a didactic form, designed to draw in its readers through a compelling story and appealing, even cute, characters, and to teach important lessons through allegory. It is this consistency, within a general pattern of evolution, that this chapter will trace.

There are good reasons for regarding fables as the first children's literature. They were written down as early as two thousand years BCE on the cuneiform tablets used by the Sumerians in what is now Iraq and Iran. According to Gillian Adams, the fact that fables were written on unbaked clay tablets in relatively unformed writing demonstrates that they were used by children in school lessons.[2] Fables were used for education from a very early period in India too. A collection called the *Panchatantra* had been composed at least as early as the sixth century BCE, and certain fables were later extracted into a separate collection for use by children, usually known as the *Fables of Bidpai* (or *Pilpay*). Bidpai is a learned Brahmin who tries to overcome the stupidity of three princes by encasing their lessons in short narratives. They were widely translated – into Arabic, then Greek (which was the version which circulated widely in medieval Europe), and, by the eighteenth century, English. Most famous in the West are the fables associated with the name Aesop. Aesop was probably a real historical figure, a slave living somewhere in Asia Minor in the sixth century BCE who may later have moved to Greece. He is mentioned by Plato, Plutarch, Herodotus and other Greek writers, and there is a record of a collection of his tales, by Demetrius of Phalerus, now destroyed, being in the Great Library of Alexandria in the fourth century BCE. But the first collection of fables attributed to Aesop that still exists dates only from the Roman period, a collection assembled by the poet Phaedrus in the first century CE. Fables were apparently central to the education of Roman children. As well as Phaedrus' collection of Aesop (called the *Romulus*), they might have read another by Babrius (also first century CE, written in Greek verse) or by Avianus (compiled in around CE 400). All these continued to be read by children throughout medieval Europe.

The relationship between all the different fable traditions is incestuous, with versions of the same narratives, characters and morals cropping up in Indian, Greek, Roman and other later collections, such as the French 'Reynard the Fox' series (c.1175–1250). However, by the later medieval period in Britain, almost all fables were being marketed as having come from Aesop. Sir Roger L'Estrange nicely summed up the situation in his important edition of 1692:

> the Story is come down to us so Dark and Doubtful, that it is Impossible to Distinguish the *Original* from the *Copy:* And to say, which of the Fables are *Aesops*, and which *not;* which are *Genuine*, and which *Spurious*.[3]

From the fifteenth century many different collections were published under Aesop's name, mostly, apparently, for a sophisticated, adult audience. William Caxton's 1484 translation (one of the first books printed in Britain) was in large format and expensive; Robert Henryson's *The Morall Fabillis of Esope in Scottis Meter* (1570) was addressed to 'worthie folk' and 'lordis of prudence'; and John Ogilby's *The Fables of Aesop* (1651) and Jean de La Fontaine's French *Fables Choisies* (1668–93) were written in stylish and sophisticated verse. But throughout the Renaissance period in Britain, Aesop's *Fables* was also the text most commonly used in schools to teach elementary English.[4] Indeed, Sir Roger L'Estrange admitted that he had started to amass his late seventeenth-century collection by pilfering 'the Common *School-Book*'.

More importantly, L'Estrange redesigned the fable to suit children's abilities and needs, as he saw them. He complained that fables had previously been,

> Taught in All our Schools; but almost at such a rate as we Teach *Pyes* [magpies] and *Parrots*, that Pronounce the Words without so much as Guessing at the Meaning of them: Or to take it Another way, the Boys Break their Teeth upon the

Shells, without ever coming near the Kernel. They Learn the
Fables by *Lessons*, and the Moral is the least part of our Care
in a Childs Institution.

For L'Estrange, the potency of the fable lay in the way instruction
could be combined with the pleasure of a short narrative: 'it is
beyond All Dispute,' he wrote, 'that the Delight and Genius of
Children, lies much toward the Hearing, Learning, and Telling of
Little Stories'. The writer for children should therefore always be
'Indulging and Cultivating of This *Disposition*, or *Inclination*, on the
One hand, and the Applying of a Profitable *Moral* to the *Figure*, or
the *Fable*, on the *Other*'. By these means, 'These very Lessons
Themselves may be Gilt and Sweeten'd, as we Order Pills and
Potions; so as to take off the Disgust of the Remedy.'[5] This provides
another reason for believing that fables should be regarded as the
earliest form of modern children's literature, for L'Estrange's
theory of the fable foreshadows the 'instruction and delight' strategy proudly employed fifty years later by John Newbery, so often
regarded as the first publisher to offer children entertainment inter-
twined with education.

Perhaps equally beholden to L'Estrange and the fable tradition
was the educational theory so influentially advocated by John Locke
in his *Some Thoughts Concerning Education* of 1693, only a year after
the publication of L'Estrange's Aesop. Locke practically para-
phrased L'Estrange's ideas. He famously likened the child to a
tabula rasa (blank tablet or slate), but this was merely a restatement
of L'Estrange's view that '*Children* are but *Blank Paper*, ready
Indifferently for any Impression'. And Locke's lament at the lack of
safe and useful reading matter for children, although there was so
much 'perfectly useless trumpery', recalls L'Estrange's even more
contemptuous assertion that his fables replaced nothing better than
'Insipid *Twittle-Twattles*, Frothy *Jests*, and Jingling *Witticisms*'.
Even more strikingly, Locke maintained that there were only two
books available that were suitable for the education of children:
Raynard the Fox and *Aesop's Fables*.[6] Although some were to com-
plain that because fables were 'a palpable Falsehood, and a mere
Fiction', they accustomed children to deceit (which, *ipso facto*, was
a bad thing, but also 'abates much of the Pleasure of reading the

Story')[7], Locke's endorsement ensured that the fable flourished throughout the eighteenth century and beyond. Reworked collections appeared every few years.[8]

Increasingly, these new collections were designed solely for children. Joseph Jackson justified his own 1708 venture into print by claiming that L'Estrange's collection 'seems rather designed for part of the furniture of a statesman's closet, than the satchel of a school-boy' so that the fables have 'not so fully attained the chief aim of their publication viz. the Instruction of Youth.' His, by contrast, would be concise, direct and well-illustrated so as to enable 'an easier reception into the understanding, or at least root it deeper in the memory of every juvenile reader'.[9] A century later, in his *Fables Ancient and Modern* (1805), William Godwin repeated the Lockean position, that 'fables were the happiest vehicle which could be devised for the instruction of children in the first period of their education', but argued that, if they were to be appealing and effective, revisions were necessary. He developed the characters of the animal protagonists and introduced humans to interact with them. Attempting 'to make almost all my narratives end in a happy and forgiving tone', he replaced the customary abrupt manner and pithy morals with a more discursive style and protracted lessons. 'The Ass in the Lion's Skin' exhibits his method very well. Godwin's fable is around five times as long as the traditional version, with a beginning, middle and end to the narrative, and it is buttressed by geographical notes ('All this happened in a country where lions lived; I suppose in Africa'). Moreover, whereas in the standard version, an ass dons a lion's pelt to scare his master and other animals, Godwin's ass uses the pelt to punish boys who have been tormenting him. The moral comes some way before the fable's end and is also made more relevant to children: 'Cheats are always found out.' The narrative closes not with the ass being beaten, but with a much more tender rapprochement with the children, bordering on sentimentality: 'now, instead of running away the moment they came in sight, he would trot to meet them, would rub his head against them to tell them how much he loved them, and would eat the thistles and the oats out of their hand: was not that pretty?'[10]

Many later writers sought to make their fables more directly appealing to children by abridgement not extension. Walter Crane's

Baby's Own Aesop (1887) distilled them into limericks, and the morals into snappy maxims, and relied heavily on his beautiful full-page illustrations to fascinate the reader. Here is 'The Crow and the Pitcher' for example:

> How the cunning old Crow got his drink
> When 'twas low in the pitcher, just think!
> Don't say that he spilled it!
> With pebbles he filled it,
> 'Till the water rose up to the brink!

Crane's moral is 'Use your wits'.[11] Each generation makes its own refinements. The attempt to contemporise fables is evident for example even in the (rather clunky) title of *Aesop's Funky Fables* (1997). Its publishers trusted jointly to Korky Paul's 'wild and inventive illustrations' and Vivian French's 'catchy rap-rhythms and witty retelling' to 'make these the funkiest fables around!' Here is the start of 'The Lion and the Mouse':

> Squeak squeak
> Nibble nibble
>   Rummage rummage
>   Pitter patter
>   Pitter patter
>   Pitter –
> EEEEEEEEEEEEEEEEEEEEEEEEEEEK!
> Oh no no no no no no no!
> Oh my pitter patter heart oh my whiskers
> That are trembling!
> Mr Lion
> Please don't eat me!
> Let me go!

Aesop's Funky Fables are much less didactic than most previous versions too. Indeed the morals are entirely omitted.[12]

Comparing L'Estrange to Godwin to Crane to *Aesop's Funky Fables* reveals some fairly obvious changes in style, format, language and tone. What are often even more revealing about society's changing attitudes to childhood and children's literature are slight variations in the content of the fables and the sometimes subtle shifts of emphases in the morals. The well-known 'The Boy Who Cried Wolf' is an interesting example. In Michael Morpurgo's 2004 version the lesson is that 'No one believes a liar even when he is telling the truth.'[13] But three hundred years earlier, for L'Estrange, the moral had been 'He must be a very Wise Man that knows the True Bounds, and Measures of Fooling [sic]'. His further 'Reflexion' explains that the boy's error was not in joking about the danger of wolves, but in taking the joke too far. Despite its hazards, L'Estrange insists that raillery remains 'the very Sawce of Civil Entertainment': an important part of how society functions smoothly and how the individual relates to the community.[14] By 2004 (and well before, in fact) the fable's moral had become much more straightforward and more literal: more 'childish' one might say. According to the critic David Whitley this is because in the mid-eighteenth century authors influenced by Locke began to see that fables were the perfect medium for encouraging children to work out the lessons for themselves, decoding the allegory or the illustrations to discover simple lessons. Fables were regarded as 'a testing ground for ideas about what children needed from a story and the most appropriate ways for this to reach them', Whitley concludes.[15] Yet if the morals have been simplified since the eighteenth century, we cannot say for certain that the fables themselves have become more 'childish'. It is now a standard part of 'The Boy Who Cried Wolf' that the boy ends up being eaten along with his sheep, and this is what happens in Morpurgo's apparently very traditional 2004 retelling. We might be tempted to regard the bland conclusion of the version in *Aesop's Funky Fables* – with the boy climbing a tree to escape the wolf but being forced to spend the rest of his days feeding the chickens and chopping wood so that he 'never had time to play' – as a modern palliation of Aesop's savagery, perhaps in deference to parental anxieties about violence in books for the young.[16] In fact, though, the boy is not eaten in most seventeenth- and eighteenth-century versions, and it is likely that the wolf's consumption of the boy is actually a contamination from fairy tales such as 'Little Red Riding Hood'. Aesop's fables have evolved in fascinating, but not predictable, ways.

By the end of the nineteenth century new, post-Aesopic collections of fables were appearing. Probably the most successful are Joel Chandler Harris's *Uncle Remus* stories (from 1879) and the *Just So Stories* (1902) and *The Jungle Books* (1894–95) by Rudyard Kipling. These are not so obviously didactic as the Aesopian fables, and they are bound together into much more sophisticated framing narratives, but they retain the same basic format: short narratives about individual animals representing a particular type of person or behaviour. An alternative tradition was the novel-length animal story designed to illustrate more substantial lessons through more sustained narratives. Early examples include Dorothy Kilner's *The Life and Perambulations of a Mouse* (1783) and Edward Kendall's *Keeper's Travels in Search of his Master* (1798), but the form came of age in the late Victorian and Edwardian periods with books like Anna Sewell's *Black Beauty* (1877), Richard Jeffries' *Wood Magic* (1881) and Jack London's *The Call of the Wild* (1903). For the critic John Goldthwaite what these books represent is 'the beast fable suddenly shedding its ancient moralizing intent and taking on the affective weight of modern prose fantasy.'[17]

But in fact there had always been a substantial crossover between the fable and the animal story. Sewell's intention in *Black Beauty: the Autobiography of a Horse* was to reveal the mistreatment that horses receive from humans. But even if it was not designed exclusively for children, it retains many of the characteristics of the fable. Much of the text concentrates on the best methods to train and manage a horse, but the same lessons are allegorically applicable to humans. The advice given to Black Beauty by his mother, the reason why he lives a more or less contented life that ends happily, is decipherable in the same way as Aesop's warning not to cry wolf: 'do your work with a good will, lift your feet up well when you trot, and never bite or kick even in play.'[18] Likewise, the abuse Sewell chiefly complains of is the 'bearing rein', and although this was genuinely a nineteenth-century practice designed to enhance horses' appearance but causing them discomfort and shortening their lives, it also functions as part of the fable. Black Beauty and his fellow horses rebel against it, causing damage and preventing their mistress from getting to the Duchess' garden party. Sewell did not append a moral, but it is evident nonetheless: brutally to impose restrictions, especially if just for the sake of appearances, will always be resented and counterproductive (or, more Aesopically: 'So violent Threat and Rigour often fail, | Where milder courses oftentimes prevail').[19] Sewell means the lesson to be applied to children as well as to horses, and even perhaps to wives, for it is Lady W—— who favours the bearing rein, and Black Beauty's groom complains bitterly that it is the job of her husband to prevent her cruelty: 'if a woman's husband can't rule her . . . I wash my hands of it.'[20]

In fact, a century before *Black Beauty*, Sarah Trimmer had already happily planted fable elements into a sustained animal story in *Fabulous Histories* (1786). It tells the parallel stories of a family of birds and another of humans: hence its alternative title, *The History of the Robins*, under which it remained in print until well into the twentieth century. Trimmer was adamant that her novel should be considered not 'as containing the real conversations of birds (for that it is impossible we should ever understand), but as a series of FABLES, intended to convey moral instruction'. The two human children, Harriet and Frederick, and the four nestlings, Robin, Dicky, Flapsy and Pecksy, learn roughly the same general lessons: that 'In a family every individual ought to consult the welfare of the whole, instead of his own private satisfaction' and that God has created the world so that all animals are interdependent and that to hurt or kill other creatures without reason is to transgress against the *'divine principle* of UNIVERSAL BENEVOLENCE'. There were more specific lessons too, often taught through inset fable-like vignettes. The robins meet many other birds, learning from their various failings how one ought to behave. The magpies talk all at once so no-one can understand what they say; the chaffinch is condemned for telling tales; the cuckoo denounced for stealing other birds' nests. In another Aesopian episode, the young robins learn that appearances can be deceptive when they find that a man spreading seeds on the ground for them is no philanthropist, but a bird-catcher. Meanwhile Harriet and Frederick learn from other humans: Mrs Addis, who dotes on her pets to the neglect of her own children, and Edward Jenkins who tortures animals, eventually being killed by his own horse. But as in the conventional fable, nature has much to teach humans too. A visit to a beehive leads his mother to ask whether Frederick would fight as well for his monarch as the bees do for their Queen?[21]

The cosmological role of animals, and the relationship between animals and humans, naturally became a frequent subject for these expanded fables. Trimmer's Christianity dictated that mankind had dominion over animals, but although no animal rights campaigner or vegetarian, she insisted that God was in all animals and that they should be treated kindly ('I often regret that so many lives should be sacrificed to preserve ours,' says the children's mother, 'but we must eat animals, or they would at length eat us').[22] Two centuries later, the same pantheistic theme was taken up by Ted Hughes in his *What is the Truth? A Farmyard Fable for the Young* (1984), though with the environmentalist implications brought much further to the fore. The book is composed of the animal poems that an assortment of humans recite to God and his Son when they visit Earth one night. Each is beautiful and moving in its way. But, God insists, they miss the Truth, which is that 'I was those Worms . . . I was that Fox. Just as I was that Foal. . . . I am each of these things. The Rat. The Fly. And each of these things is Me. It is. It is. That is the Truth.'[23]

If Trimmer and Hughes emphasised the interconnectedness of human and animal life, many modern fabulists have preferred to show animals and humans at war. The fundamental lesson of these fables has been that humans are beasts, both in the sense that we are part of the natural world too and should seek to preserve it, and that humans can be as cruel and uncaring as any animal. Roald Dahl's extended fable, *Fantastic Mr Fox* (1970), is typical in its representation of the way in which 'civilisation' has alienated humans from their natural state, a happier and (ironically) more humanitarian way of life that Dahl's animals still inhabit. Boggis, Bunce and Bean are three repulsive farmers who decide to kill a fox who has been poaching their poultry. With their guns and their mechanical diggers they drive him and his family underground, laying waste to the landscape and forcing all the local animals to the brink of starvation. Mr Fox saves the animals' lives by tunnelling to Boggis's chicken shed, Bunce's storeroom and Bean's cider cellar, and the animals live happily in a new underground utopia while the farmers camp in vain at the foxhole ('And so far as I know, they are still waiting.'). What has happened, the reader realises, is that the humans have become rude, nasty and unpleasant, as only Dahl could make them, and as savage as any wild beast, while the animals have become civilised. Mr Fox is convivial, inviting all the animals to his feast. He is chivalric, treating his wife courteously (if somewhat patronisingly). And he is moderate, taking only what he needs from the unlimited stores he has obtained. While the farmers and their employees are outside in the rain ('armed with sticks and guns and hatchets and pistols and all sorts of other horrible weapons') Mr Fox's tunnels have led him physically and symbolically closer to human habitation, until he ends up in the basement of Bean's own house. Morally he is far more civilised too. When a badger questions him about his theft of the farmers' food Mr Fox replies 'My dear old furry frump . . . do you know anyone in the *whole world* who wouldn't swipe a few chickens if his children were starving to death?' By the end of the book, Mr Fox even talks of his poaching as 'shopping'. Besides, the farmers are trying to *kill* the animals, he points out, 'But *we're* not going to stoop to *their* level.' *Fantastic Mr Fox* marries the characters and satire of Aesop with Dahl's uniquely grotesque misanthropy to produce a playful fable about a kind of 'progress' that has brought little but greed, vindictiveness and natural devastation.[24]

John Goldthwaite attributes the rise of the animal story in the late nineteenth century to the advent of 'empire, electricity, and later the automobile, and, perhaps most importantly, of urbanization'.[25] These developments severed people's links with nature but simultaneously encouraged a nostalgic Arcadianism that created the demand for books like Beatrix Potter's *The Tale of Peter Rabbit* (1901) or Kenneth Grahame's *The Wind in the Willows* (1908). Critics have seen the latter in particular as depicting nature threatened equally by technology (Toad's motor car) and the lower classes (the stoats and the weasels who invade Toad Hall), but offering a consoling fantasy in which the 'good' animals (Badger, Rat, Mole) finally rally round to save 'Toad from his extravagances, and the aristocracy from the masses' and 'the English countryside from the forces of industrialisation and exploitation.'[26] But if nostalgia for the rural was often an essentially conservative impulse, by the 1960s the desire 'to get ourselves | Back to the garden', as Joni Mitchell put it in her 1969 song 'Woodstock', had become more politically radical. This new Arcadiaism was still derived from anxiety about the ills of modern, urban, consumerist society, but its fables attack rather than defend existing power structures. Increasingly inflected with environmentalist concerns, they are often more dystopian than consoling. A fine example is David Macaulay's picturebook *Baaa* (1985) in which sheep move into the city after the last humans have somehow disappeared. When over-population results in shortages, their leaders can only pacify the flock by feeding them a product called 'Baaa'. We gradually discover that this must be made of sheep. The population necessarily declines until only two are left: 'one day they met for lunch', the book chillingly concludes.[27] *Baaa* is a satire on the logic of the consumer society and, more generally, is designed to demonstrate how quickly civilisation can alienate creatures – ovine and human – from their true nature.

This is also the basic theme of one of the most complex and successful modern children's fables, Robert O'Brien's *Mrs Frisby and the Rats of* NIMH (1971). It tells of a colony of rats captured for research in a scientific institution ('NIMH': probably based on the American N.I.H. – National Institutes of Health). The injections they are given render them super-intelligent and long-lived, and they escape. Once free, they build for themselves a new society, reading human books, harvesting a share of the crops of the farmer Mr Fitzgibbon, and even harnessing his electricity supply. They help Mrs Frisby, a mouse, by moving her home out of the way of Farmer Fitzgibbon's plough. Like Trimmer long before him, O'Brien was happy to draw attention to the fable-like nature of his novel. Chapter three, 'The Crow and the Cat', recalls Aesop's 'The Mouse and the Lion', with Mrs Frisby saving Jeremy the crow from Dragon the cat by gnawing through the string in which Jeremy is tangled. It is a synecdoche of the whole novel, for eventually Mrs Frisby is integral to the survival of the rats too, warning them of the arrival of the pest exterminators.

This description might make *Mrs Frisby and the Rats of* NIMH sound twee, but the book is actually exceptionally intelligent and surprisingly powerful. Despite their abilities, the rats are rather pitiful creatures, unsure of who they are. By the experiment they 'were set apart from even our own kind', recalls Nicodemus, their leader. Should they 'go back to living in a sewer-pipe . . . eating other people's garbage' just because 'that's what rats do', he asks?

'Where does a group of civilized rats fit in?' Their answer is extraordinary, taking the novel much further beyond its satire on animal experimentation. Their plan, inspired by reading about the rise and fall of the ancient Egyptians, Greeks and Romans, is to establish a new civilisation, but unlike all previous rat societies, it will not be based on stealing food, but on their own farming of the land in an area remote from human habitation. This utopianism emphasises how the novel as a whole functions as a much larger fable than anything in Aesop. There is perhaps the implication that all human societies are based on theft too, but above all, it is the foolish vanity of human civilisation that is emphasised. It is sign-posted by the farmer's name: 'Fitz', from the French 'fils', meaning son (usually associated with illegitimate descent), and 'gibbon', pointing to mankind's simian ancestry. An equivocal attitude to progress permeates the whole novel, from the arrogance of the NIMH scientists (whose treatment of animals would have been roundly condemned by Trimmer or Sewell) to the attitude of Jenner's break-away group of rats who want to live like humans, stealing whatever is necessary from them and threatening to 'find out where they keep the dynamite and use it on them.' It is best summed up in a short, inset fable that Nicodemus tells. Mrs Jones keeps her house clean with a broom and mop until she buys a vacuum cleaner which does the job quicker. Soon all the neighbouring houses have vacuum cleaners and a factory opens up. Its pollution makes the houses dirtier than they were before, so that Mrs Jones has to work twice as long to keep her house *almost* as clean as it had been before she had bought the vacuum cleaner.[28] In its way, *Mrs Frisby and the Rats of* NIMH is as political a fable as George Orwell's *Animal Farm*.

Such a strong political slant in a fable was nothing new. Seventeenth- and eighteenth-century collections of Aesop had been very specific in their satire, offering commentaries on recent political events and controversies. One of Aesop's fables tells how the pigeons were so harassed by a kite that they asked a hawk to be their protector, only to find that the hawk 'makes more Havock . . . in Two Days, than the *Kite* could have done in Twice as many months.' The Tory L'Estrange easily converted this into a attack on the 'Glorious Revolution' of 1688–89 when the English had invited

William III to take the throne from James II.[29] Samuel Croxall managed to use the same fable to argue a contrary political point of view in 1722. James Thurber's *Fables for Our Time* from 1940 are the direct descendants of these, combining historical specificity with a general moral application. Here is 'The Rabbits Who Caused All the Trouble':

Within the memory of the youngest child there was a family of rabbits who lived near a pack of wolves. The wolves announced that they did not like the way the rabbits were living. . . . One night several wolves were killed in an earthquake and this was blamed on the rabbits, for it is well known that rabbits pound on the ground with their hind legs and cause earthquakes. On another night one of the wolves was killed by a bolt of lightning and this was also blamed on the rabbits, for it is well known that lettuce-eaters cause lightning. The wolves threatened to civilize the rabbits if they didn't behave, and the rabbits decided to run away to a desert island. But the other animals, who lived at a great distance, shamed them, saying, 'You must stay where you are and be brave. This is no world for escapists. If the wolves attack you, we will come to your aid, in all probability.' So the rabbits continued to live near the wolves and one day there was a terrific flood which drowned a great many wolves. This was blamed on the rabbits, for it is well known that carrot-nibblers with long ears cause floods. The wolves descended on the rabbits, for their own good, and imprisoned them in a dark cave, for their own protection.

When nothing was heard about the rabbits for some weeks, the other animals decided to know what had happened to them. The wolves replied that the rabbits had been eaten and since they had been eaten the affair was an internal matter. But the other animals warned that they might possibly unite against the wolves unless some reason was given for the destruction of the rabbits. So the wolves gave them one. 'They were trying to escape,' said the wolves, 'and, as you know, this is no world for escapists.'
Moral: Run, don't walk, to the nearest desert island.[30]

In America in 1940 this might have been read as an anti-appeasement fable designed to bring the USA into the Second World War by allegorising the Nazi conquest of Austria, Czechoslovakia and Poland. From our perspective it is difficult not to read it as a veiled representation of the persecution of Jews in Nazi Germany. One critic has (anachronistically) suggested that the subject is the Soviet takeover of Hungary in 1956.[31] The multiplicity of possible meanings is a symptom of the fable's universality. Certainly it works as a general statement about the ease with which minorities can be blamed for disasters. The very slightly feasible allegation that the rabbits caused the earthquake quickly descends into the absurd contention 'that carrot-nibblers with long ears cause floods'. The mordant humour (the 'internal matter' – a play on the rabbit's edibility) adds to the effect. At their best, then, irrespective of the links with their original context, Thurber's fables are as generally relevant as Aesop's. He did not originally write his fables for the young, but as the distance from the specific events and attitudes that they satirise has increased, so too has their suitability for children.

It might be argued that Thurber, Orwell, O'Brien, Dahl and most other modern authors were, with their fables of toleration, cooperation and conservation, maintaining what was basically a progressive, liberal tradition dating back to Aesop. Aesop's world had been one of competition and predation, but the small or slow often triumphed over the big or fast ('The Hare and the Tortoise'), animals thrived by mutual aid ('The Lion and the Mouse') and selfishness was roundly condemned ('The Dog in the Manger'). Tolerance of difference has also been a traditional concern of fables. Sewell's *Black Beauty* has been read as an attack on slavery as much as cruelty to animals.[32] More obviously engaged with the politics of race are Harris' 185 *Uncle Remus* stories (from 1879), although they are not now much read, at least in the original versions, because of their white author's ventriloquism of what he affected to think were the speech patterns of black slaves. This can certainly be regarded as extremely patronising and insulting, yet when we consider that Harris was writing about an astute black narrator who tells his own stories to the son of his white owners, and thereby is perhaps able to influence the future of the plantation, the picture becomes more complicated. In any case, the stories themselves, mostly recounting the victories of the trickster Brer Rabbit over his more powerful enemies, seem to offer a coded account of resistance to authority. As Harris put it in his introduction to *Songs and Sayings* (1881), the fables he collected were 'thoroughly characteristic of the Negro',

> and it needs no scientific investigation to show why he selects as his hero the weakest and most harmless of all animals, and brings him out victorious in contests with the bear, the wolf, and the fox. It is not virtue that triumphs, but helplessness; it is not malice, but mischievousness.[33]

Likewise, the language used by Rudyard Kipling in his account of why the 'Ethiopian' – 'really a negro, and so his name was Sambo' – is black is unpalatable now, but can be read as an attempt to explain and play down – or perhaps celebrate – racial difference. Just as the leopard with whom he shares this *Just So Story* chooses his own spots, so the 'Ethiopian' devises for himself his 'nice working blackish-brownish colour, with a little purple in it, and touches of slaty-blue' so that he too may hunt more effectively.[34]

One of the moral lessons that fables have traditionally been intended to teach is about the difference between surface and substance, appearance and reality, and this may help to explain why race – frequently represented in terms of skin colour – has always been a subject for them. Samuel Croxall's 'The Blackamoor', for instance, included in his 1722 collection, tells of a foolish man's wish to wash his black slave white. The attempt attracts derision, and the valuable 'Æthiopian' is killed in the process.[35] One of Ted Hughes' fables, 'How the Polar Bear Became' (1963), written in the manner of Kipling's *Just So Stories* and in some ways a corrective to 'How the Leopard Got His Spots', offers a more complex investigation of the politics of appearance. The Polar Bear routinely wins the animals' beauty contest on account of her beautiful white fur. This makes her increasingly vain and she longs to get away from the other animals who dirty her coat. The Peregrine Falcon, who usually comes second in the contests, devises a plot to remove his rival. He tells her of a country that is 'so clean it is even whiter than you are' and he shows her the way.

She lives at the North Pole still, with the company of only her sycophantic admirers, the seals. In some ways, this is a piece of whimsy, gently teasing Darwinism, and lacking a clear moral. It might be read as a satire on vanity. But because of the Polar Bear's whiteness there is a political dimension too. The other animals did not win the contest because they were 'all the wrong colour . . . black, or brown, or yellow, or ginger, or fawn, or speckled'. But when the Polar Bear's pride in her whiteness and her purity leads her to exile herself to the barren icecap, it is all the other animals who inherit the fruitful world. Racial arrogance is sterile, isolating and self-destructive.[36]

If Hughes, Kipling and Croxall tackled issues of race indirectly, other fabulists aimed to make their fables more overtly about racial politics. One of the best examples is *The Country Bunny and the Little Gold Shoes* (1939), a picturebook written by DuBose Heyward (a white author best known for his depictions of black culture in the American South of the 1920s) with illustrations by Marjorie Flack. It tells of the five rabbits who deliver all the Easter eggs. When one of them grows old, the Grandfather Bunny chooses a replacement, always wise, and kind, and swift. It is the dream of the book's heroine, 'a little country girl bunny with brown skin and a little cotton-ball of a tail', to become one of them, but 'all of the big white bunnies who lived in fine houses, and the Jack Rabbits with long legs who can run so fast' laughed at her chances. Their scorn is only deepened when she gives birth to twenty-one babies and has to spend all of her time rearing them. But then when a replacement Easter Bunny is needed, it is she who impresses the Grandfather with her wise, efficient and kind household management. She becomes the Easter Bunny and is even given the hardest job of all, to deliver an egg to a boy who has been ill for a year but never complained, and who lives beyond rivers and hills at the top of the tallest mountain. Her perseverance in this almost impossible task wins her the magic golden shoes, which allow her to complete the delivery, and she returns home to her happy family. *The Country Bunny* celebrates the triumph of poverty over affluence, the country over the town, the female over the male, and the small over the big. Above all, it is a fable about race, telling of the eventual victory of the 'country girl bunny with a brown skin' over the 'big white bunnies'. The only element that jars with this ideological positioning is the affluence, whiteness and maleness of the Grandfather Rabbit and of the uncomplaining child (at least in the illustrations), especially since they seem to represent God and Christ respectively.[37]

It is possible, then, to argue that the fable is an inherently liberal or even radical genre. But there is a strong streak of conservatism too. Many of Aesop's fables seem designed to teach readers to be happy with what they have. In Michael Morpurgo's twenty-first century version, for instance, the moral of 'The Town Mouse and the Country Mouse' is 'Better to be happy with what you need than risk everything for more.'[38] In earlier periods, especially times of social upheaval, this kind of warning against ambition was often more explicitly political. The Reverend H. G. Keene's *Persian Fables, for Young and Old* (1833), published by the evangelical Society for Promoting Christian Knowledge in the year after the Great Reform Act, openly advocated resignation, humility and contentment with one's lot. 'The Ambitious Crane', wrote Keene, teaches that 'The wisest thing we can do, is to follow the pursuits that belong to our station', while the moral of 'The Greedy Cat' was 'Poverty may have its hardships; but wealth and greatness have their troubles and alarms.'[39] Today, this advocacy of passive contentment remains in place, but it is often presented, much less politically, as self-actualisation: be happy with who you are, rather than be content with your rank in life. Morpurgo's moral for 'The Wolf and the Donkey', for instance, is 'Stick to what you know and be true to yourself.'[40] Indeed, a number of recent fabulists have moved away from traditional moral and social didacticism, preferring fables that read like Zen parables and that advocate personal awareness and fulfillment. The closing tale in Arnold Lobel's Caldecott-winning *Fables* (1980), 'The Mouse at the Seashore', is a good example. It tells of a young mouse's determination to see the sea despite his parents' warnings of the danger. On his journey, he is duly attacked by cats, dogs and birds, but finally arrives:

> The moon and the stars began to appear over the ocean. The Mouse sat silently on the top of the hill. He was overwhelmed by a feeling of deep peace and contentment.

Lobel's moral is 'All the miles of a hard road are worth a moment of happiness.'[41] More mystical than moral or practical, this represents another stage in the evolution of the fable. Yet the basic form of the fable has remained the same: the anthropomorphism, the economy of expression, the single precept, the small story teaching a wider truth. What is striking about the fable is both how little the form has changed over the many centuries of its existence, but how easily it has been adapted to suit the attitudes, anxieties and priorities of different periods.

SUMMARY OF KEY POINTS

- Fables can be regarded as the earliest form of modern children's literature, used by children in ancient Sumer, India, Greece and Rome, and throughout medieval Europe.
- Fables can take many forms, and vary widely in length and sophistication, but they have consistently been used to teach important lessons using an engaging, allegorical story with appealing characters.
- Familiar fables have been constantly reworked and re-presented to suit changing cultural and political values, and changing ideas about the nature of childhood and children's literature. New fables have also been devised to express new anxieties.
- Fables have often been used to teach both specific and generalised political lessons.
- Perhaps because of their traditional use of animal characters, fables have frequently addressed environmental concerns.
- Perhaps because they have traditionally taken the difference between surface and substance as a theme, fables have often investigated questions of racial and ethnic difference.

NOTES

1. G. A. Henty, 'To the Reader', *Those Other Animals* (London: Henry and Co. [1892]), p. v.

2. Gillian Adams, 'Ancient and medieval children's texts', in *International Companion Encylopedia of Children's Literature*, ed. Peter Hunt, 2nd edn, 2 vols (London: Routledge, 2004), vol.1, pp. 225–38 (p. 226).

3. Sir Roger L'Estrange, *Fables of Æsop and Other Eminent Mythologists with Morals and Reflexions* (London: R. Sare *et al.*, 1692), p. i.

4. See Adams, 'Ancient and medieval children's texts', pp. 233–4 and 'Medieval children's literature: its possibility and actuality', *Children's Literature*, 26 (1998), 1–24. See also Nicholas Orme, *English Schools in the Middle Ages* (London: Methuen, 1973), Edward Wheatley, *Mastering Aesop: Medieval Education, Chaucer and his Followers* (Gainesville, FL: University Press of Florida, 2000), and *The Norton Anthology of Children's Literature*, ed. Jack Zipes *et al.* (New York: W. W. Norton, 2005), pp. 387–8.

5. L'Estrange, *Fables of Æsop*, pp. 7 and 2–3.

6. John Locke, *Some Thoughts Concerning Education* (London: A. and J. Churchill, 1693), section 148, pp. 183–4; L'Estrange, *Fables of Æsop*, p. 3.

7. John Marchant, *Puerilia: Amusements for the Young* (London: P. Stevens, 1751), p. iv. Jean-Jacques Rousseau made the same point later in *Julie; ou, La Nouvelle Héloïse* (1761): *Eloisa: or, a Series of Original Letters*, 4 vols (London: R. Griffiths, T. Becket and P. A. De Hondt, 1761), vol. 3, p. 288.

8. For more details see Jayne Elizabeth Lewis, *The English Fable: Aesop and Literary Culture, 1651–1740* (Cambridge: Cambridge University Press, 1996), and Anja Müller, 'Picturing Æsops: re-visions of Æsop's Fables from L'Estrange to Richardson', *1650–1850*, 10 (2004), 33–62.

9. Joseph Jackson, *A New Translation of Æsop's Fables, Adorn'd with Cutts; Suited to the Fables* (London: Thomas Tebb, 1708), pp. vii–viii.

10. William Godwin (writing as 'Edward Baldwin'), *Fables Ancient and Modern. Adapted for the Use of Children* (London: Thomas Hodgkins, 1805), pp. iii–iv.

11. Walter Crane, *The Baby's Own Aesop* (1887), rpt in *Norton Anthology of Children's Literature*, p. 401.

12. Vivian French and Korky Paul, *Aesop's Funky Fables* (London: Puffin, [1997] 1999), back cover and pp. 24–5.

13. 'The Wolf and the Shepherd's Son', Michael Morpurgo, *The Orchard Book of Aesop's Fables*, illustrated by Emma Chichester Clark (London: Orchard Books, 2004), p. 96.

14. 'The Boy and false Alarms', L'Estrange, *Fables of Æsop*, pp. 73–4.

15. David Whitley, 'Samuel Richardson's *Aesop*', *Opening the Nursery Door: Reading, Writing and Childhood 1600–1900* (London: Routledge, 1997), pp. 65–79 (pp. 75 and 79).

16. French and Paul, *Aesop's Funky Fables*, p. 23.

17. John Goldthwaite, *The Natural History of Make-Believe: A Guide to the Principal Works of Britain, Europe and America* (New York: Oxford University Press, 1996), p. 253.

18. Anna Sewell, *Black Beauty, his Grooms and Companions; the Autobiography of a Horse. Translated from the Original Equine* (London: Puffin, [1877] 1994), p. 4.

19. 'Of the Sun and the North-Wind', Anon. *Æsop's Fables, With Their Morals: in Prose and Verse* (London: J. Hodges, 1741), p. 132.

20. Sewell, *Black Beauty*, p. 113.

21. Sarah Trimmer, *Fabulous Histories. Designed for the Instruction of Children, Respecting Their Treatment of Animals* (London: T. Longman *et al.*, [1786] 1798), pp. vii–viii, 69, 172, 110–12, 144, 119–20.

22. Trimmer, *Fabulous Histories*, p. 115.

23. Ted Hughes, *What is the Truth? A Farmyard Fable for the Young*, with drawings by R. J. Lloyd (London: Faber & Faber, 1984), p. 121.

24. Roald Dahl, illustrated by Quentin Blake, *Fantastic Mr Fox* (London: Puffin, [1970] 1996), pp. 80, 58–9 and 79.

25. Goldthwaite, *Natural History of Make-Believe*, p. 251.

26. Tess Cosslett, *Talking Animals in British Children's Fiction, 1786–1914* (Aldershot: Ashgate, 2006), p. 180.

27. David Macaulay, *Baaa* (1985), rpt in *Norton Anthology of Children's Literature*, pp. 1068–96, pp. 1095–6.

28. Robert C. O'Brien, *Mrs Frisby and the Rats of* NIMH (London: Puffin, [1971] 1975), pp. 124, 118–19, 137, 151 and 146.

29. L'Estrange, *Fables of Æsop*, p. 21.
30. James Thurber, *Fables for Our Time and Famous Poems Illustrated* (London: Hamish Hamilton, 1940), p. 69.
31. Marie Fernandes, *The Animal Fable in Modern Literature* (New Delhi: B. R. Publishing Corporation, 1996), p. 137.
32. Moira Ferguson, 'Breaking in Englishness: *Black Beauty* and the politics of gender, race and class', *Women: A Cultural Review*, 15 (1994), 34–52.
33. Joel Chandler Harris, *The Complete Tales of Uncle Remus*, ed. Richard Chase (New York: Houghton Mifflin, [1955] 2002), p. xxv. See Goldthwaite, *Natural History of Make-Believe*, pp. 251–86, for a long and enthusiastic discussion of the Uncle Remus stories.
34. 'How the Leopard Got His Spots', Rudyard Kipling, *Just So Stories* (London: Puffin, [1902] 2004), pp. 45–6.
35. Samuel Croxall, *Fables of Aesop and Others Newly Done into English* (London: Thomas Astley, [1722] 1728), pp. 315–16.
36. Ted Hughes, *How the Whale Became and Other Stories* (London: Puffin, [1963] 1982), pp. 40–6.
37. DuBose Heyward, with pictures by Marjorie Flack, *The Country Bunny and the Little Gold Shoes. As told to Jenifer* (London: Collins, 1956), pp. 2–4.
38. Morpurgo, *Orchard Book of Aesop's Fables*, p. 89.
39. Rev. H. G. Keene, *Persian Fables, for Young and Old* (London: John W. Parker, 1833), pp. 68 and 87.
40. Morpurgo, *Orchard Book of Aesop's Fables*, p. 75.
41. Arnold Lobel, *Fables* (New York: HarperCollins, 1980), p. 40.

CHAPTER 2

Poetry

This chapter is intended as a concise overview of the development of verse for children since the late seventeenth century. The first problem to confront is the difficulty of determining what children's poetry actually is. It is a problem that has defeated many poets and critics.[1] Is it a question of subject matter? Or language, tone, form or style? Or is it a question of the audience that the poet intended to reach? If so, what about those poems that were written for adults, but have since become 'anchored to the children's verse tradition by a kind of gravitational pull' as one recent anthologist puts it?[2] Certainly, anthologies of children's verse have always been full of poems that were originally intended for adults, like James Greenwood's compilation *The Virgin Muse* (1722), designed for 'young gentlemen and ladies' but providing them with the work of Milton and Dryden. Indeed, some anthologies, like Coventry Patmore's *The Children's Garland* (1862), have made a boast of excluding any poem first written for children. And many children have enjoyed 'adult verse'. Anne of Green Gables, for instance, particularly loved 'poetry that gives you a crinkly feeling up and down your back' by eighteenth-century poets now read by few adults let alone children.[3] Then of course gender, class, location and age will have played a part in determining what constitutes children's poetry, and its definition will have changed over time. Probably the majority of the verse that was once thought perfectly suited to the needs or wants of children would now be neither enjoyed by them nor prescribed for them by adults.

This is certainly the case with almost all the verse written for children before the Victorian period. Modern anthologies sometimes include a smattering of eighteenth-century and Romantic-era poems, but they generally get into their stride only with Robert Browning ('The Pied Piper of Hamelin', 1842) and Edward Lear (*A Book of Nonsense*, 1846), or in America, Henry Wadsworth Longfellow (*The Song of Hiawatha*, 1854). Earlier children's poetry is generally now characterised as 'concerned with religious and moral education', with the corollary 'that actual childhood is being completely bypassed'.[4] Even Morag Styles, whose history of children's poetry champions several early texts, takes this line. She contends that until Robert Louis Stevenson's *A Child's Garden of Verses* (1885), 'Children's verse was still weighed down by adults' determination to instill a code of good manners, conventional behaviour and religious observance in the young.'[5] Pre-nineteenth-century children's poems, as the introduction to *The Oxford Book of Children's Verse in America* puts it, 'appear to twentieth-century eyes wholly impossible for children.'[6]

The earliest verse written solely for children was undeniably extremely devout. John Bunyan's *Country Rhimes for Children* (1686), more often known as *Divine Emblems* or *A Book for Boys and Girls*, and Isaac Watts' *Divine Songs Attempted in Easy Language for the Use of Children* (1715) are the best-known examples. Both writers were concerned primarily with children's inherently sinful nature and used their poetry to remind readers about the imminence of death. They were determined to discipline and educate the reader, using poetry as the vehicle. But if Bunyan and Watts emphatically do not participate in our modern concept of childhood, they do share many of our poetic values. Styles, for instance, commends Bunyan's 'lyrical use of language', and Patricia Demers speaks highly of Watts' 'graceful prosody and sweetness of tone' and 'inimitable gentleness'. Their conscious fashioning of their verse to suit children's tastes and abilities has also been admired. Heather Glen is impressed by Bunyan's efforts to see the world as a child might see it; Styles congratulates Bunyan on understanding 'children's need for play'. Demers argues that 'only a poet of great

compassion and delicacy' – like Watts – 'would have attempted to
relate the major events of Christian salvation in the form of a
lullaby', as he does in 'A Cradle Hymn':

> Hush, my dear, lie still and slumber!
>   Holy angels guard thy bed!
> Heavenly blessings without number
>   Gently falling on thy head.
>
> . . .
>
> 'Twas to save thee, child, from dying,
>   Save my dear from burning flame,
> Bitter groans, and endless crying,
>   That thy blest Redeemer came.[7]

Both texts, but most obviously Bunyan's, derive from the tradition
of the emblem book in which the verse 'epigram' was supposed to
explicate an accompanying picture. Although emblems were widely
used during the Catholic Counter-Reformation to elucidate the
bible and theology, in the Protestant tradition it was important that
the pictures should be taken from the natural world and from ordinary life. This helps to explain the friendly and familiar tone of
Bunyan's and Watts' verse.[8] The direct engagement with the child
reader links Bunyan and Watts with the work of many of today's
children's poets who are also usually anxious to speak of real life to
real people, and who often use verse and illustration in conjunction,
much like the emblem books. Indeed, Bunyan's and Watts' poetry
lasted much longer than the strict Puritan religiosity from which it
had arisen. After a steady start, Watts' verse sold well even into the
nineteenth century, inspiring William Blake's *Songs of Innocence
and Experience* (1789 and 1794) and remaining well enough known
in the 1860s for it to be parodied in Lewis Carroll's *Alice* books.
Imitations proliferated during the eighteenth century, authors generally offering their work as an addition to Watts' verses not as a
replacement. Perhaps the best was Christopher Smart's final work,
written from prison, *Hymns for the Amusement of Children* (1770), a
collection of emblems chiefly remarkable, critics have suggested, for
a syntactical difficulty that forces the reader actively to engage with
the text.[9] Smart's *Jubilate Agno* ('Rejoice in the Lamb', composed

1758–63), written from the madhouse, is probably his best known piece, and some see it as an important harbinger of the 'golden age' ushered in by *Alice's Adventures in Wonderland* a century later in 1865. Amongst other strange verse it contained Smart's poem in praise of his cat, Jeoffry, still sometimes anthologised despite its very eccentric religious fervour: 'For he is of the tribe of Tiger. . . . For he is a mixture of gravity and waggery . . . . For the divine spirit comes about his body to sustain it in complete cat. . . . For by stroking of him I have found out electricity'.[10]

By and large, though, this kind of devotional verse has been marginalised from the standard histories of children's books because of its ardent and, to some, oppressive piety. But there is certainly a case for saying that early collections of poetry for children, such as John Marchant's two-hundred page *Puerilia: or, Amusements for the Young* (1751), ought to be considered as just as important in the history of children's literature as the much more celebrated mid-eighteenth-century innovations in prose produced by John Newbery. One definition of children's literature might be that it concerns itself with children's lives and views the world from their point of view. Marchant said he would do just that, providing verse for children that is 'adapted to their own Way of thinking, and to the Occurrences that happen within their own little Sphere of Action', as well as being composed 'in as pleasant and humorous a Stile' as he could manage. Hence his poems are about dolls and cricket, ice-skating and new dresses, though they remain devout.[11] John Wright's even earlier *Spiritual Songs for Children* (1727) is also interesting. One poem, 'A Poetical Exercise on the Author's Journey into Middlesex, and to the famous City of London', is a scathing attack on the impiety of metropolitan life, but also offers a description of the city that must have been intriguing to many children:

> *London*! What's *London*? Tis a World of Pride,
> Frizels and Furbelows on ev'ry Side;
> Patches like Moles, and powder'd Wiggs like Snow,
> Ladies like Peacocks with their Gallants go.[12]

With its talk of the 'Beasts and Birds, Fishes and Serpents keen' that can be seen in the natural history collections at Gresham

College, the armour at the Tower of London, the 'Mad, Distracted, and . . . Lunatick' at Bedlam, and the '*Jews* and *Gentiles*' who 'worship their own Way, | Some chant with Organs, and with Whirlgigs pray', the poem is a sort of a travelogue in the tradition of Thomas Boreman's slightly later *Gigantick Histories* books about the 'Curiosities of London' (1740–43) or even modern picture-books like Richard Scarry's, or the *Curious George* series (1941–66) by H. A. and Margret Rey.

However, it is a mistake to imagine that early modern children's encounters with verse were limited to the religious and moral poetry designed especially for them. In fact, verse was everywhere in seventeenth- and eighteenth-century Britain and America, and it would have permeated children's lives in a way that, perhaps, poetry has not done since. It is surely not an overstatement to say that most children led a much richer poetic life in the seventeenth and eighteenth centuries than they do today. The availability of secular and irreligious verse to children is hinted at in Watts' preface to *Divine Songs*. 'Verse was at first design'd for the service of God,' he argued, but 'it hath been wretchedly abused since.'[13] Likewise, Marchant's preface gives an insight into what verse was available to children and how they may have used it: 'no sooner can they read,' he wrote, 'but they are furnished with the most filthy Ribaldry, which they are instructed to con and get by Heart, and when they can sing it to some ordinary Tune, they are made to thrill it with their little Voices in every Company where they are intro-duced'.[14] As for Bunyan, he ashamedly admitted that his boyhood reading had included many ballads.[15] We can only understand the devotional and moral children's poetry that Bunyan, Watts, Marchant and others produced if we recognise it as a reaction to children's immersion in much more profane verse.

Ballads were part of oral culture, but by the sixteenth and seven-teenth centuries in England a great many were in print, either in small anthologies ('garlands'), singly in short pamphlets, or on single large sheets of paper illustrated with simple woodcuts ('broadsides'). Although some were religious, others contained accounts of legendary figures (like Robin Hood), commemorated topical events (such as murders or political scandals), or offered short verse narratives. Some were perfectly designed to appeal to children. For example, *The Friar and the Boy*, in print since the sixteenth century, tells of a mistreated boy's sudden empowerment when he acquires a magical charm that makes people break wind uncontrollably. He uses it without compunction to gain vengeance against his cruel stepmother:

> And then a cracker she let fly,
>   That almost shook the ground.
> She blush'd as they made merry sport,
>   The little boy reply'd,
> My mother has a good report
>   You hear at her backside,
> Sure had there been a cannon-ball,
>   With such a force it flew,
> It would have beaten down the wall,
>   Perhaps the chimney too.[16]

The Friar and the Boy is characteristic of many ballads in its coarseness, as well as its longevity. But it is also typical for its clear narrative and its use (in most eighteenth-century versions) of the simple but compelling 'ballad metre': organised in quatrains, rhyming a-b-a-b, and with four accented syllables in the first and third lines, and three in the third and fourth.

Besides their encounters with ballads many early modern children would have come across a great deal of poetry in their education. John Locke, in *Some Thoughts Concerning Education* (1693), had recommended *Aesop's Fables* and *Reynard the Fox* as the books most likely to draw children into learning and both these, by the eighteenth century, were generally published in verse. The educational programme set out half a century later by John Vowler in 'The Young Student's Scheme' (1743) was much more demanding, but retained a place for poetry and was itself set out in verse form. 'I'll tell you, Sir, how I design | My Point in Learning to attain', the poem begins, before listing the details of the self-imposed curriculum: scripture, history, geography, astronomy and, on '*Thursdays* I'll Poetry rehearse, | Those Songs and Hymns I've learnt in Verse.'[17] If from the social elite, it is likely that this conscientious student's Thursday lesson would have included mostly Greek and

Latin poetry, although by the middle of the eighteenth century many educationalists were insisting that 'boys should begin with the *English* poetry' (usually the work of Edmund Spenser and John Milton, James Thomson and Alexander Pope).[18] Vowler wrote in verse, he said, because it 'was easier learnt and longer retain'd by Children than Prose'.[19] In accordance with this widely-held view, it is quite likely that pupils would have found some of their textbooks for geography, history and many other subjects (not to mention religion) also set out in verse. By the early nineteenth century, children's books were teaching almost every subject through poetry. Charlotte Finch's *The Gamut and Time-Table in Verse*, for instance, sets out to explain the theory of music through cheerful lines like these: 'Then of Demisemiquavers, thirty-two in a line, | With the Ten and six semiquavers make even time.'[20] It was not only children from affluent backgrounds who were receiving an education through poetry. Thomas Gills's *Useful and Delightful Instructions by Way of Dialogue Between the Master and his Scholar . . . Composed in Verse* (1712) was 'recommended to the Use of Children of both Sexes, train'd up in the Charity-Schools'.

Besides its use in school, there is evidence that mothers were using poetry in the more informal education of their children at home. The classic example is Jane Johnson, the wife of a Buckinghamshire clergyman, who, in the 1740s, produced a collection of home-made cards and books to help teach her children to read. On one card, for instance, Johnson meticulously drew two women and one man in very elegant dress, placing above them these verses, presumably her own invention, designed to amuse and instruct (in national prejudices, if nothing else):

> Such short Gowns as these, are much used in France,
> And the Men and the Women cut capers and dance.
> The Ladys they Paint, and their backsides they show.
> The Men hop and skip, and each one is a Beau
> Would you see men like monkeys, to France you must go.[21]

It is not unlikely that many other elite and middle-class mothers (and fathers) also wrote verse for their own children. Certainly, many eighteenth-century women writers included poetry directed at their children in their published collections. Part of her 1734 *Poems on Several Occasions*, for instance, was Mary Barber's 'Written for My Son, and Spoken by Him at His First Putting on Breeches' (boys wore petticoats, like their sisters, until they were 'breeched' at around five or six years old).

Even children unlucky enough to lack poetic parents would still have encountered verse at home through, if nothing else, what we now call nursery rhymes. Their history is extremely obscure, largely because they originally circulated in oral form, but what is known has been very clearly set out by Iona and Peter Opie. As they explain, the earliest published references to such still familiar verses as 'Boys and Girls Come Out to Play' and 'The Lion and the Unicorn' are often in eighteenth-century mock-serious discussions of their supposed political or philosophical meanings. Only towards the end of the century were they being collected by scholars genuinely interested in this poetry as folklore. Seventy-nine nursery rhymes were collected into *Gammer Gurton's Garland, or, the Nursery Parnassus* in 1784 by the antiquarian Joseph Ritson. Nursery rhymes had been published especially for children well before this though. Mary Cooper's *Tommy Thumb's Pretty Song Book* (c.1744) had contained 'Bah, Bah, a black sheep', 'Who did kill Cock Robin' and many other nursery classics. *Mother Goose's Melody, or Sonnets from the Cradle*, probably first published in the mid-1760s, by John Newbery or his nephew, was advertised as containing 'the most celebrated songs and lullabies of the old British nurses; calculated to amuse children, and to excite them to sleep.'[22] Other similar collections rapidly followed, becoming popular in both Britain and America. Some verses that were apparently original, written especially for these volumes but very much in the style of the traditional nursery rhymes, were also included. In *The Top Book of All, for Little Masters and Misses* (c.1760), for instance, this satire on boastfulness appeared, under the title 'Telling *Tommy Thumb* a Story':

> Little, pretty, Jacky Nory,
> Telling Tommy Thumb a Story,
> How he's gotten into Breeches,
> And his Pockets full of Riches,

And how he shall on Cock-horse ride,
With Sword and Gun girt by his Side,
And that he will with his great Gun,
Kill all the French when they do run,
And with his Sword he will them cut,
As small as Herbs for Porridge Pot;
Nay more he vows, and which is worse,
He'll cut them smaller than a Horse,
And with one Blow cut off a Head,
And send the Backside for to beg.
But pray, says Tom, first kill that Mouse,
That eats my Cakes, and stinks the House.
Not I, says Jack, Lud, how it frights,
Let's run away before it bites.[23]

Jacky Nory's insistence that he has 'gotten into Breeches' would have spoken specifically to a boy's pride at going through that rite of passage. Moreover, even though some slight moral warning against vanity does remain, it was clearly designed primarily to amuse. Evidently by the 1760s and '70s, the market could accommodate poetry that was both especially for children and more or less exclusively entertaining.

By the end of the eighteenth century then, child readers had an enormous range of verse available to them, some of it written especially for them, some of it 'inherited' from adults; some of it derived from folk traditions, much of it newly-minted; some designed to instruct, some to entertain. Access to these different kinds of verse would have been dependent on age, affluence, gender, religion, education, literacy and location. The number of volumes of children's poetry began to increase in the early nineteenth century. New varieties developed too: amongst others, nonsense verse, narrative poems and sentimental verse. Fundamentally, though, the children's poetry of the nineteenth and twentieth centuries, even these ostensibly new kinds of verse, may be regarded as continuations of traditions that had emerged in the eighteenth century. Religious verse certainly survived. Not only were Bunyan and Watts still read, but much more of a similar style was produced. Most of it is now forgotten, save only, perhaps, those poems that lived on as hymns:

Cecil Frances Alexander's 'All Things Bright and Beautiful' and 'Once in Royal David's City', for example, first published in 1848 in her *Hymns for Little Children* (likewise Christina Rossetti's 'In the Bleak Midwinter', 1872, and Eleanor Farjeon's 'Morning Has Broken', 1931). The sort of simple rhymes that featured in *Tommy Thumb's Pretty Song Book* and *Gammer Gurton's Garland* provide another example of a verse tradition that has survived from the early modern period (or before) into the present. They have continued to evolve, through what Iona Opie calls 'the process of fission and fusion . . . the alteration of words and phrases through misunderstanding, failure of memory, or deliberate innovation', so that children still recite versions, or at least modern counterparts, as playground rhymes.[24] The cadences, colloquiality and jumbled (and often subversive) values of this kind of children's popular or 'street' poetry have also been self-consciously taken up by a variety of modern poets. Eleanor Farjeon sought to replicate the feel of nursery rhymes in much of her early twentieth-century children's poetry (*Nursery Rhymes of London Town*, 1916–17), and a good proportion of A.A. Milne's verse is in the same tradition: 'I think I am a Muffin Man. I haven't got a bell, | I haven't got the muffin things that muffin people sell'.[25] More recently, authors of so-called 'urchin verse', popular, especially in Britain, since the 1970s, have set out to reproduce the voices, subjects and general spirit of playground rhymes. This is from Allan Ahlberg's *Heard it in the Playground* (1989):

> We seen 'em in the cloakroom, Miss –
> Ann Cram and Alan Owen
> Tryin' to have the longest kiss –
> They had the stopwatch goin'!'[26]

This kind of poem, written by an adult in imitation of children's own 'street' verse, deliberately carnivalesque but still just noticeably infused with an adult's sensibility, is a direct descendent of the account of 'Jacky Nory, | Telling Tommy Thumb a Story' published over two centuries earlier.

Another verse tradition that began early but continues still is the cautionary tale. Many were included in the most successful collection of the early nineteenth century, *Original Poems for Infant Minds* (1804–5), written largely by the sisters Ann and Jane Taylor. Here boys who play truant from school end up being torn apart on mill-wheels, and girls who raise false alarms are burned in raging fires. The aim is instructive of course, but the lack of proportion between the calamitous punishment and the minor crime is ludicrous today and may well have been laughable to many readers even when these verses were first published. The neatness of the verse that contains these moral fables only emphasises their absurdity. It is no surprise, then, that parodies were produced, most famously Heinrich Hoffmann's *Struwwelpeter*, translated from the German as *Shock-Headed Peter* in 1848. What is more curious is that others – Hilaire Belloc (*Cautionary Tales for Children*, 1907) and Roald Dahl (*Revolting Rhymes*, 1982), for example – were eager to write similar parodies long after the original moral verses had become extinct. They were, it seems, expecting that many of their readers were still being berated in verse. Moreover, however tongue-in-cheek their poetry was, it was not wholly lacking a didactic dimension. Hoffmann admitted that he wrote such poems as 'The Dreadful Story of Harriet and the Matches' to impress the reader 'more than hundreds of general warnings', as well as to amuse.[27] Similarly, the Oompa-Loompas' songs, gloating over the fate of each sinning child in Dahl's *Charlie and the Chocolate Factory* (1964), are very droll but also expressive of the author's genuine disdain for over-indulged children: 'Augustus Gloop! Augustus Gloop! | The great big greedy nincompoop!', sing the Oompa-Loompas as he is apparently drowned in a lake of molten chocolate. They explain:

> How long could we allow this beast
> To gorge and guzzle, feed and feast
> On everything he wanted to?
> Great Scott! It simply wouldn't do![28]

With its vestigial didactic impulse, and its celebration of salutary violence, Dahl's poetry is not so very different from original cautionary verse of the early nineteenth century, which itself owed much to Puritan warnings of the wages of sin: 'There is a dreadful

Hell, | And everlasting Pains, | There Sinners must with Devils dwell | In Darkness, Fire, and Chains.'[29]

The history of nonsense verse reveals another pattern of gradual evolution rather than sudden innovation by iconoclastic geniuses.[30] Edward Lear and Lewis Carroll were undeniably brilliant, but there were many antecedents. Whimsical anthropomorphic poems like William Roscoe's *The Butterfly's Ball and the Grasshopper's Feast* (1806), or verses based on folk characters, such as Sarah Catherine Martin's *The Comic Adventures of Old Mother Hubbard and her Dog* (1805), are two possible sources. And, as Styles notes, even in the eighteenth century, nonsense 'was already a thriving form in chapbook culture'.[31] One such chapbook was *The World Turned Upside Down*, in which verses and images depicted such inversions as fish turned anglers and stags turned huntsmen. The verse could be comic. In an early nineteenth-century version, a man attempting to eat himself remarks 'If I once get my legs in | As far as my knees, | The rest will slip down | With a great deal of ease'.[32] It was also somewhat subversive, proffering that fantasy that the disempowered might one day become dominant. Being largely subordinate themselves, children may well have enjoyed *The World Turned Upside Down* long before a version was published especially for them in 1810. This was *Signor Topsy-Turvey's Wonderful Magic Lantern* by Ann and Jane Taylor. Although the subversion was constrained – the power inversions being presented as slides projected by a comical travelling showman – a rebellious element did remain. The hare in 'The Cook Cooked', enraged by the idea that '*hares* should be nutrition', 'brew'd sedition' and fomented a conspiracy of all the other animals in the larder. Other episodes were more in the tradition of moral literature. 'Children at War, and Cats and Dogs at Peace' attempted to shame children into good behaviour by demonstrating that their petulance was just as ludicrous as a fish wanting to live out of water, say.[33] Although both the subversion and the morality are lacking from Lear's verse, the foundations of the nonsense, especially in his early work, remain largely the same: the distortion, exaggeration or inversion of reality. His Jumblies (*Nonsense Songs, Stories, Botany, and Alphabets*, 1870), for instance, go to sea in that least watertight of objects, a sieve, while the Owl and the Pussycat – an unusual ménage in itself – buy, for a shilling, the metal loop put through a pig's nose for their wedding ring, though which one of them wears it, and how, is not made clear. What Lear added to the formula, and Carroll developed further, were more and madder logic reversals, the inclusion of ludicrously irrelevant characters and objects, many neologisms and bad puns, and much linguistic experimentation. The technique was to reach its zenith in the two Alice books (1865 and 1871) with poems like 'The Lobster Quadrille' and 'Jabberwocky'.

Curiously, in the 1870s, both Lear and Carroll seem to have retreated from their earlier playfully experimental verse, preferring to encase their nonsense within longer narratives. Lear's 'The Dong with the Luminous Nose' (from *Laughable Lyrics*, 1876) is a self-pitying account of a heartbroken creature who fashions for himself a nose like a lamp so that he may search for his lost Jumbly Girl. The nonsense of Carroll's *The Hunting of the Snark* (1876) is more like the world of Samuel Beckett's *Waiting for Godot* (1952) than *Through the Looking-Glass*. Carroll called it 'An Agony in Eight Fits', and he sends his miscellaneous characters on a grim, apparently dangerous and largely unexplained quest to find a Snark. The poem's final statement (the single line that came suddenly to Carroll, inspiring him to write the poem), 'For the Snark *was* a Boojum, you see', somehow conveys both their fear and frustration at the futility of the voyage.[34] Whether light or dark in tone, it was Carroll's and Lear's technical ability to write really compelling verse that allowed such flights of nonsense. The rhythm, rhyme and pace of the poetry carries the reader on even when the words themselves make no sense. This is the paradox at the heart of good nonsense poetry: that the apparent freedom, and even randomness, have to be carefully restrained and regulated within firm verse structures if they are not to disorientate the reader. Only the best nonsense verse written since – by A. A. Milne, Mervyn Peake and Spike Milligan in Britain, say, or Ogden Nash and Shel Silverstein in America – can match these two halves of Carroll's and Lear's achievement: the poetic proficiency, and the linguistic inventiveness and inversion of the normal.

With roots in the early modern period, but its most celebrated and enduring examples materialising in the mid-nineteenth century, the history of the children's narrative poem parallels the history of nonsense verse. Longfellow's *The Song of Hiawatha* (1855) or 'Paul Revere's Ride' (1863) are classic examples, and their strong narratives and driving rhythms clearly show their antecedents in the ballad tradition. The former derived its complicated metre from ancient, orally transmitted Finnish verse-narratives. The latter plainly signalled its author's aspiration to the ballad tradition with its first stanza:

> Listen, my children, and you shall hear
> Of the midnight ride of Paul Revere,
> On the eighteenth of April, in Seventy-five;
> Hardly a man is now alive
> Who remembers that famous day and year.[35]

As in the early modern period, many of the nineteenth- and twenti-eth-century ballads best loved by children were not necessarily orig-inally written for them. Somehow, at least as far as anthologists of children's poetry have been concerned, they have crossed an invisi-ble divide and become part of children's literature. Thus, not only are poems such as Robert Browning's 'How They Brought the Good News from Ghent to Aix' (1845) and John Masefield's 'Sea Fever' (1902) now more likely to be found in collections of children's than adult verse, but, apparently purely because of their strong narrative, melodramatic tone, and driving rhythm, children's anthologies feature more recondite and even disturbing material such as Samuel Taylor Coleridge's 'Rime of the Ancient Mariner' (1798) or Alfred Noyes's intense account of a woman tied up, sexually assaulted and killing herself, 'The Highwayman' (1913). Other poets have delib-erately set out to capture the spirit of early modern popular litera-ture. For example, some of the poetry of Charles Causley, celebrated as 'probably the greatest exponent of the modern ballad', is very much in the tradition of texts like *The Friar and the Boy*, both in its playfulness and delight in bodily function:

> King Foo Foo sat upon his throne
> Dressed in his royal closes,
> While all around his courtiers stood
> With clothes-pegs on their noses.

'This action strange,' King Foo Foo said,
'My mind quite discomposes,
Though vulgar curiosity
A good king never shoses.'

But to the court it was as clear
As poetry or prose is:
King Foo Foo had not had a bath
Since goodness only knoses.[36]

The ballad form is extremely adaptable, and, if it is less popular than it once was, good examples were still being published even in an age when free verse and 'street poetry' celebrating the quotidian above the extraordinary, have come to dominate. Mick Gowar's 'Rat Trap' (1992), for example, is a reworking of Browning's 'The Pied Piper of Hamelin' (1842), promising to reveal what actually happened. In this version, the plague of rats is invented by the mayor to distract the townspeople from his rapacious regime. The Pied Piper – more usually employed for 'Street theatre, kid's parties' – is hired to exterminate the rats, which he does by arming all the boys with sticks and leading them in a 'Rat-killing Bash-up, and barbecue'. In part, this is conventional postmodernism, using the intertextuality for humour, voicing the reader's likely scepticism about the sort of supernatural events Browning describes, and generally trying to destabilise the authority of traditional narrative poetry. It might also be taken as a wry fable, commenting on the propensity of corrupt men to blame nature for their failings. But it is more sinister too. After the massacre of the rats, 'A taste for bloodletting started to grow', and the Piper threatens to lead the boys against the city elders: 'Let's finish the job we started today: | Cleanse Hamelin Town properly!':

A forest of sticks was raised in salute.
In reply, the Piper lifted his flute . . .
'I give in,' said the mayor. 'I'll pay you your fee.
But first, our dear children. You must set them free
From this terrible spell.
Just look at them – there!

How their lips seem to snarl,
How their eyes seem to stare.'
The Piper just grinned: 'Some things can't be undone:
We've taught them the pleasure of killing for *fun*.[37]

Much may be read into the poem's description of the scapegoating of an innocent group described as vermin, and the ability of a charismatic leader to beguile a mob into mass violence and the overthrow of the legitimate, if incompetent, government. For more astute readers, the parallels with the rise of Nazism in 1930s Germany will be inescapable.

Given its worldly cynicism, it is surprising to find that Gowar's 'Rat Trap' ends like this:

> And so saying, the Devil
> went
> back
> down
> to
> Hell.[38]

It might be said that the sudden introduction of the supernatural neutralises the poem's political satire. But it is the arrangement of words to resemble steps that seems most curious. Playing with layout and typography is characteristic of much modern children's poetry: Benjamin Zephaniah's 'According to My Mood' (1994), for example, mixes different fonts and upper and lower case letters, and adds punctuation marks and misspellings, to argue that 'I have *poetic* license, i WriTe thE way i waNt.'[39] But Gowar's device is rather twee and resembles nothing so much as A. A. Milne at his most saccharine – the sort of poem that was satirised with pitiless precision by J. B. Morton:

> Hush, hush, nobody cares,
> Christopher Robin
> has
> fallen
> downstairs.[40]

Opinion is divided on Milne's two books of poetry, *When We Were Very Young* (1924) and *Now We Are Six* (1927). Although they were and remain hugely successful, both in terms of sales and their absorption into popular culture, some critics have derided what they see as their sentimentality, whimsicality, idealisation of childhood and the cosy world they present of upper middle class British life. Others (including Milne himself) have sought to defend the poems by pointing out how easy it is to misread them. 'Vespers', for instance, depicts Christopher Robin kneeling at the end of his bed, piously praying for his mother, father and nursemaid. This might be thought a corny representation of what Humphrey Carpenter has called the 'Beautiful Child', a Victorian idealisation of a child 'distinguished . . . by an almost heavenly innocence'. But, as Carpenter goes on to say, although Christopher Robin 'occasionally repeats one of the formulas he has been taught', he is not actually praying, and is constantly being distracted by the material world around him:

> *God bless Mummy*. I know that's right.
> Wasn't it fun in the bath to-night?
> The cold's so cold, and the hot's so hot.
> Oh! *God bless Daddy* – I quite forgot.

Carpenter argues that the poem reveals Milne's hostility to formal religion, and that its ending – an emphatic '*God bless me*' – reveals the natural and ruthless egotism of children, exploding any notion of childhood innocence or holiness.[41] Certainly 'Vespers' is an extremely sensual poem, for it is always the child's delight in what he has seen, heard or touched that distracts him from his prayers.

Childhood angst is also quite often observable in Milne's poetry, lurking behind the façade of sentimentality. It is tempting to read the famous poem 'Disobedience', for example, as an expression of a boy's Oedipal anxiety. It begins by telling the reader that James James Morrison Morrison Weatherby George Dupree 'Took great | Care of his Mother, | Though he was only three.' When she disobeys his injunction not to go down to the end of the town 'if you don't go down with me', she goes missing and, despite the reward offered by King John (who somehow enters the poem from another compartment of the boy's imagination), 'She hasn't been heard of since.' The poem dramatises a boy's fear that his mother will desert him for the adult world (she wears a 'golden gown' to make her disobedient trip, both its goldenness and gowniness being more likely to appeal to men than boys). The curious final stanza, which the reader is instructed to recite 'very softly', is a funeral dirge for lost mothers (it even replaces the term itself with 'M*****'). Only with its very final word does the poem offer reassurance, especially if it is being read aloud by a child in the company of a parent, reaffirming the child's centrality with a capitalised, shouted, 'ME!'[42]

Neither the sentimentality of Milne's verse, nor its attempt to recapture what it was like to be a child, was entirely new. The poetry of Robert Louis Stevenson, whose *A Child's Garden of Verses* was published in 1885, is a clear influence, so too perhaps was the work of Christina Rossetti (*Sing-Song: A Nursery Rhyme Book*, 1872) and their American counterpart, Eugene Field (*Love Songs of Childhood*, 1896). With their direct address to the child reader, and idealisation of childhood, all were the heirs of the best eighteenth-century poets like Christopher Smart and William Blake. Neither subject matter, nor form, nor tone would rule out Smart's 'Hymn for Saturday' (1770), for example, from *A Child's Garden of Verses* or *Now We Are Six*:

> Now's the time for mirth and play,
> Saturday's an holiday;
> Praise to heaven unceasing yield,
> I've found a lark's nest in the field.[43]

What Stevenson did pioneer, and Milne developed, was the representation of the individual child's anxieties, particularly the worries of sensitive and solitary children. Many of Milne's poems deal with loneliness and isolation ('Halfway Down', 'Come Out With Me', 'Solitude'), which seems to reflect a perception on Milne's part that childhood is a state in which one is largely ignored – requiring the compensation of imaginary friends perhaps, such as Winnie-the-Pooh. An entire section of Stevenson's *A Child's Garden of Verses* (1885) is called 'The Child Alone'. They too tell of imaginary friends ('The Unseen Playmate') and make-believe worlds ('The Little Land', 'Block Cities'). They also exhibit a frustration that parents cannot or will not understand the world of childhood. Instead, 'They sit around a home and talk and sing, | And do not play at anything', which leaves the child isolated and, on occasion, imagining themselves to be their parents' enemies:

> I see the others far away
> As if in firelit camp they lay,
> And I, like to an Indian scout,
> Around their party prowled about.[44]

Superficially the poems seem to be happy accounts of childhood games, but they simultaneously articulate a child's horror of being abandoned. They plead for somebody to join in the game, or at least to notice it. What is more, they betray a fear that childhood must end. This is the beginning of final poem in the collection:

> As from the house your mother sees
> You playing round the garden trees,
> So you may see, if you will look
> Through the windows of this book,
> Another child, far, far away,
> And in another garden, play.
> But do not think you can at all,
> By knocking on the window, call
> That child to hear you.

Titled 'To Any Reader', this was designed to show young readers that the author had himself once been a child, and that his adulthood is a fate that awaits them too.[45] From the adult point of view, it is a lament that childhood has passed and cannot be regained and a rebuke to those who do not value it, a familiar refrain in nineteenth-century poetry from Wordsworth to Carroll's more succinct lament:

> I'd give all wealth that years have piled
> The slow result of life's decay

To be once more a little child
For one bright summer day.[46]

Carroll may not have written this specifically for children, but the
self-pity of grown-ups is at the heart of much Victorian children's
verse too.

It is largely because of this rather creepy idealisation of childhood that many critics now regard *A Child's Garden of Verses* with
ambivalence if not hostility. John Goldthwaite complains that 'No-
one has ever lied up a stereotype so sweetly'.[47] And Stevenson's
attempt to ventriloquise the children's voices provides a perfect
illustration of Jacqueline Rose's contention that children's literature is necessarily an adult fantasy of how they would wish childhood to be, artfully designed to seduce children into compliance.[48]
There is no doubt, though, that Stevenson changed the history of
children's poetry. Poems written from the point of view of the child,
and representing their games, imaginings and attitudes, prepon-
derated throughout the first half of the twentieth century, appearing in single-authored, volume-length sequences, loosely grouped
round one or two themes or motifs. Noteworthy British examples
include Walter De la Mare's *Songs of Childhood* (1902) and *Peacock
Pie* (1913) and Eleanor Farjeon's many volumes (her most famous
collection was *The Children's Bells*, 1957), as well as Milne. Peter
Hunt has characterised the children's poetry of this period as 'conservative and regressive'.[49] Anthologists prepared to look beyond
the usual suspects can show this not to be the case – in *The New
Oxford Book of Children's Verse* (1996), for instance, experimental
children's poems by the likes of Ezra Pound, Gertrude Stein,
Wilfred Owen, e. e. cummings, Langston Hughes and Stevie Smith
are interspersed with the more traditional output of Milne, Noyes
and Kipling. Nevertheless, all this material can look rather dowdy
and unadventurous when compared with the new wave of children's
verse that began in the 1970s.

This 'new wave' is now commonly known as 'urchin verse'. It is
poetry that purports to be about modern children and their ordinary lives: playground fights, friendships made and broken, abusive
families, boredom at school and so on. It is set in the present, not a
romanticised past. Its protagonists are lower- and middle-class

children: not actual street-urchins, but not brought up by nurse-maids, and not the owners of extensive private grounds, and certainly not adults. It is written, by and large, in free verse, rather than in traditional metres and rhyme structures. Slang, the vernacular, and children's authentic speech-patterns have replaced more self-consciously poetic language. All this sounds radical, an impression supported by the criticism that 'urchin verse' has provoked. Commentators have worried that the price of accessibility is ephemerality and disposability, and that the squibbishness of modern children's poetry will dissuade young readers from ever graduating onto 'real', 'classic' poetry that is (they say) beautiful and multifaceted in a way that urchin verse is not.[50] The most perceptive critics have remarked that this new kind of verse is, more than anything else, a response to the way that childhood has been culturally constructed. Poetry is regarded as being 'profound and static, delicate and reflective', says Peter Hunt, while children are now generally imagined to be the opposite: 'shallow and dynamic, robust and outgoing'. It is from this disjunction that this new form of poetry has emerged, full of 'quick, flip gags that adults assume that children will like, precisely (and demeaningly) because it is junk in adult terms.'[51] For Alison Lurie too, the danger is that by providing children with 'easier' verse, modern poets may be writing to fit a false construction of modern childhood (short attention span; low-brow tastes) and that this will be self-perpetuating, making the false construction real and infantilising generations of readers.[52]

There is probably no need to worry. For one thing, the best authors of 'urchin verse' – amongst others, Gareth Owen, Allan Ahlberg, Benjamin Zephaniah and Michael Rosen (whose collection, *Mind Your Own Business*, is sometimes said to have begun the trend in 1974) – have produced poetry which is colloquial, quotidian and accessible, but which is also thought-provoking and multi-layered, sensitive and artistic. Here, for instance, is Roger McGough capturing the feelings of a child on his or her first day at school:

A millionbillionwillion miles from home
Waiting for the bell to go. (To go where?)
Why are they all so big, other children?

So noisy? So much at home they
must have been born in uniform.
Lived all their lives in playgrounds.
Spent the years inventing games
that don't let me in. Games
that are rough, that swallow you up.
And the railings.
All around, the railings.
Are they to keep out wolves and monsters?
Things that carry off and eat children?
Things you don't take sweets from?
Perhaps they're to stop us getting out
Running away from the lessins. Lessin.
What does a lessin look like?
Sounds small and slimy.
They keep them in glassrooms.
Whole rooms made out of glass. Imagine.

I wish I could remember my name
Mummy said it would come in useful.
Like wellies. When there's puddles.
Yellowwellies. I wish she was here.
I think perhaps my name is sewn on somewhere
Perhaps the teacher will read it for me.
Tea'cher. The one who makes the tea.[53]

If the wordplay here is a little feeble, blatantly introduced to tickle
young readers (or listeners), there is ample compensation in the
careful creation of a mood of bewilderment and suppression. The
uniforms, the railings, the loss of identity (except through a sewn-on
label) make the school into a prison camp, but in which even fellow
inmates seem agents of oppression. All readers will be able to associ-
ate with this child, stuck half-way between the cosiness of mother,
home and yellow wellington boots, and the strangeness of school
with its strange lexicon and new social networks. This is a poem that
might defamiliarise the surroundings of those who have already
become habituated to school, prompt a sense of autobiography, or
even encourage empathy with those just arriving. Like many of the

best of these poems, it somehow manages to be menacing and cheerful, instructive and fun.

In any case, 'urchin verse' has not dominated late twentieth- and
early twenty-first century children's poetry as much as its critics
contend. Other, more traditional forms have co-existed. Notable
British children's poets of the same period include Ted Hughes
(*What is the Truth*, 1984) and John Mole (*Boo to a Goose*, 1987). And
'urchin verse' is, in any case, largely a British development. Shel
Silverstein (*A Light in the Attic*, 1981) and Jack Prelutsky (*The New
Kid on the Block*, 1986), amongst a few others, have provided a
sort of American equivalent, but Glenna Sloan, in her survey of
American verse, has found that most American children's poetry
'stays well within its traditions'.[54] Moreover, new forms of verse
have already developed out of, and away from, the kind of poetry
being written by Rosen, McGough and others in the 1970s and '80s.
Jackie Kay, for example, uses the colloquial language, free verse
forms and everyday subjects of the 'urchin' school – probably to an
even greater extent than McGough or Rosen, for she employs Scots
dialect and takes racism and broken families as two of her principal
themes. But the jokiness has faded, replaced by an exploration of
the complications of modern life and their effects on the developing consciousness. Her verse is still wry but is no longer whimsical.
Here is part of 'What Jenny Knows' from Kay's first collection,
Two's Company (1992):

> 'I didn't come out of my mummy's tummy.
> No I didn't,' I says to my pal Jenny.
> But Jenny says, 'you must have,
> How come?' And I replies,
>
> 'I just didn't. Get it. I didn't.'
> 'Everybody does' says Jenny,
> who is fastly becoming an enemy.
> 'Rubbish,' I say. 'My mummy got me.
> She picked me. She collected me.
>
> I was in a supermarket,
> On the shelf and she took me off it.'
> 'Nonsense,' says Jenny. 'Lies.'

The speaker explains to Jenny that she is adopted:

> 'I know That!' says Jenny,
> 'But you still came out
>
> Somebody's tummy. Somebody
> had to have you. Didn't they?'
> 'Not my mummy. Not my mummy,' I says.
> 'Shut your face. Shut your face.'[55]

It is an everyday conversation between two friends in which nothing is resolved or revealed, but in which a world of conflicting emotions and loyalties are exposed. It is poetry of the street, or the playground, about real children and their real concerns, but it is not jokey or ephemeral. Like all of the best children's poetry of recent decades, it has not reacted to Victorian and Edwardian sentimentality with a too ardent commitment to earthiness and obviousness. Just as Watts or Smart could be gentle and engaging while remaining religious, or Lear and Carroll absurd while remaining decorous and controlled, so Kay and the best contemporary children's poets combine subtlety with immediacy, and realism with weightiness.

In the mid-1980s, Donald Hall wrote in his introduction to *The Oxford Book of Children's Verse in America* that 'contemporary fashions in children's verse, which favour humor and nonsense, will one day seem as quaint as pieties about dead children.'[56] The poetry of the 'urchin' school does not yet seem quaint, and much fine humorous and nonsense verse continues to be written. But the poetry of Kay, and of most of the other poets discussed in this chapter, show how inappropriate it is to organise children's verse into fashions and fads that come and go. The question of what makes good children's poetry has been much discussed and never resolved. For some the key characteristic is the immediate appeal to the senses, without the need for reflection, memory or learning.[57] For others, good children's poetry must have 'simplicity without stupidity'.[58] Some might think that the most important thing is for poems to see things from a child's point of view (even if others point out the impossibility of the endeavour). What is clear, though, is that good children's poetry has been written throughout the last three centuries, and that it is the continuities that are more striking than the changes.

SUMMARY OF KEY POINTS

- Verse was more pervasive in pre-modern culture than today and children would have encountered poetry in almost all aspects of their daily lives: at school, in their devotions, in their homes and on the streets. By the mid-eighteenth century, much of this poetry was being published especially for children and was designed to entertain them.
- Much children's poetry has been condemned as sentimental and twee, but it is sometimes more cynical and satirical about childhood than it first appears, and can explore children's (and adult's) anxieties in surprising depth.
- Poetry written recently to be more accessible and relevant to children has been condemned by some critics as unsophisticated and ephemeral, but the best of this verse is as subtle and weighty as it is punchy and immediate.
- What actually constitutes children's poetry has always been uncertain, and subject matter, original intended audience, language and genre do not offer certain guidance.
- Changing constructions of childhood have affected ideas of children's verse, but formal, tonal and stylistic continuities are often more striking than the innovations.

NOTES

1. For some thoughts on definition see John Mole, 'Questions of Poetry', *Signal*, 74 (1994), 86–92 and Glenna Sloan, 'But is it poetry?', *Children's Literature in Education*, 32 (2001), 45–56.
2. Neil Philip, 'Introduction', *The New Oxford Book of Children's Verse* (Oxford: Oxford University Press, 1996), p. xxv.
3. L. M. Montgomery, *Anne of Green Gables* (Wordsworth Classics, [1908] 1994), p. 45.

4. Peter Hunt, *Children's Literature* (Oxford: Blackwell, 2001), p. 295.
5. Morag Styles, *From the Garden to the Street. An Introduction to 300 Years of Poetry for Children* (London: Cassell, 1998), p. 1.
6. Donald Hall (ed.), *The Oxford Book of Children's Verse in America* (New York: Oxford University Press, 1985), p. xxiv.
7. Styles, *From the Garden to the Street*, p. 9; Patricia Demers, *From Instruction to Delight: An Anthology of Children's Literature to 1850*, 2nd edn (Don Mills, Ontario: Oxford University Press Canada, 2004), p. 77; Heather Glen, *Vision and Disenchantment* (Cambridge: Cambridge University Press, 1983), pp. 10–11; Isaac Watts, *Divine Songs Attempted in Easy Language, for the Use of Children* (London: Richard Ford, [1715] 1727), pp. 47–50.
8. Christopher Hill, *A Turbulent, Seditious and Factious People: John Bunyan and his Church 1628–1688* (Oxford: Clarendon Press, 1989), pp. 267–74.
9. Mark Booth, 'Syntax and Paradigm in Smart's *Hymns for the Amusement of Children*', in *Christopher Smart and the Enlightenment*, ed. Clement Hawes (New York: St. Martin's Press, 1999), pp. 67–81.
10. Smart, *Jubilate Agno* (written 1758–63, published 1939), in *From Instruction to Delight*, ed. Demers, pp. 273–4.
11. John Marchant, *Puerilia: or, Amusements for the Young* (London: P. Stevens, 1751), pp. v–vi.
12. John Wright, *Spiritual Songs for Children: or, Poems on Several Subjects and Occasions* (London: Joseph Marshall, 1727), pp. 7–11.
13. Watts, *Divine Songs*, p. [xv].
14. Marchant, *Puerilia*, p. vi.
15. John Bunyan, *A Few Sighs from Hell, or The Groans of a damned Soul* (London: Ralph Wood, 1658), pp. 156–7.
16. *The Friar and Boy . . . Part the First* (no publication details but c.1760), pp. 11–12.
17. John Vowler, *An Essay for Instructing Children on Various Useful and Uncommon Subjects* (Exeter: printed for the author, 1743), p. 38.

18. James Barclay, *A Treatise on Education* (Edinburgh: James Cochran, 1743), p. 131.
19. Vowler, *An Essay for Instructing Children*, p. viii.
20. Charlotte Finch, *The Gamut and Time-Table in Verse* (London: Dean and Munday, c.1825), p. 35.
21. Set 21, no. 9, Jane Johnson MSS., Lilly Library, Indiana University, Bloomington, Indiana, online at http://www.dlib.indiana.edu/collections/janejohnson/ [accessed 16 August 2007].
22. *The Oxford Dictionary of Nursery Rhymes*, ed. Iona and Peter Opie (Oxford: Oxford University Press, [1951] 1997), pp. 28–36.
23. *The Top Book of All, for Little Masters and Misses* (London: R. Baldwin and S. Crowder, c.1760), pp. 7–9.
24. Iona Opie, 'Playground Rhymes', *The Cambridge Guide to Children's Books in English*, ed. Victor Watson (Cambridge: Cambridge University Press, 2001), pp. 570–1.
25. Milne, 'Busy', *Now We Are Six* (London: Egmont, [1927] 1989), p. 7.
26. Allan Ahlberg, 'The Longest Kiss Contest', *Heard it in the Playground* (London: Puffin, [1989] 1991), p. 13.
27. Humphrey Carpenter and Mari Prichard, *The Oxford Companion to Children's Literature* (Oxford: Oxford University Press, 1984), p. 502.
28. Roald Dahl, *Charlie and the Chocolate Factory* (Harmondsworth: Penguin, [1964] 1975), p. 74.
29. Watts, 'Heaven and Hell', *Divine Songs*, p. 16.
30. Noel Malcolm, *The Origins of English Nonsense* (London: Harper Collins, 1997) and Kimberly Reynolds, *Radical Children's Literature: Future Visions and Aesthetic Transformations in Juvenile Fiction* (Basingstoke: Palgrave Macmillan, 2007), pp. 45–67.
31. Styles, 'Poetry', in *International Companion Encyclopedia of Children's Literature*, ed. Peter Hunt, 2nd edn, 2 vols (London: Routledge, 2004), vol. 1, pp. 396–417 (p. 405).
32. *The World Turned Upside Down* (York: J. Kendrew, c.1830).
33. Jane and Ann Taylor, *Signor Topsy-Turvy's Wonderful Magic Lantern; or, the World Turned Upside Down* (London: Tabart, 1810), pp. 8 and 40.

34. Lewis Carroll, *The Hunting of the Snark* (1876), in *Alice in Wonderland*, ed. Donald J. Gray (New York: W. W. Norton, 1992), p. 234.

35. *The New Oxford Book of Children's Verse*, p. 29.

36. Peter Hollindale and Zena Sutherland, 'Internationalism, Fantasy, and Realism', pp. 252–88 in *Children's Literature. An Illustrated History*, ed. Peter Hunt, (Oxford: Oxford University Press, 1995), p. 284. Charles Causley, *Figgie Hobbin* (Harmondsworth: Penguin, [1970] 1979), p. 43.

37. Mick Gowar, 'Rat Trap', from *Carnival for the Animals, and Other Poems* (1992), in *The New Oxford Book of Children's Verse*, p. 325.

38. Gowar, 'Rat Trap', p. 326.

39. Benjamin Zephaniah, 'According to my mood', from *Talking Turkeys* (1994), in *The New Oxford Book of Children's Verse*, p. 334.

40. J. B. Morton, 'Now We Are Sick' (1931), quoted in *The Faber Book of Parodies*, ed. Simon Brett (London: Faber & Faber, 1984), p. 258.

41. Humphrey Carpenter, *Secret Gardens: The Golden Age of Children's Literature* (London: George Allen and Unwin, 1985), pp. 107 and 196. A. A. Milne, *When We Were Very Young* (London: Egmont, [1924] 1989), pp. 99 100.

42. Milne, *When We Were Very Young*, pp. 30–3.

43. Smart, 'Hymn xxxiii: For Saturday', in *The New Oxford Book of Children's Verse*, p. 1.

44. Robert Louis Stevenson, 'The Land of Story-Books', *A Child's Garden of Verses* (London: Wordsworth, [1885] 1994), pp. 97–8.

45. Stevenson, *Child's Garden of Verses*, pp. 139–40.

46. Lewis Carroll, 'Solitude' (1853), *The Complete Works of Lewis Carroll*, ed. Alexander Woollcott (London: Nonesuch, 1939).

47. John Goldthwaite, *The Natural History of Make-Believe* (New York: Oxford University Press, 1996), p. 28.

48. Jacqueline Rose, *The Case of Peter Pan or The Impossibility of Children's Fiction* (London: Macmillan, 1984).

49. Hunt, *Children's Literature*, p. 297.

50. Summarised in Styles, *From the Garden to the Street*, pp. 262–70.

51. Peter Hunt, 'The New Oxford: "Poetry Alive"', *Children's Literature Association Quarterly* 22 (1997), 149–50 (p. 149).
52. Alison Lurie, *Boys and Girls Forever: Children's Classics from Cinderella to Harry Potter* (Harmondsworth: Penguin, 2003), p. 157.
53. Roger McGough, 'First Day at School', from *In the Glassroom* (1976), in *The New Oxford Book of Children's Verse*, ed. Philip, p. 290.
54. Glenna Sloan, 'But is it poetry?', p. 52.
55. Jackie Kay, 'What Jenny Knew', from *Two's Company* (1992), in *The New Oxford Book of Children's Verse*, p. 336.
56. Hall, *The Oxford Book of Children's Verse in America*, p. xxiv.
57. Neil Philip, 'Introduction', *The New Oxford Book of Children's Verse*, p. xxv;
58. Styles, *From the Garden to the Street*, p. 156.

CHAPTER 3

Moral and Instructive Tales

In an essay written in 1980, Nina Bawden, the author of many successful children's books including *Carrie's War* (1973) and *The Peppermint Pig* (1975), wrote a strongly worded essay attacking what have been called the 'problem novels' of the 1970s. These were books designed mainly for teenagers in which (she said) 'fashionable social problems' were 'dragged in to satisfy some educational or social theory.' She lamented that this was what 'superficial critics consider realism to be'. Since they were part of life, Bawden accepted, such subjects as poverty and divorce, learning disabilities and racism, should certainly not be ignored by children's literature. But focusing on this kind of issue did not in itself make a book good, and it ought not to be a book's only *raison d'être*. Nor should children's books 'be used as a kind of therapy'. Why should a poor child have to read of poverty? Why should anyone think that a child from a one-parent family would feel better after reading about other children from one-parent families? 'The most important realism that children need,' she insisted, 'is the realism of the emotional landscape in which the book is set'. A children's book, she concluded, 'should be judged for the pleasure it gives, for its style and its quality', not according to how well it serves 'factions and interests and ideologies'.[1]

Bawden's essay is a good place to start this chapter since it brings up the two issues of realism (the accurate depiction of everyday life) and didacticism (instruction for a specific purpose) which will link together the very various texts discussed here. This is not to say that some fairy tales or fantasies are not didactic, nor, say, that school stories or adventure tales cannot be realistic. But there is an important and distinct tradition of children's literature, visible from the seventeenth century to today, that deals with ordinary children in ordinary situations being taught to deal with ordinary problems. It is the endurance of this tradition across centuries that can make Bawden's comments seem rather curious. What was wrong with the problem novels, she was essentially arguing, was that they tried to teach specific lessons in a context that readers would recognise as their own. In other words, they attempted to fuse didacticism and realism. But authors have always sought to do just this. 150 years before Bawden's attack, Catherine Sinclair, author of what is sometimes thought of as 'the first modern children's novel', *Holiday House* (1839), had railed against moral children's books which tried to 'stuff the memory' with 'ready-made opinions', leaving no room 'for the vigour of natural feeling, the glow of natural genius, and the ardour of natural enthusiasm.'[2] Charles Lamb similarly attacked 'the cursed Barbauld crew' (by which he meant the authors of late eighteenth-century moral tales, like Anna Laetitia Barbauld) for their dreary didactic realism which had supplanted, he said, those 'wild tales which made the child a man'.[3] This desire for 'real stories' rather than real life, and for subtly imparted values rather than explicit instruction, has been a constant theme of children's literature criticism. But just as constant, and more productive, has been the steady disregard of this criticism.

A comparison of some specific realistic, didactic texts from across the last three centuries will show more clearly exactly how durable this particular form of children's literature has been. Perhaps the most archetypal of all the teenage problem novels of the 1970s is Judy Blume's *Forever* (1975). It was the most controversial, and successful, in a sequence of books which she had began with *Are You There God? It's Me, Margaret* (1970) and continued with *Then Again, Maybe I Won't* (1971), *It's Not the End of the World* (1971), *Deenie* (1973) and *Blubber* (1974). These had dealt with boyfriends and bras (eleven-year-old Margaret prays for both), menstruation and masturbation, divorce and disability, bullying (the persecution of overweight Linda in *Blubber*) and, in *Forever*, sex. Its story is simple. At a party, the narrator, a seventeen-year-old called Katherine, meets Michael, a boy of her own age. They begin a relationship, gradually becoming more and more intimate until they become fully sexually active. They promise to stay together forever. By the end of the novel, though, Katherine, and perhaps Michael, have begun relationships with other people. Even if the book is not exactly erotic, it has undoubtedly been the book's descriptions of sex which have kept it so popular with young readers, and which have drawn so much condemnation. That *Forever* was still, in the US in 2005, in the top ten of books 'challenged' as being unsuitable for children shows how controversial its subject remains.[4]

On the surface *Forever* could not be more dissimilar from what we might call the 'classic' moral tales produced in great numbers in the late eighteenth and early nineteenth century by women such as Barbauld, Maria Edgeworth and Mary Wollstonecraft. These were generally short stories, rather than full-length novels, though many of them are about the same characters and trace their growth over a number of years. They are usually told by an omniscient third-person narrator, or sometimes given as dramatic dialogues, whereas *Forever* is narrated by Katherine. Another difference is these books' intended audience. *Forever* was designed for teenagers. Barbauld and Edgeworth wrote some of their tales for children as young as two or three, though later sequels were for readers who might, anachronistically, be described as teenagers. Above all, one might think, it is the subject matter that distinguishes the eighteenth-century moral tale from the twentieth-century problem novel. Edgeworth, for example, was careful to reassure parents in the preface to a collection of stories about the ten-to-thirteen-year-old Rosamond that she had not 'attempted to give what is called a knowledge of the world, which ought not, cannot be given prematurely'.[5] This demonstrates how keen Edgeworth was to please parents and to explain to them why her books were suitable for their children. She clearly intended the tales to be read by children and adults together. By contrast, Blume deliberately wrote about subjects which parents and children seldom discussed (a point she forcibly made with the title she chose for a collection of letters readers had sent her: *Letters to Judy: What Your Kids Wish They*

Could Tell You, 1986). Yet if we turn to Wollstonecraft, the similarities with Blume are much more striking than the differences. She had wanted to include lessons about 'chastity and impurity' in one of her collections of moral tales, for, she wrote, 'impurity is now spread so far that even children are infected'. She added that she was,

> thoroughly persuaded that the most efficacious method to root out this dreadful evil . . . would be to speak to children of the organs of generation as freely as we speak of other parts of the body, and explain to them the noble use which they were designed for, and how they may be injured.

Wollstonecraft left out such material only after being convinced that her views would 'not have sufficient weight with the public to conquer long-fostered prejudices.'[6] But it is noticeable that, like Blume two hundred years later, Wollstonecraft felt that to talk openly about taboo subjects was the best way to encourage healthy development.

Edgeworth, more prim that Wollstonecraft, did not make reference to sex in her moral tales, but nor did she escape criticism. The deeply conservative Sarah Trimmer wrote in 1803 that Edgeworth's books were not sufficiently religious and added that parents sometimes have to impose good behaviour and enforce discipline rather than always letting children come to their own conclusions.[7] Again, these were the same criticisms as would be levelled at Blume's work, and it is the centrality of this idea that children should teach themselves that gives the moral tale its coherence across two centuries. The most famous of Edgeworth's moral tales is 'The Purple Jar' (1796). This short fable begins with Rosamond out shopping with her mother. Her eye is caught by a purple jar on display in the window of an apothecary's shop and she begs her mother to buy it. Her mother will purchase only one item and, because Rosamond's shoes are very worn, she steers her towards a new pair instead of the jar. Rosamond ponders her choice, but the lure of the jar proves too strong. When she returns home, she is disappointed to find that the jar itself is not purple at all, but was simply filled with an odorous purple liquid. Later, Rosamond's distress is compounded when her father withdraws his offer to take her to see a glasshouse full of exotic plants because her shoes are in such a disgraceful state. She bitterly regrets her choice. 'O mamma,' she says, 'I am sure – no not quite sure, but I hope I shall be wiser another time.'[8] Several modern critics have been appalled that, even though Rosamond's shoes hurt her feet, her mother did not intervene in her choice.[9] But the idea that children should learn their lessons on their own is every bit as central to Edgeworth's writing as it is to Blume's. Just as Rosamond's mother did not impose the lesson about value, or the importance of distinguishing between appearance and reality, so, in *Forever*, Katherine's parents trust her to find out about sex for herself (although her mother cuts out relevant articles from the paper for her and her grandmother sends her leaflets on contraception, abortion and sexually transmitted diseases). In fact the main tension of *Forever* comes from Katherine's certainty that she will always love Michael versus her parents' awareness that the relationship will falter. They are adamant that Katherine's relationship should not govern her important decisions, such as her choice of university. For the most part they allow her to work this out for herself, although on one occasion, without her knowledge, her father does autocratically arrange for Katherine to take a good job at a summer camp (where she meets her next boyfriend). Like Rosamond, Katherine eventually comes to see the wisdom of her parents' attitudes.[10] But this one instance of parental authority exposes the power relationship within the text. Despite the illusion of freedom, Blume's teenagers are in fact still subservient to their parents, just as Rosamond was to hers. What both Edgeworth and Blume actually provide is a parental fantasy in which children are allowed to learn their own lessons, but always come to the conclusions which their parents would wish.

Older and newer moral tales are also linked by their determination to appear almost hyper-realistic. Typical in its gritty and graphic subject matter, and in its attempt to heighten immediacy by carefully deploying references to such things as current television programmes, pop music hits and school text books is Richard Peck's *Are You in the House Alone?* (1976) – the book which Nina Bawden was probably attacking when she wrote against a book congratulated for 'being the first children's book with a rape in it'.

Blume's similar use of shock tactics, and teenage argot, is evident right from *Forever's* first, shocking sentence: 'Sybil Davison has a genius I.Q. and has been laid by at least six different guys.'[11] Although there is nothing like this in Edgeworth, she too strove hard for a verisimilitude which would anchor her didacticism in everyday life. *Forever* describes in detail the process of getting into university; 'The Purple Jar' gives a detailed description of the shops Rosamond visits. Both authors immerse their protagonists in material culture. In *Forever*, Blume deploys references to the purchase of new clothes, of finding bargains, of visits to cinemas and cafes, of the whole process of saving and spending money, as a way of stapling the narrative to the real world with real teenage concerns. Surprisingly, Edgeworth's tales are even more concerned with children's purchasing power. As Marilyn Butler has pointed out, 'it would usually be possible to name the exact sum in the pocket of any of Maria Edgeworth's twelve-year-olds.'[12] Edgeworth and Blume also tried as hard as they could to give realistic representations of child psychology. Edgeworth has been applauded for portraying 'the first living and breathing children in English literature since Shakespeare'.[13] She manages to give this impression by representing her characters' faults and limitations. Rosamond is solipsistic, motivated by strong but fleeting desires, and, at the end of the tale, is still appealingly unsure that she will be able to reform. Blume's Katherine is just as self-absorbed and impulsive, just as angry at her parents' refusal to see things her way, then as willing to admit that they were right.

All this ostentatious realism has several purposes. First, Edgeworth and Blume were both trying to emphasise that literature is not removed from real life and to enable the reader to see him or herself in the text. Second, they were attempting to establish a division between the young reader and adults and to give the impression that the book is somehow on the reader's side. In *Forever* this is achieved by Katherine's first-person narration, a characteristic of the majority of post-War Young Adult fiction, much of which shows the influence of J. D. Salinger's *The Catcher in the Rye* (1951). The confessional mode of these books allows readers to feel complicit in the plot and to share the narrator's resentment at adult superciliousness and interference. In a very similar way in

'The Purple Jar', the reader participates in all Rosamond's deliberations, anticipation, disappointment and regret. Indeed, when Rosamond's father refuses to let her accompany him to the glasshouse, Edgeworth does not attempt to mitigate the harshness of his edict. The sense of injustice she creates cements the bond between the reader and Rosamond. But above all, the sense of realism developed by both Edgeworth and Blume was designed to smooth the passage of the didacticism.

However, both *Forever* and Edgeworth's moral tales are more than mere vehicles for didacticism. One critic, for example, has argued that Edgeworth's tales focus on 'issues of adult authority and child empowerment', exploring 'what it's like for juveniles who seek both separation and relation' in a society in which children 'must develop their own sense of self, yet maintain the affiliative network that defines social being.'[14] Many critics have been more sceptical about Blume's place in the history of children's literature, but *Forever* is a sophisticated and satisfying text, much more than simply a 'problem novel'. It has dated quite badly, as the fact that it is now marketed as 'a teenage classic' acknowledges, but for several different reasons simultaneously. On the one hand, its attempt to capture teenage demotic language now seems rather quaint. On the other, it now seems the product of a specific historical period, after the advent of the contraceptive pill and before the onset of AIDS.

Certainly many modern readers will find it shocking that one of Katherine's friends is encouraged to go on the pill by her mother even before she has had sex: 'she said she'd feel better if she knew that I was prepared for college, in every way', recounts her rather bemused daughter.[15] Yet sex is not really the issue at the core of *Forever*. The book is principally about change and the illusion of permanence. The action of the novel takes place at the moment when Katherine is poised between one phase of life and the next, about to graduate from high school and depart for university. Many other smaller shifts make up the fabric of the book, also disturbing her previous comfortable life: her sister's arrival at puberty, the desertion of some of her friends, her grandfather's death and so on. Most obviously the disruption of the past is caused by her relationship with Michael and the commencement of her sex-life. She is desperate for the relationship always to endure, her conviction symbolised by a silver disk Michael buys her, engraved with the word 'forever' and hanging from a (heavily metaphorical) chain. The novel, then, is an account of Katherine coming to understand that however secure the past has been, she must break her self-imposed ties, freeing herself to enter a new stage of her life. Moreover, Blume suggests that what Katherine is experiencing on a personal level, society as a whole is also going through in the late 1960s and early 1970s. The permissive society's break with the past cannot be resisted, she argues. Rather, it has to be embraced, even by parents whose instinct is to protect their daughters from adult sexuality. And its consequences have to be faced, even when they are as difficult as the unwanted pregnancy of Sybil Davison, whose promiscuity Blume introduced in the novel's first sentence. *Forever* can seem morally conservative, arguing that sex should always take place within a loving environment. But it is also a novel of liberation, making the case for the acceptance of change, both personal and social.

The classic moral tales of the late eighteenth and early nineteenth centuries could also incorporate a progressive agenda within their fundamentally conservative moral universe. Almost all of them were opposed to racism and slavery, for instance, and not only because so many were written and published by religious non-conformists. Some critics have argued that moral tales often present a feminist programme. Mary Wollstonecraft's *Original Stories from Real Life* (1788), for example, can certainly be regarded as representing the sort of rational education for girls that its author would later demand in *A Vindication of the Rights of Woman* (1792). Christine Wilkie-Stubbs has claimed that Wollstonecraft 'was using her writing for children to subvert and interrogate the role of women in society'.[16] But the principal connection between these early moral tales and the new moral tales of the later twentieth century is their commitment to realism and rationalism. Indeed, the classic moral tale developed in conscious opposition to fiction which had included supernatural elements. The warnings of John Locke's *Some Thoughts Concerning Education* (1693) were foundational. He had been adamant that nursemaid's stories used to frighten children into good behaviour did much more harm than good. Sarah Trimmer was paraphrasing him when she argued against fairy stories, claiming that 'the terrific images, which tales of this nature present to the imagination, usually make deep impressions, and injure the tender minds of children, by exciting unreasonable and groundless fears.'[17] Fiction was produced to dramatise this effect. 'The History of Francis Fearful', published in about 1774, explained to its child readers how the stories of Goody Senseless, his nurse, put all sorts of superstitious terrors into Francis' head. When he was sent to school, his fear of bats and scarecrows made him the laughing stock of the other pupils.[18]

This same concern for realism determined what went into the late eighteenth-century moral tales as well as what was left out. Arnaud Berquin, a French children's author whose work became almost immediately popular in translation, and an important influence on many British writers, clearly explained his principles. 'Instead of those wild fictions of the Wonderful, in which their understanding is too commonly bewilder'd,' he wrote, in his books children would:

> see only what occurs or may occur within the limits of their families. The sentiments with which the work abounds, are not above the level of their comprehension. It introduces them, accompanied by none, except their parents, the companions of their pastimes, the domestics [servants] that surround them, or the animals they are accustomed to behold. 'Tis in their own ingenuous language they express themselves: And, interested in the several events the work describes, they are directed by the impulse of their little passions. They are punish'd when they happen to do wrong, and find a recompense resulting from their commendable actions. Every thing concurs to lead them on to virtue, as their happiness, and give them a distaste of vice, by representing it a source of sorrow and humiliation.[19]

The key points here are that readers will meet only those things which they find around them in their own lives, and that it is on these that the didacticism will be based. This is essentially a manifesto for the moral tale.

Key to the reformatory purpose of the British moral tale was the reader's ability to recognise him or herself in the text. Although a few moral tales took poor children as their protagonists, by far the majority were set in affluent, middle-class families in which either leisured parents superintend their children's education or a surrogate, usually a governess, has been appointed. Although some were set in the city, most were located in a bucolic rural environment. These tales mirror, even if they also somewhat idealise, the families of the books' intended consumers. This is naturalistic realism then – striving for an accurate representation of one segment of real life – not the realism of the nineteenth-century novel which attempted to depict the conditions, speech and attitudes of the working classes. It was above all important that readers should be able to identify themselves in the characters they were reading about, their desires and fears, and their errors. Thus Mary Ann Kilner's *Jemima Placid* (c.1783) is really a series of children's everyday faults cast into narrative form. Two sisters fight over the toy furniture for their dolls' houses, smashing their dolls in the process; a boy puts a spider down his sister's neck and she overturns the furniture in her fright; a girl is so excited by the prospect of going to a ball that she vomits in the coach, ruining her own and her companions' dresses. The book's method is clearly explained in its sub-title: *The Advantage of Good-Nature Exemplified in a Variety of Familiar Incidents*. Its aim, though, was not simply to *exemplify*, but to encourage its readers to repent and reform. 'If the characters you meet with in any way resemble your own,' Kilner wrote, 'and if those characters disgust and offend you, instead of throwing the book aside with resentment, you should endeavour to improve the failings of which you are conscious, and then you will no longer meet with your own portrait in that which the Author has described.'[20]

It would be impossible to list all the specific lessons taught by all the moral tales, but they can perhaps be rolled up into one or two basic dicta. First, children must honour and obey adults, especially their parents. Beyond this, they should always be sensible and prudent, planning for the future and assessing their options rationally (unlike Rosamond with her purple jar), and not impetuous, clumsy, temperamental, jealous or selfish. In other words, most classic moral tales urged children not to be childish. This is very clear in *Virtue and Vice: or, the History of Charles Careful, and Harry Heedless* (c.1780). Some children, the narrator declares, 'learn early to act like men and women, while there are other people, who may be said to be boys and girls for the whole course of their lives.' The former, like Charles, are the book's heroes; the latter, like Harry, its villains. It is as a reward for his precocious maturity that Sir Robert becomes Charles' patron, gratifying him by treating him 'rather like a little man, than a child'. In the terms of this book, and most late eighteenth-century moral tales, to be good is to renounce one's childhood, for a 'virtuous child' is almost a contradiction in terms.[21]

One surprise about the lessons of the moral tale are that they are not always especially moral. John Aikin and Anna Laetitia Barbauld's *Evenings at Home* (1792–96), for example, contained many scientific sections, teaching children about botany, say, and manufacturing processes.[22] More frequently, the moral tales seem designed to encourage and enable social and economic advancement rather than any more abstract moral improvement. 'The Purple Jar', for instance, can be read as a fable about the difference between appearance and reality, but it also teaches children more banal lessons such as how to shop successfully. Edgeworth acknowledged that she wrote many tales 'to excite a spirit of industry' and 'to point out that people feel cheerful and happy whilst they are employed.'[23] Overall, the principal drive was to inculcate thrift, honesty, diligence and prudence – what might be termed 'commercial virtues' – and to give a strong sense of the value of things. Even when charitable giving is promoted, as it often is, only a judicious, means-tested philanthropy was countenanced. Charity had become a fiscal transaction rather than moral duty, commendable because it signified a child's economic rationalism rather than any open-hearted benevolence.[24]

The most nakedly commercial of all moral tales were the novels of Barbara Hofland, mostly published in the 1810s and 1820s. Like Edgeworth, she saturates her novels in the financial details of her protagonists' lives. Her two most celebrated novels, *The Son of a Genius* (1812) and *The Daughter of a Genius* (1823), single out for attack those who possess talent but lack financial responsibility. The two 'geniuses' are condemned because they spend extravagantly when they are rich, and make few efforts to earn money when they are poor. Other lessons Hofland urgently teaches are the value of compound interest in *Daughter of a Genius* and the importance of keeping receipts in *Son of a Genius*. When the genius claims that it is beneath his dignity as an artist to ask for a receipt, Hofland's mouthpiece character disagrees: 'a great mind can take in petty cares, an aspiring genius stoop to petty details; since it is impossible to be virtuous and pious without it'. Words like 'virtue' and 'piety' are common in the moral tale, but Hofland's deployment of them here acknowledges that, for her, business rectitude is in itself actually pious and virtuous. It is immoral, and even an affront to God, to despise economic good practice. Piety, morality and commercial probity had become one and the same thing.[25]

Perhaps the principal ambition of the classic moral tale then was to teach children how to prosper. This was a lesson directed at the individual child reader, and perhaps more especially his or her parents who, after all, were likely to making the investment in the child by buying the book. But many moral tale authors also envisaged their books as possessing the power to reform, even perfect, society as a whole. According to some readings, the moral tale was essentially an ideological weapon wielded by the bourgeoisie, used to endorse middle-class principles over both aristocratic and plebeian value systems. When they attacked showiness, languor or economic fecklessness, Andrew O'Malley has argued, they were targeting an aristocratic, dilettante philosophy. When they urged the importance of hard work they were aiming at the putatively lower-class conviction that good fortune came out-of-the-blue, rather than as the result of planning and industry.[26] This supposedly lower-class 'lottery mentality' had been embedded in tales of the supernatural (such as Locke had said servants were fond of telling children). The moral tale was designed to replace such chapbook tales and fairy stories. After all, as one writer put it, they give children 'an erroneous idea of the ways of Providence' by suggesting that God will reward those who are virtuous, even if they do not help themselves.[27] Viewed in another light, though, eighteenth-century moral tales can seem much more conservative, advocating a restrictive acquiescence to things as they are. The concluding moral of Kilner's *Jemima Placid* is 'Unavoidable disasters are beyond remedy, and are only aggravated by complaints. By submitting with a good grace to the disappointments of life, half its vexations may be escaped.'[28]

The moral tale's determination to affect public as well as private morality makes it something of a utopian genre. A useful comparison can be made with the children's literature produced in the heyday of the Soviet Union. This was socialist not bourgeois of course – compulsorily so after the first congress of Soviet writers in 1934 had made socialist realism the only permissible mode for all literary production – but it was similarly unashamed in its ideological agenda. All Soviet children's books had to propagate doctrinally correct thinking, to show the forces of progress triumphing, and to depict all right-minded characters co-operating in the cause of the general good.[29] Children were defined in terms of what they would become – the citizens of the future – not as beings who should be left free from political concerns. 'These principles', it can be said, 'bear a close resemblance to those upon which the English eighteenth-century moral tale was constructed.'[30] In eighteenth-century Britain there was no legislation forcing the moral tale to promote a particular ideological programme, and political and religious differences certainly existed between its ideologically disparate authors. But in their optimistic conviction that children's literature could improve both the individual and society, authors of the moral tale were asserting the right that Maxim Gorky claimed for Soviet writers at the 1934 congress, 'to participate directly in the construction of a new life, in the process of "changing the world"'.[31]

If Gorky's maxim applies to eighteenth-century moral tales, how much more does it fit the realist children's fiction produced from the late twentieth century? Blume's *Forever* was one amongst 'adolescent novels of ideas', as one critics has called them, which sought to make the personal political, trying simultaneously to improve the individual reader and to engineer a better society through the realistic representation of everyday life and its problems.[32] Several books tackled the problem of racism in urban Britain, for example. Bernard Ashley's *The Trouble with Donovan Croft* (1974) wove a story around the adoption of a black boy from a Jamaican background into a white family. Jan Needle's *My Mate Shofiq* (1978) was even more viciously realistic, showing a recession-hit Lancashire mill town as an urban wasteland where racism was endemic. At times it tips over into a sort of hyper-realism, the exaggerated winter weather being designed to emphasise the brutality of life and perhaps, rather awkwardly, the discomfort of the Pakistani families who live there: 'They ought to feel it more, by rights, being as how they came from a hot country', says the book's chief character, Bernard. In both books, the reader is shown the ugliness of children's racism, so vividly, in fact, that Needle in particular was criticised for his accurate representation of his characters' racially offensive language.[33] The passage in which Shofiq explains to his new friends that he does not want to be called a 'Paki' is typical, meant to be shocking in its realism, but ending up rather clumsy because it is so clearly propagandistic:

'I can't rightly explain,' he said, 'but it's horrible. I mean I don't call you lot all Whities, or something. There's just something . . . it sounds . . .'

'Ah rubbish, lad,' said Terry. 'Everyone calls Pakis Pakis. It stands to reason. I mean, my dad calls Pakis Pakis; and blackies. Like West Indian kids gets called niggers and Chinese is Chinkies. I mean, it's just what you get called, it don't mean nowt.'

'It does, it does!' said Shofiq. 'I'll tell you, it means . . .'

He was helpless. He couldn't explain.

'I just wish you wouldn't, that's all,' he ended lamely.

'Rubbish!' said Terry firmly. I'll call you what I like, and you're a Paki, so there.'

Shofiq started to roll up his sleeves.

'All right then, Smelly White Pig,' he said grimly. 'Take your coat off, lad, 'cause I'm going to batter you.'

Maureen solved it in the end by pointing out that no one was allowed to call Bernard Bernie. Bern was all right, or even Slobberchops. But not Bernie. They discussed as to why, but he couldn't rightly say. But he hated it, and that was that. Terry, who wasn't thick, agreed that he'd not call Shofiq a Paki.

'It's not just me, though,' said Shofiq. 'Everybody hates it, it's rotten. But thanks, Terry.'

'Well I won't call any of 'em – you – Pakis in future,' said Maureen. 'Pakistanis is good enough for me.'

Shofiq giggled: 'Or Indians, or Bangladeshies, or Bengalis, eh? How about British? It's on me birth certificate!'

But that just got them confused.

What is also evident here is something that differentiates *My Mate Shofiq* from many eighteenth-century moral tales but links it to Soviet propaganda: the idea that the attitudes and values of previous generations should be dispensed with, and the hope that children will be able to make a better world on their own. Terry's father is the villain here as much as the bullies who pick on Shofiq at school. So too is Bernard's father who has to impose redundancies at his mill and has decided to sack the Pakistani workers because, he claims, they are 'always stopping work for religion, some festival do or sommat' and they don't 'try to do it our way'.[34] If there is hope, Needle insists, it lies with the children. This is dramatically restated at the end of *The Trouble with Donovan Croft*. Traumatised by his sense of alienation, Donovan has been entirely mute for the duration of the novel. His friendship with his white foster-brother Keith has been gradually developing though, and he suddenly shouts out to save Keith from an oncoming car. What has overcome society's racism and broken Donovan's silence is not politicians, parents, teachers or social workers, but the friendship of two boys.[35]

Some problem novels can seem more personal than political. Betsy Byars' *The Summer of the Swans* (1970) focused on a boy with learning difficulties; Richard Peck's *Don't Look and It Won't Hurt* (1972) was about unmarried motherhood; Katherine Paterson's *The Great Gilly Hopkins* (1979) was about a fostered girl with behavioural problems who longs to find her real mother but finally learns, when her birth mother rejects her, that it has been this dream that has been preventing her from finding happiness in her life. Others successfully combine both. Shocking as Gail's rape is in Peck's *Are You in the House Alone?* (1976) much of the book's horror derives from the reactions of the snobbish, misogynistic inhabitants of her Connecticut suburb. Her assailant comes from an established, patrician family, while many of her neighbours believe that Gail has been asking for trouble because of her previous sexual relationship with a local boy from a less affluent family. 'Why does the law protect the rapist instead of the victim?', Gail's experiences lead her to demand, to which the only answer the book offers is 'Because the law is wrong'.[36]

Increasingly these modern moral tales have shied away from offering any simple, confident solution to the problems they represent. An excellent example is Berlie Doherty's *Dear Nobody* (1991), a novel with teenage pregnancy at its centre. It reads almost like a deliberate re-writing of Blume's *Forever*, but designed for more cynical times. Like Blume's Katherine and Michael, Doherty's Helen and Chris are in their final year of school, are working towards their places at university, and are experimenting with sex. In *Dear Nobody*, though, the novel's only sex-scene occurs on the second page, is wholly unplanned, and is described in only a single line. Helen becomes pregnant and the rest of the novel takes the form of a complicated narrative, split between Chris's memories of that year, written down on the evening before he leaves for university, and Helen's letters to her unborn child, 'Nobody'. Many of the novel's episodes seem intended to undercut the cosy optimism of *Forever*. Both Helen's and Chris's families are dysfunctional. Chris's mother has left home, and his attempts to find her and build a relationship help set the context for his other concerns. Helen's mother is emotionally distant. She offers Helen no support and almost forces her to have an abortion. Eventually we find that this is because of her guilt and resentment at her own illegitimate birth. Indeed, in *Dear Nobody* there are few if any emotionally stable figures who can dispense wisdom and love in the way that so many of Blume's characters do. In contrast with Katherine's wise and loving grandmother in *Forever*, Helen's has withdrawn from the world to her darkened bedroom. When Helen visits the family planning clinic, she finds not the solicitude and good advice that Katherine had benefited from, but 'young women sitting there, most of them smoking, most of them looking fed up and tired and lonely' and she leaves without seeing anyone.[37]

In fact, despite her emotional confusion, the only composed figure in the book is Helen herself. It is she who knows she must keep her baby and, shockingly, who decides to end her relationship with Chris, much against his wishes, at least partly in order to allow him to take his place at university. She and Chris were 'a pair of kids having fun together', she writes to her unborn child. 'And now we've been catapulted into the world of grown-ups. I'm not ready for forever. I'm not ready for him, and he's not ready for me.' It seems a deliberate rejoinder to Blume's *Forever*, with Helen taking the rational role of Katherine's parents. What Doherty has done is to destabilise the idea of maturity. Gone is the fantasy, so consoling for both young readers and adult authors, that teenagers simply have to learn to accept the wisdom of their elders in order to turn out as happy human beings. It is the younger people – Helen, and even her daughter Amy – from whom we can learn most. The book concludes with the four generations of women in Helen's family sitting together with Amy 'a fine thread being drawn through a garment, mending tears.'[38] *Dear Nobody* could be called a feminist book perhaps, and there may be a suggestion of an anti-abortion agenda. It warns readers about the fragility of relationships and about their social responsibilities. But beyond this, it is difficult to determine precisely what lessons are being taught. Ultimately, Doherty suggests that life is full of emotional complexity but that there is no simple way of dealing with it. People have to deal as best they can with their problems and to welcome rather than fear the richness of life. In a way, this recalls the lessons of some of the eighteenth-century moral tales. 'Unavoidable disasters are beyond remedy, and are only aggravated by complaints', wrote Mary Ann Kilner at the end of *Jemima Placid*. 'By submitting with a good grace to the disappointments of life, half its vexations may be escaped.'[39]

One important question remains: what happened to the moral tale between its early nineteenth-century heyday and what might be thought of as its reincarnation in the problem novels of the 1970s? According to some histories of children's literature moral tales had died out by the Victorian era, superseded by a proliferation of new sub-genres: adventure stories, nonsense verse, Carrollian fantasies, family stories, newly re-popular fairy tales, and so on. It is certainly tempting to think of Catherine Sinclair's *Holiday House* (1839) as the moral tale's death-knell. Its preface savagely attacked didactic children's literature. The book itself seems calculated to undermine the moral tale. For most of its course it celebrates, rather than castigates, the mischievous behaviour of Harry and Laura, even when they do something as dangerous as setting the house on fire. The disciplinarian Mrs Crabtree can be regarded as a vicious caricature of the sternly rational female teachers who had peopled the late eighteenth-century moral tale, and she is ruthlessly mocked. The book becomes much more pious towards its close, and much darker too when Harry and Laura's brother dies. But this cannot quite banish the memory of the anti-morality of its first half, nor of the way that Sinclair seemed to deride the whole notion of the moral tale by having Uncle David sententiously tell the children that he has 'only one piece of serious, important advice to give', which turns out to be 'never crack nuts with your teeth!' It is, as David Rudd points out, 'an aphorism rarely found stitched into samplers.'[40]

However, it would be more accurate to say that the moral tale evolved than that it become suddenly extinct. Most obviously, it became imbued with an Evangelical Christianity, in which form it thrived at least until the end of the nineteenth century.[41] The process of transition can be observed in the work of Mary Martha Sherwood. Her early works were moral tales in the Edgeworthian manner. Sarah Trimmer commended *The History of Susan Gray* (1802), for example, because 'all the arguments which Reason and Religion can furnish [are] enforced by the most striking examples of *persevering Virtue*'.[42] But thirteen years later, Sherwood reissued her book in a much more Evangelical form, editing out what she had come to consider as the book's doctrinal faults. Her change from rational moralist to Evangelical Christian had happened in India, where she had followed her husband, a soldier. It was her concern at the speed with which British children assimilated into a non-Christian culture that persuaded her of the need for a children's literature which emphasised religious orthodoxy not abstract morality. The result was dozens of tracts and some immensely successful novels, notably *Little Henry and his Bearer* (1814), a neo-Puritan tale describing the boy's pious death after having converted his Indian servant to Christianity, and *The Fairchild Family* (first part, 1818). Perhaps the most appealing today is *The Little Woodman, and His Dog Cæsar* (1818), an extremely enjoyable fusion of fairy tale, animal story and religious tract. It describes how six sinful boys plan to kill their youngest brother William by abandoning him in the forest because only he has heeded their dying father's religious advice. He is saved by a combination of divine intervention and his dog, who fights off wolves and eventually leads him to an isolated cottage which turns out to belong to his pious grandmother. The book ends when his six brothers reappear, their health and fortunes ruined by their wicked lives. William takes them in and puts them on the road to repentance. Sherwood's moral, directed at both children and their parents, explains the importance she ascribed to books that could reach the young: 'Fathers and mothers, you should lead your children to love God while they are little, and while their hearts are tender. And you, little children, lose no time, but give yourselves up to God before you become hard and stubborn, like William's brothers.'[43]

It was both direct authorial interventions like this, which shattered any pretence of realism, and the strict, disciplinary nature of Sherwood's writing, to which the next generation of children's writers objected. Charlotte Yonge and Mary Louisa Stewart (universally known as Mrs Molesworth), for instance, had read Evangelical stories by Sherwood and others when children, and were adamant that, in their own writing, no child should 'be taught the religion of fear', as Mrs Molesworth put it.[44] Yonge was clearly aware of the tradition of didactic fiction, and of her own position within and beyond it. She wanted to provide 'something of a deeper tone than the Edgeworthian style, yet less directly religious than the Sherwood class of books'.[45] It is this careful positioning that has resulted in both Yonge and Molesworth being congratulated for the realism of their characters and settings, and for their role in diminishing the prominence of didacticism. For Roger Lancelyn Green, Mrs Moleworth's writing is characterised by 'the complete absence of any direct moral teaching'. For Marghanita Laski, Yonge's characters, especially Ethel May in *The Daisy Chain* (1856), are drawn with such 'sympathetic realism' that it must have been a huge relief to Victorian children to encounter them. 'To have someone *like ourselves* conquer her faults and reap the reward of her virtues was a conception altogether new in children's literature', Laski writes. This diminishes the achievement of the Edgeworth generation, who also tried to enable readers to recognise themselves in the text, but it stresses again the parallels with twentieth-century didactic fiction.[46]

Yonge and Molesworth are very different authors, the former standing at the forefront of a revised Evangelical tradition, the latter becoming successful with more secular books. Her first hit was *Carrots: Just a Little Boy* (1876), about the youngest of six children, mothered by his older sister Floss when his mother falls ill, who gets into trouble when he unintentionally steals a half-sovereign, so innocent is he about money. It includes the phonetic reproduction of 'baby-talk' which most critics agree makes the books almost unreadable now, although it was one of their most popular features when they were first published. The Evangelical fiction of Yonge and her successors is just as little likely to be popular with modern children and just as easy to mock. Louisa Charlesworth's *Ministering Angels* (1854) recounts at tedious length the good deeds performed by the Clifford family children, a formula inverted by E. Nesbit in *The Wouldbegoods* (1906) in which all the Bastable children's benevolent schemes go horribly awry. Even Margaret Nancy Cutt, who named her study of Victorian children's literature after Charlesworth's book and devoted a chapter to speculating why it was so hugely popular, concludes that 'Judged by the standards of Arthur Ransome, Laura Ingalls Wilder and others of today, this book is hopeless.'[47] Many of its successors were worse, published by various Tract Societies who insisted on the 'basic requirements of a repentance, a conversion, and a Christian death scene'.[48] The description of one of these given by Janey, a twelve-year-old, working-class, Lancashire girl in Frances Hodgson Burnett novel *Haworth's* (1879) is only slightly exaggerated:

> she had th' asthma an' summat wrong wi' her legs, an' she knowed aw th' boible through aside o' th' hymn-book, an' she'd sing aw th' toime when she could breathe fur th' asthma, an' tell foak as if they did na go an' do likewise they'd go to burnin' hell where th' fire is na quenched an' th' worms dyeth not.

'It's a noice book,' Janey adds, 'an' theer's lots more like it in th' skoo' libery – aw about Sunday skoo' scholars as has consumption an' th' loike an' reads th' bible to foak an' dees.'[49]

What is clear is that by prioritising didacticism over realism these Victorian Evangelical children's books were echoing the Puritan books of the seventeenth-century, such as James Janeway's *A Token for Children* (1672). The link is emphasised by the Evangelicals' emphasis on personal amendment and individual salvation rather than general social reform. The good deeds performed by the Clifford children in *Ministering Angels* are important not because they will improve society, but because they will ensure the children's places in heaven. As Gillian Avery has put it, in Charlesworth's moral universe, 'God has created a world where the poor exist to train the consciences and charitable instincts of those better off.'[50] Likewise, Mrs O. F. Walton's *Christie's Old Organ, or Home Sweet Home* (1875) is about life on the streets of Victorian London with the street urchin Christie looking after the ailing street-musician Treffy. But the plot of the novel concerns only Christie's conversion of Treffy to Christianity and Treffy's consequent happy death. This emphasis on individual reform, often with child characters in the role of missionary, is important for two reasons. First it shows how little these later-nineteenth-century didactic texts are concerned with the possibility of social mobility, a substantial shift from the moral tales of a century before. There is never any suggestion that Christie's virtues might enable him to rise from the gutter, nor does he hope to do so. Some of the so-called 'waif-stories' or 'street-arab' tales are different in this regard, Hesba Stretton's *Jessica's First Prayer* (1867) and *Little Meg's Children* (1868), for example, and their American counterparts *Ragged Dick; or, Street Life in New York* (1867) and *Tattered Tom; or, the Story of a Street Arab* (1871) by Horatio Alger. These were written partly to encourage piety and partly to draw attention to the poverty of children in urban slums (both Stretton and Alger were in fact active campaigners against the exploitation of children), but these were exceptions. And the second reason why what might be called the solipsism of the Evangelical texts is important is because it argues that virtue is not to be taught, but is somehow found within oneself, having simply to be wakened. This is evident even in Frances Hodgson Burnett's more secular novels. In *Little Lord Fauntleroy* (1886) the young boy transplanted from the streets of New York to the English aristocracy soon finds himself acting as if he had always belonged there. Sarah Crewe's fortunes change in the opposite way in *A Little Princess* (1905; originally published as *Sara Crewe* in 1887). Having plummeted from affluence on her eleventh birthday when she learns that her father has died after losing all his money in diamond-mine speculation, Sara begins the life of a drudge. Only by imagining herself to be a princess, who must always behave with courage and nobility, does she endure her new life, until she is rescued from poverty by the arrival of her father's business partner with the news that the diamond mines have succeeded.

The point of *The Little Princess* is that Sara found the means of tolerating poverty inside herself. She had not needed to be *taught*. Not only had Hodgson Burnett's novels departed from realism then, but in a sense, they had dispensed with didacticism too. *The Little Princess* seems a moral tale because it tries to show children what virtues are needed to deal with adversity. But it simultaneously undermines the use of didactic literature by showing that these virtues are already within everyone, and even that they can best be wakened by the imagination. This dwindling of faith in the potential and necessity of didactic literature no doubt helped to hasten the decline of the moral tale in the early twentieth century. Coupled with the formulaic severity of Evangelical fiction, the whole idea of realistic, didactic children's literature fell into disrepute. It was not to be revived until the problem novel reinvented the form half a century or more later.

SUMMARY OF KEY POINTS

- Using realism to instruct has been a central aim of children's fiction from the eighteenth-century moral tale to the modern problem novel.
- Overt didacticism became less popular in late nineteenth- and early twentieth-century children's fiction; lessons were supposed to be intuited rather than imposed.
- Early moral tales traditionally aimed to inculcate mature behaviour in children (rationality, forethought, selflessness), but from

the later nineteenth century children's own values (as perceived by adults authors) were often presented as more beneficial than adult attitudes.

- In the later twentieth century the didactic novel for children began to confront political and social questions very directly.
- While early moral tales showed that most problems could be solved by better behaviour or more sensible thinking, the modern 'adolescent novel of ideas' seldom offers simple solutions to the problems it presents.

NOTES

1. Nina Bawden, 'Emotional Realism in Books for Young People', *The Horn Book Magazine*, 56 (1980), 17–33.
2. Catherine Sinclair, *Holiday House: a Series of Tales* (Edinburgh: William Whyte and Co., 1839), p. vi.
3. Charles Lamb to Samuel Taylor Coleridge, 23 October 1802, in *The Letters of Charles and Mary Anne Lamb*, ed. E.W. Marrs Jnr (Ithaca, NY: Cornell University Press, 1976), vol. 2, pp. 81–2.
4. A challenge is a 'formal, written complaint, filed with a library or school requesting that materials be removed because of content or appropriateness'. See the American Library Association, 'Challenged and Banned Books', online at <http://www.ala.org/ala/oif/bannedbooksweek/challengedbanned/challengedbanned.htm> [26 November 2007].
5. Maria Edgeworth, *Rosamond*, 2 vols (London: R. Hunter, 1821), vol. 1, p. v.
6. Mary Wollstonecraft, 'Introductory Address to Parents', *Elements of Morality, For the Use of Children . . . Translated from the German of the Rev. C. G. Salzmann* (London: J. Johnson, 1790), pp. xii–xiii.
7. *Guardian of Education* 2 (1803), 175–82.
8. Maria Edgeworth, 'The Purple Jar', *From Instruction to Delight. An Anthology of Children's Literature to 1850*, ed. Patricia Demers 2nd edn (Don Mills, Ontario: Oxford University Press, 2004), pp. 176–81.

9. F. J. Harvey Darton, *Children's Books in England*, revised by Brian Alderson, 3rd edn (Cambridge: Cambridge University Press, 1982), p. 141; John Rowe Townsend, *Written for Children* (London: Pelican, [1965] 1976), p. 42.

10. Judy Blume, *Forever* (London: Young Picador, [1975] 2005), pp. 93, 100, 128 and 139.

11. Blume, *Forever*, p. 1.

12. Marilyn Butler, *Maria Edgeworth: A Literary Biography* (Oxford: Clarendon Press, 1972), p. 163.

13. P. H. Newby, *Maria Edgeworth* (Denver: Alan Swallow, 1950), p. 24.

14. Mitzi Myers, 'Impeccable Governesses, Rational Dames and Moral Mothers: Mary Wollstonecraft and the Female Tradition in Georgian Children's Books', *Children's Literature*, 14 (1986), 31–59 (p. 34).

15. Blume, *Forever*, p. 124.

16. Christine Wilkie-Stubbs, 'Childhood, didacticism and gendering', in *International Companion Encyclopedia of Children's Literature*, ed. Peter Hunt, 2nd edn, 2 vols (London: Routledge, 2004), vol. 1, p. 355.

17. *Guardian of Education*, 2 (1803), pp. 185–86.

18. *The Lilliputian Magazine; or, Children's Repository*, 6 vols (London: W. Tringham, c.1774), vol. 2, pp. 55–67.

19. Arnaud Berquin, trans. Rev. Anthony Meilan, *The Children's Friend; Consisting of Apt Tales, Short Dialogues, and Moral Dramas*, 8 vols (London: 'Printed for the Translator', 1786), vol. 1, pp. 16–17.

20. Mary Ann Kilner, *Jemima Placid*, 3rd edn (London: J. Marshall & Co., [c.1783] c.1785), pp. 28–9, 63–4, 39 and 89.

21. Anon., *Virtue and Vice* (London: J. Harris, [c.1780] 1815), pp. 28–9 and 24.

22. See Aileen Fyfe, 'Science for young readers' in *Books and the Sciences in History*, ed. M. Frasca-Spada and N. Jardine, (Cambridge: Cambridge University Press, 2000), pp. 276–90.

23. Maria Edgeworth, 'Preface Addressed to Parents', *The Parent's Assistant; or, Stories for Children* (London: MacMillan and Co., [1796] 1897), p. 3.

24. See M. O. Grenby, ' "Real Charity Makes Distinctions": Schooling the Charitable Impulse in Early British Children's Literature', *British Journal for Eighteenth-Century Studies*, 25 (2002), 185–202.
25. Barbara Hofland, *The Daughter of a Genius* (London: J. Harris, [1823] 1828), p. 111; *The Son of a Genius* (London: John Harris, [1812] 1827), pp. 117–18.
26. Andrew O'Malley, *The Making of the Modern Child: Children's Literature and Childhood in the Late Eighteenth Century* (New York: Routledge, 2003), pp. 1–65.
27. Catharine Macaulay, *Letters on Education* (London and New York: Garland Publishing, [1790] 1974), p. 53.
28. Kilner, *Jemima Placid*, p. 90.
29. Ben Hellman, 'Russia', in *International Companion Encyclopedia of Children's Literature*, vol. 2, p. 1179.
30. Humphrey Carpenter and Mari Prichard, *The Oxford Companion to Children's Literature* (Oxford: Oxford University Press, [1984] 1995), p. 464.
31. Maxim Gorky, 'Soviet Literature,' in *Soviet Writers' Congress 1934: The Debate on Socialist Realism and Modernism in the Soviet Union* (London: Lawrence and Wishart, 1977), p. 67.
32. Peter Hollindale, 'The Adolescent Novel of Ideas', *Only Connect: Readings on Children's Literature*, ed. Sheila Egoff, Gorden Stubbs, Ralph Ashley and Wendy Sutton, 3rd edn (Toronto: Oxford University Press, 1996), pp. 315–26.
33. See Elaine Moss, 'The Seventies in British Children's Books', *The Signal Approach to Children's Books* (Harmondsworth: Kestrel, 1980), pp. 48–80 (p. 63).
34. Jan Needle, *My Mate Shofiq* (London: Lions, [1978] 1979), pp. 10, 88–9 and 98–9.
35. Bernard Ashley, *The Trouble with Donovan Croft* (Harmondsworth: Puffin, [1974] 1977), p. 187.
36. Richard Peck, *Are You in the House Alone?* (New York: Laurel-Leaf, [1976] 1989), p. 137.
37. Berlie Doherty, *Dear Nobody* (London: Collins, [1991] 1997), pp. 1–2 and 47.
38. Doherty, *Dear Nobody*, p. 200.
39. Kilner, *Jemima Placid*, p. 90.

40. Sinclair, *Holiday House*, p. 19; David Rudd, 'The Froebellious Child in Catherine Sinclair's *Holiday House*', *The Lion and the Unicorn*, 28 (2004), 53–69 (p. 61).
41. See Margaret Nancy Cutt, *Ministering Angels. A Study of Nineteenth-century Evangelical Writing for Children* (Wormley: Five Owls Press, 1979) and J. S. Bratton's *The Impact of Victorian Children's Fiction* (London: Croom Helm, 1981).
42. *Guardian of Education*, 1 (1802), 267.
43. Mary Martha Sherwood, *The Little Woodman, and his Dog Cæsar* (Wellington: F. Houlston and Son, [1818] c.1825), pp. 10–11. See M. Nancy Cutt, *Mrs. Sherwood and her Books for Children* (London: Oxford University Press, 1974).
44. Carpenter and Prichard, *Oxford Companion to Children's Literature*, p. 355. See Jane Darcy, ' "Worlds not realized": The work of Louisa Molesworth', in *Popular Victorian Women Writers*, ed. Kay Boardman and Shirley Jones (Manchester: Manchester University Press, 2004), pp. 111–34.
45. Charlotte Yonge, 'Preface', *Scenes and Characters or Eighteen Months at Beechcroft* (London: Macmillan, [1847] 1889), p. viii.
46. Roger Lancelyn Green, *Mrs Molesworth* (London: Bodley Head, 1961), p. 56; Marghanita Laski, *Mrs. Ewing, Mrs. Molesworth and Mrs. Hodgson Burnett* (London: Arthur Baker, 1950), p. 27.
47. Cutt, *Ministering Angels*, p. 68.
48. Ibid., p. 170.
49. Frances Hodgson Burnett, *Haworth's*, 2 vols (London: Macmillan, 1879), vol. 1, pp. 52–3.
50. Gillian Avery, *Nineteenth Century Children: Heroes and Heroines in English Children's Stories 1780–1900* (London: Hodder and Stoughton, 1965), p. 90.

CHAPTER 4

The School Story

Writing in 1940, George Orwell argued that the school story was fundamentally socially and politically conservative and, second, 'a thing peculiar to England.'[1] Both of these judgments are open to question. First, if the genre is inherently conservative, it seems odd that several of the most canonical of its texts were greeted by widespread opprobrium on their first appearance. Rudyard Kipling's *Stalky & Co.* (1899), Robert Cormier's *The Chocolate War* (1974) and Melvyn Burgess' *Doing It* (2003) are all good examples. Second, school stories have existed outside Britain. In Germany *Schulromane* were popular in the nineteenth and twentieth century. Many were being published in the Soviet Union around the time Orwell was writing. And since then, it has been in the United States that many of the most celebrated school stories have appeared – John Knowles' *A Separate Peace* (1960) for example. Indeed, in calling the school story an English genre, Orwell was overlooking many earlier north American classics too, such as Susan Coolidge's *What Katy Did At School* (1873), Louisa May Alcott's *Little Men* (1871) and L. M. Montgomery's *Anne of Avonlea* (1909).

On the other hand, the classic tradition of the school story – narratives in which the school features almost as a character itself, and in which children fit happily into their school, each helping to form the character of the other – does seem to be rooted in British culture. Interestingly, Coolidge's, Alcott's and Montgomery's books were all part of longer series, almost as if these authors had chosen to write about school simply because it was a convenient new theatre for their heroine's operations. As for the German and Russian versions, the former 'appear to be written for an adult rather than a schoolboy audience' one critic has noted, and they usually demonstrate how school adversely affects the development of the individual, rather than how school can be an enjoyable and character-forming experience, whereas many Soviet school stories tended to be written to show how 'an individualistically minded pupil gets corrected by the class collective'.[2] This chapter will reflect the quintessentially British identity of the school story, focusing on texts published first in Britain, although many went on to achieve international popularity. It will be best to point out at the outset that in Britain, a 'public school' actually denotes the most exclusive kind of private school, institutions generally founded in the nineteenth century or earlier and drawing their pupils from the social elite. It should also be noted that most British public schools, as well as other, less prestigious private schools, were single-sex. This resulted in the development of major differences between the traditions of boys' and girls' school stories, differences which will be discussed here as they arise rather than in separate sections. In fact, in recent times, the traditions of boys' and girls' school stories have begun to coalesce, as is evident in the most striking reoccurrence of the form, J. K. Rowling's Harry Potter novels.

Literature designed for children has been set in schools from very early times. Compositions inscribed onto clay in about 2000 BCE have survived which recount school anecdotes amongst the Sumerians of Mesopotamia. One, entitled 'School Days', tells of a boy being late for school because he has overslept and loitered on his way, then getting into further trouble by talking in class and failing to complete his homework. He is beaten, but complains to his father, who invites the headmaster to dinner. Having been treated well and bribed by gifts, the headmaster softens his attitude and praises the boy.[3] This is a remarkable document in itself, but all the more so because of its close similarity to texts being used in medieval England. These *colloquia scholastica*, schoolbooks from which spoken Latin or polite English was to be learned, were produced in substantial numbers from the fifteenth century. They were often composed of dialogues between a master and a pupil, or between fellow schoolboys.[4] A fairly late example is *Pueriles Confabulatiunculae: or Children's Dialogues*, probably written in Latin by Evaldus Gallus in the mid-sixteenth century and which had appeared in English by 1617. Most of its episodes are set in school. Although seriously intentioned, its dialogues are sprightly and even subversive. Somehow the book manages to give a full flavour of a Renaissance schoolroom but also to connect smoothly with the classic school stories of the nineteenth and twentieth centuries. Most of the book's episodes revolve around the laziness of the boys and the perpetual threat of being beaten. But these are pupils who are willing to stand up for themselves, cheekily getting the upper hand over their elders. When the master arrives to beat all the boys who were late to school, for instance, one defends himself by saying that his father had commanded him to check on his crops:

M. [the master] Your father hath command at home, I in the schoole.
A. [Andrew, the pupil] But my father commanded me at home.
M. But I forbad any man to do otherwise, than here I will & command.
A. Will you not, that we obey our parents?
M. Yea, altogether.
A. Why then am I blamed for doing this?

To which the master can only reply, clearly frustrated by the casuistic manoeuvres of his pupil, 'Get thee gone, get thee gone: we spend the time by this strife.' Another boy explains his lateness by pleading that he was forced to help his parents entertain guests who refused to leave until midnight – he escapes the rod, but only if he promises that the master will be invited next time! Beyond such duelling between masters and pupils, there is also much banter and bullying between the boys. They steal one another's property and sneak on each other's wrongdoings: 'Peter hath beaten mee with his fists. . . . He talks of a scurrilous matter. . . . He suffereth me not to study. . . . He hath made water upon my shooes.' And the book ends with a jape straight out of *Billy Bunter* or *The Beano*. When Gisbert is charged by his father to take a sealed letter to the school-master he rightly suspects that it contains instructions for his punishment. Gisbert deftly switches it with one from a school-mate's much more lenient father. The master is thereby instructed never to beat Gisbert but to inflict severe punishment on his innocent but molly-coddled friend.[5]

Although principally a book of instruction, *Pueriles Confabulatiunculae* fulfils what might be thought the three basic criteria of the school story: it is set almost entirely in school; it takes the relationships between the scholars and their teachers as its primary focus; and it contains attitudes and adventures which are unique to school life. These are certainly the hallmarks of the early classics of the genre: Harriet Martineau's *The Crofton Boys* (1841), Thomas Hughes' *Tom Brown's Schooldays* (1857), F. W. Farrar's *Eric, or Little by Little, a Tale of Roslyn School* (1858) and Talbot Baines Reed's *The Fifth Form at St. Dominic's* (first serialised in the *Boy's Own Paper*, 1881–82). The same definition works for the many series which became so popular in the golden age of the girls' story, by L. T. Meade (beginning with *A World of Girls*, 1886), Angela Brazil (from *The Fortunes of Philippa*, 1906), Dorita Fairlie Bruce (from *Dimsie Goes to School*, 1920), Elinor Brent-Dyer (from *The School at the Chalet*, 1925) and Enid Blyton (from *The Twins at St. Clare's*, 1941, and *First Term at Malory Towers*, 1946). Several commentators have felt that this kind of traditional school story was, as Geoffrey Trease put it, 'petering out in the sand' by the mid-twentieth century. Isabel Quigly concurred, calling the final chapter of her study of the genre, *The Heirs of Tom Brown* (1982), 'The decline and fall'.[6] But they were incorrect. Traditional school stories continued to be published, albeit sometimes with a twist. Anne Digby's girls' school stories, from *First Term at Trebizon* in 1978, were conventional in many ways, though, notably, sex was introduced in *Boy Trouble at Trebizon* (1980). The Grange Hill books, based on a British television series, dealt with sex, racism, dyslexia, drugs and many other 'problem issues' from their inception in 1980 with Robert Leeson's *Grange Hill Rules OK?* – but the traditional school story format remained in place. Most remarkably of all, J. K. Rowling's *Harry Potter* series (1997–2007) reused the conventions of the classic school story to great popular acclaim, setting the action at Hogwarts, a school for magicians but in all other respects a reiteration of the traditional British public school.

Many other stories may be set largely in school, but either do not show the school from the pupils' point of view – *The History of Goody Two-Shoes* (1765), for example – or use the school only as a backdrop. Frances Hodgson Burnett's *A Little Princess* (1905) is typical in this regard. Its heroine, Sara Crewe is the victim of her teacher's cruelty, but her retreat into an imaginary world in which she is a princess, takes her well away from the world of school. Louise Fitzhugh's *Harriet the Spy* (1964) similarly relies on a school setting, but its subject is Harriet's personal growth. When the note-books in which she records her scathing opinions of her school-friends are discovered, she realises that she must try to empathise with, rather than condemn, other people. The school setting merely provides the context. Indeed, since the later nineteenth century, almost all Western children have attended school, meaning that writers seeking to represent contemporary children's lives realisti-cally have been more or less forced into one of three courses: to show their protagonists at school, to show them after school or in the school holidays (with the threat of school usually hanging over them), or to somehow remove them from school artificially. This is what the narrator of Roald Dahl's *Danny the Champion of the World* (1975) inadvertently termed 'the problem of school'. 'It was the law that parents must send their children to school at the age of five,' says Danny, 'and my father knew about this.' But Dahl was writing a book about a boy's relationship with his father, so Danny's start at school is delayed for years while he is taught to be a mechanic at home, and then Danny's truancy is connived at by his father when the day of their great poaching adventure comes round. School intrudes occasionally, and we hear of the alcoholism or brutality of the teachers, but Danny always thinks of it in terms of its inferior-ity to his education at home. Whenever he enters the 'squat ugly red-brick' school, he always imagines that the engraved stone cemented into the brickwork commemorating its foundation in the year of Edward VII's coronation – the symbol of its dignity and authority – would have been put to better use if his father was allowed to vandalise it with a series of daily educational but amusing and subversive adages (for instance, 'I'LL BET YOU DIDN'T KNOW THAT IN SOME BIG ENGLISH COUNTRY HOUSES, THE BUTLER STILL HAS TO IRON THE MORNING NEWSPAPER BEFORE PUTTING IT ON HIS MASTER'S BREAKFAST-TABLE'). Moreover, he obstinately resists his father's suggestion that he should invite schoolmates home, not, he says, 'because I didn't have good friends' but 'because I had such a good time being alone with my father.'[7]

Dahl's fantasy of a son's greater love for his father than his friends flies in the face of most school stories, where fellowship between the pupils is key. Indeed, a great many school stories deal directly with the gradual integration of new pupils into the school community. Angela Brazil's *For the School Colours* (1918), for instance, as well as including an episode with the unmasking of a German spy, centres around the entrance into snobbish Silverside of girls from a less prestigious school. Over the course of the novel, Aveline, with the advice of her friend Mrs Lesbia Carrington, teaches the established Silverside pupils to accept the incomers, and the new girls to fit into Silverside's traditions. However, the majority of school stories focus on the integration of the individual not the group. In Blyton's *First Term at Malory Towers*, the semi-autobiographical Darrell Rivers arrives at the school, worried about fitting in. She chooses badly at first, but ultimately finds the friends who will accompany her for the rest of the series. It is not difficult to see why this process of friend-gathering is so central to many school stories. First, it provides a frame for the narrative. Second, it was often designed to reassure nervous pupils that they would soon find friends. After all, school stories have often been written for the benefit of scared school entrants, from *Tom Brown's Schooldays*, written, as Thomas Hughes said, to convey to his eight-year-old son 'what I should like to say to him before he went to school', to Janet and Allan Ahlberg's more obviously didactic *Starting School* (1988), deliberately designed to help children settle in to this new phase of their lives.[8] And third, the acquisition of friends is central to one of the key themes of the school story, what we might call socialisation, or, to borrow a term from psychoanalysis, individuation. This, according to Carl Jung, is the way in which the wholeness of the self is established by integrating the individual psyche and the collective unconscious of the community, or at least its collective identity. School settings clearly offer a perfect opportunity to depict children learning to balance their sense of self and of community, to mature by integrating themselves into society.

Even some of the very earliest school stories address this theme. *School Occurrences: Supposed to Have Arisen Among a Set of Young Ladies, Under the Tuition of Mrs. Teachwell* (1782), by 'Mrs. Lovechild' (probably Ellinor Fenn), is largely an account of the social negotiations between the four pupils, Miss Sprightly, Miss Pert, Miss Cheat and Miss Pry.[9] Similarly, but about boys, Maria Edgeworth's 'The Barring Out; or, Party Spirit' (1796) is a moral tale with the clear aim of dissuading pupils from forming themselves into gangs. In psychological terms, it is about the boys' *over-*identification with the group, Edgeworth attempting to steer readers back towards a sense of their own individual identity. The story begins conventionally with the arrival of a new boy, Archer. It is he who brings the idea of 'parties' to Dr Middleton's small village school. Seeing another popular boy, De Grey, as a rival, Archer divides the school into two factions, the Archers and the Greybeards. To cement his popularity, he leads his gang in a 'barring-out': an eighteenth-century English schoolboy custom which involves locking themselves into the classroom with enough food and drink to survive a siege by their teacher. Their hope is that they will be able to extract greater privileges from him. In Edgeworth's story, the barring-out goes awry, with food running out and mutiny amongst the conspirators. The situation is saved only when De Grey volunteers as a hostage, and by Archer's belated realisation that De Grey and he should be friends not rivals. Dr Middleton ends the story by commending Archer's decision: 'one such friend is worth two such parties'. In fact, though, as the school story genre developed Edgeworth's warnings against gangs would go unheeded, for close-knit, exclusive friendships would become a frequent feature of school stories. They might be slightly subversive, as with Stalky, Beetle and M'Turk in Rudyard Kipling's *Stalky & Co.* (1899), or mawkishly sanctimonious, as with the 'Secret Society of Fairbank' in L. T. Meade's *The School Favourite* (1908) with its strict four-rule code: 'Love, Obedience, Work, Do a little deed of kindness to some one every day' ('Then, you see, having sworn to love, to obey our teachers, to work, and to do kindnesses, we are formed into a band . . . and I don't think all through our lives this band of fellowship can ever be broken.').[10] But overall, even those school stories which centred on a gang of friends would continue to echo Edgeworth's demand for a balance between individual and community, self-reliance and camaraderie.

It is extraordinary that Edgeworth's eighteenth-century text already contained many of the standard features of the classic boys' school story. As early as 1796, it seems, Edgeworth was operating within a well-defined set of literary conventions, rather than attempting to represent actual school life. The new boy, the stern but kindly master, the midnight feast, the bully, the gluttonous buffoon (named Fisher in 'The Barring-Out', a clear prototype of the famous Billy Bunter who first appeared in 1908 in *The Magnet*) – all these would become very familiar motifs. So too would be the apparent rarity of actual lessons, the sense of school-boy honour, the way in which a chorus of pupils gathers round each protagonist, swayed by their oratory to take one side or another. They play a role much like the mob in Shakespeare's Greco-Roman plays, something recognised by Archer: 'O ye Athenians,' he says to his party, 'how hard do I work to obtain your praise.'[11] Above all, it is Edgeworth's presentation of the power-struggles being waged in the fictional boys' schools that would endure. The rivalry between individual pupils would receive its definitive treatment in the conflict between Tom and the bully Flashman in *Tom Brown's Schooldays*. But it is the continuing struggle for power between pupils and their teachers which is more interesting. 'Masters are regarded as common enemies', the seventeen-year-old Alec Waugh wrote in *The Loom of Youth* (1916), his exposé of life at Fernhurst, a thinly disguised portrait of the English public school which he had just left.[12] This is certainly the impression one gets from Kipling's *Stalky & Co.*, which represents the boys fighting an unremitting guerrilla war, based on mutual detestation, against their housemaster, Mr Prout, and Latin master, Mr King. In Anthony Buckeridge's more decorous school stories of the 1950s and '60s the hostilities have become a little less vindictive, but remain just as central to the narrative, Jennings constantly skirmishing with his teacher Mr Wilkins. Even a modern, jovial story of a co-educational school, Louis Sachar's *Sideways Stories from Wayside School* (1978), opens with Mrs Gorf, 'the meanest teacher in Wayside School', maliciously turning her class one by one into apples until they get their own back by holding a mirror up to her spell.[13]

These hostilities are interesting because they complicate the issues of authority and obedience which lie at the heart of the school story. Superficially, the teachers wield the power and the pupils are required to obey, generally coerced by the threat of severe punishment. But in fact, the children challenge this authority at every turn. In nineteenth-century novels, Gillian Avery points out, this is often because of the class divide, the children, coming from the upper orders, immediately recognising that the teachers are their social inferiors.[14] But the public school boys of children's fiction also seem to break rules on principle. Stalky and his friends seem to regard it as their duty to smoke although they know that if they are discovered they will be expelled. Tom Brown, before his reformation, plans to install 'a bottled-beer cellar under his window' and to slip out from his dormitory every night to fish.[15] Alec Waugh gave clear indications that sodomy was widely practiced and approved of by the boys at Fernhurst, although it was strictly prohibited.[16] In 'The Barring-Out' rebellion is the central theme. Archer's mutiny begins when Dr Middleton forbids the boys to use a building in the school grounds for a theatre. Archer calls this tyranny. Only later do we learn that Dr Middleton knew the building was infected with a dangerous fever. After the siege, Dr Middleton delivers a lesson about the necessary obedience of children to adults acting *in loco parentis*: 'You have rebelled against the just authority which is necessary to conduct and govern yourselves.' But more interesting is his awareness of why Archer rebelled: 'You, sir, think yourself a man . . . and you think it the part of a man not to submit to the will of another.'[17] What 'The Barring-Out' demonstrates, more transparently than most later texts, is that the school story is about children establishing a balance between the obedience of childhood and independence of adulthood. Indeed, the whole structure of the school story, particularly the boarding school story, serves to represent this. They are authoritarian places, with strict rules and harsh discipline, but they are also places of great freedom for their pupils. Teachers are generally absent from their pupils' lives, like Dr Middleton in 'The Barring-Out' or the staff of Rowling's

Hogwarts. So long as the pupils abide by the basic regulations – lesson-times, meal-times, bed-times and so on – they are largely autonomous agents, free to choose their own activities and obey their own rules. Without their decision to break the school rules, there would often be little or no narrative remaining.

Most boys' school stories, then, position their heroes in the paradoxical role of rule-bound rule-breakers. In many nineteenth-century texts this contradiction is resolved by having two levels of teachers: those the boys encounter on a day-to-day basis, regarded as the enemy, and a remote headmaster, who sits in judgment even on his teaching staff. In Kipling's *Stalky & Co.* for example, regular use is made of the pupils' right to appeal to the headmaster if they feel they have been unfairly treated by staff, as when Stalky and his friends are accused of being drunk. The headmaster sides with the boys, refusing to accede to their housemaster's demands for their expulsion. Disregarding the rules, he then administers a beating to show that discipline remains intact. It is a display of arbitrary power which the boys cheerfully accept. Then surprisingly and subversively, he shows his approval of the boys' tormenting of their teachers by allowing them to borrow from his collection of boys' adventure stories. Later, he even confides to an old boy that 'It isn't the boys that make trouble; it's the masters'. This might affirm what most school story pupils think, but to undermine the teachers' authority like this would have been unthinkable in earlier school stories, and would remain so in many later stories, perhaps especially those designed for girls.[18] The morality of such episodes is vexed. In legalistic terms, Kipling and others seem to suggest that boys should respect the judge but deplore the police. But the splitting of authority like this enables the school story to make the argument that boys develop into men by both respecting and testing authority. They mature by a combination of submission and defiance.

This fits neatly into a religious context. Kipling had based his portrait of the 'Head' on Cormell Price, his real-life headmaster at the United Services College. In this, he was following Thomas Hughes, whose *Tom Brown's Schooldays* had featured his headmaster at Rugby School, Thomas Arnold, as the 'Doctor'. Tom Brown comes to idolise him but only in the book's final paragraph, after the

Doctor's death, is the reader told that Tom's 'hero-worship' of the Doctor was a necessary precursor to 'the worship of Him who is the King and Lord of heroes'.[19] In *Stalky & Co.* the Head is literally a saviour, sucking diphtheria mucus from a sick boy's throat and restoring him to life, for which he is worshipped by Stalky and his friends. This connection between the Headmaster and God has become almost a standard feature of the school story, from Dr Middleton in 'The Barring-Out' to Professor Dumbledore in the Harry Potter books. They are loving and benevolent but just and severe, demanding obedience and ready to inflict harsh punishment, or to forgive. Each of their pupils has the free will to choose whether to abide by their teachers' commandments or not. Those who disobey can face physical chastisement, something like the torments of Hell, or worse, face expulsion from the school, their paradise, as befalls Flashman in *Tom Brown's Schooldays* or Fisher, who is 'barred-out' from Edgeworth's educational paradise. But those who sin against their teachers' authority and repent can be welcomed back into the fold – like Archer, who recognises his error and welcomes his punishment, or Tom Brown who is gradually brought away from his early bad behaviour by the subtle intervention of the Doctor. The universe of such school stories, then, is reminiscent of Puritan children's books. Each boy is urged to accept the discipline of the school voluntarily, embracing its authority, in much the same way as Protestant theology insists that each sinner should individually welcome grace into his or her heart. Like Archer before him, Tom Brown is gradually drawn into submission: 'We've always been honourable enemies with the masters', he tells his friend East, trying to convert him to his own new moral views. 'We found a state of war when we came, and went into it of course. Only don't you think things are altered a good deal? I don't feel as I used to the masters.'[20] Learning to accept authority, these boys are really reiterations of the sinners struggling to be pious in Benjamin Keach's *War with the Devil* (1673) or James Janeway's *Token for Children* (1672). In the school story, as in the Puritan world-view, their obedience is never enforced but must be the consequence of their own free-will.

In fact, once one looks for the connections between the Puritan tradition of children's literature and the school story they become increasingly evident. Perhaps the most obvious connection is to be found in the very first of the recognisably modern school stories, Sarah Fielding's *The Governess; or, the Little Female Academy* (1749). Like *Sideways Stories from Wayside School*, *The Governess* opens with apples. Here, the nine girls enrolled at Mrs Teachum's school argue about who should eat the largest apple, a dispute which immediately suggests the disobedience of Adam and Eve and their misuse of free-will. What follows is a description of the way that each of the girls comes to accept her errors and to modify her behaviour. As in so many school stories, Mrs Teachum is largely absent from the narrative. The main body of the book describes the pupils' meetings together after their lessons. Each takes it in turn to tell the story of her life and, almost as if they are on the psychoanalyst's couch, they identify the reason for their behavioural failings, and promise to reform. Mrs Teachum's surrogate is the eldest pupil, Jenny Peace. She speaks kindly to the younger girls, encouraging their introspection, and she acts as a mediator between the pupils and their teacher, asking, for instance, if it is permissible for them to tell fairy tales. In religious terms, and as her surname hints, Jenny Peace can be read as Christ, sent to save the sinners, and a representative of the godlike, remote Mrs Teachum. But Jenny Peace can also seem rather sinister, Mrs Teachum's infiltrating agent. At first, Mrs Teachum herself wanders the school gardens, occasionally dropping in on the arbour where the girls are gathered. But although she 'had a great Inclination to hear the History of the Lives of all her little Scholars . . . she thought, that her presence at those Relations might be a Balk to the Narration, as perhaps they might be ashamed freely to confess their past Faults before her'. To this end, she tells Jenny that 'She would have her get the Lives of her Companions in Writing, and bring them to her', a command which Jenny obeys (the record she keeps, one might suggest, becoming the book that Fielding wrote).[21] Such surveillance would become a feature of many school stories, with informers like Jenny frequently featuring (the role of tale-teller being given more approval in girls' than boys' stories according to Beverly Lyon Clark).[22] But on other occasions it is not quite so clear just how the teachers know what is happening throughout their school. At Rowling's Hogwarts, Professor Dumbledore's ability to be in the right place at the right time suggest an all-seeing eye, and we are left to deduce that all the school's ghosts, sentient portraits and so on act as informants. Certainly Rowling created a world in which all is known to the authorities. Harry's illegal casting of a spell in the school holidays, for example, is followed only moments later by an owl-borne reproof from the Ministry of Magic.[23]

What is significant is not how or even whether the teachers are omniscient, but that the pupils regard themselves as always being under their monitoring gaze. This is the sort of analysis Michel Foucault might have applied to the school story. Writing of prisons, and of society in general, Foucault suggested in his book *Discipline and Punish* (1975), that if someone is aware that they might be under surveillance, they begin to internalise the disciplinary code of those who watch them. In short, they begin to police themselves, meaning that authority no longer has to coerce them into compliance. Foucault's thinking illuminates *The Governess*. Its central theme might be said to be the way that the pupils learn to monitor their own behaviour and to conduct themselves as Mrs Teachum would wish, even when she is not present. They analyse themselves to find out why they disappoint their teacher. The stories they tell also reveal their internalisation of the need for submission. *The Governess* is usually celebrated for including two fairy stories at a time when such tales of the supernatural were reviled as too immoral. But what is not so often noticed is the severe discipline suggested by the longer of these, 'The Princess Hebe'. The main lesson is stated early on by the fairy who saves Hebe's life:

> it was absolutely necessary . . . that she should entirely obey the queen her mother, without ever pretending to examine her commands; for 'true obedience (said she) consists in sub-mission; and when we pretend to choose what commands are proper and fit for us, we don't obey, but set up our own wisdom in opposition to our governors – this, my dear Hebe, you must be very careful of avoiding, if you would be happy.'[24]

The rest of the tale is designed to reinforce the lesson. Certainly, by the time Jenny Peace leaves the school her fellow pupils' habit of self-monitoring is fully installed, Jenny's eye remaining upon them in her absence, as it were, so that 'if any Girl was found to harbour in her Breast a rising Passion, which it was difficult to conquer, the Name and Story of Miss *Jenny Peace* soon gained her Attention, and left her without any other Desire than to emulate Miss *Jenny's* Virtues.'[25] The same pattern frequently recurs, especially in girls' school stories. In Meade's *The School Favourite* (1908), for example, the girls have drawn up their own code of behaviour. But its discipline is far stricter that what their teachers might have imposed. When they transgress, they fine themselves: even the youngest girl, for instance, 'turning scarlet, got off her seat, flew up to Betty' – their president – 'buried her head in her neck and whispered something. Betty took twopence from the hot, chubby little hand and put it in the fundbox', the proceeds of which are given termly to the Society for the Prevention of Cruelty to Children. Because they have internalised the values of the school so thoroughly, they 'are allowed to go without any teachers, because Mrs Temple trusts us so completely.'[26]

One might even go so far as to say that the internalisation of a school's ethos was the central theme of most of the classic school stories of the nineteenth century. *Tom Brown's Schooldays*, for instance, is essentially the story of a boy gradually learning to behave as Dr Arnold would like, even – or especially – when he does not realise that the Doctor is observing his behaviour. Similarly, in Elinor Brent-Dyer's *Exploits of the Chalet Girls* (1933) a proud, aristocratic Prussian girl called Thekla von Stift learns to stifle the snobbishness which goes against the School's egalitarian ethos. This is constructed as a positive thing – 'the atmosphere of the School was doing its duty and she was already a nicer girl than the one who had come in September'.[27] It can also seem like the suppression of individuality. This, notes Debbie Pinfold, was the chief characteristic of the German school story which often 'portrays school life through the eyes of a sensitive, artistic individual who is eventually crushed by the system.'[28] But many classic British and American examples also represent what are essentially totalitarian establishments, each pupil inevitably succumbing, like Winston Smith in Orwell's *1984*, to their 'atmosphere' or 'ethos' or, to use a more loaded term, 'ideology'. Perhaps this was based in reality.

Certainly it was W. H. Auden's opinion that 'at school I lived in a Fascist state'. By deliberately appealing to 'loyalty and honour' ('the only emotion that is fully developed in a boy of fourteen') his teachers, Auden claimed, had been able to create a repressive state policed by self-censorship and informants. The consequence was a community of emotionally stunted boys whose only motivations were fear and competition.[29] Curiously, the character who exhibits this internalisation of the school ethos, and emotional stuntedness, most dramatically is J. M. Barrie's Captain Hook. In *Peter and Wendy* (1911) he agonises about what his Eton College schoolmates would have regarded as good and bad form, and even as he dies, his mind is 'slouching in the playing fields of long ago, or being sent up [for a reward from the headmaster] for good, or watching the wall-game from a famous wall.'[30] Geraldine McCaughrean took up the theme in her sequel, *Peter Pan in Scarlet* (2006), revealing that Hook's longed-for treasure is school trophies, and that the trauma which motivates his misanthropy is that his mother removed him from school before he had a chance to win them.[31]

In fact, totalitarianism has often been very deliberately brought into post-War school stories. Some of the Chalet Schools novels of the 1930s and '40s are set in the shadow of Nazism. In Cormier's *The Chocolate War*, the teacher Brother Leon accuses his pupils of turning 'this classroom into Nazi Germany for a few moments' because they do not intervene as he falsely accuses a student of cheating (a heavy irony, since it is Leon himself who tyrannically bullies his pupils).[32] More comic, but just as menacing, is the school in Gillian Cross's *The Demon Headmaster* (1982). Here the internalisation of the regime is more literal, the power-hungry headmaster hypnotising his school so that they might learn more effectively, win televised quiz competitions, and provide him with national exposure for his sinister ideas ('to have everything sorted out tidily, everything settled for you', to be 'the first properly organized, truly efficient country in the world'). His teachers and prefects are his storm-troopers ('All pupils shall obey the prefects,' they chant. 'The prefects are the voice of the Headmaster.') and those few children who can resist his hypnosis become dissidents, forced into covert operations to destabilise the regime ('I feel like Winston Smith', one of them confides).[33] But the battle for control between school and pupil is personal as well as political. In *The Chalet School and the Lintons* (1934), Thekla becomes the first pupil to be expelled. Ostensibly this is because of her vengeful animosity towards other girls, but it is also a consequence of her determination to remain herself in the face of the school's normalising regime. The same independence is characteristic of the only other girl expelled in the Chalet School novels, Betty Wynne-Davies, described in quasi-political terms as one of 'the worst firebrands the school had ever known'. Notably, Brent-Dyer also characterises both girls as more sexualised than their fellow pupils. Thekla is sixteen years old, but 'in some ways she was a good three or four years older than that', while Betty is found 'using *lipstick*'.[34] They are, it seems, expelled for much the same reason as the nylon-wearing, lipstick-using, invitation-craving Susan Pevensie is banished from Narnia in C. S. Lewis's *The Last Battle* (1956): because they have grown up.[35]

The internalisation of the school ethos is shown most deliberately by Kipling in *Stalky & Co*. His protagonists claim to despise the values which their teachers attempt to instil, especially the ideals of *Tom Brown's Schooldays*: muscular Christianity, fair play, loyalty to the 'house'.[36] But importantly, Stalky and his friends actually devote much of their energy to supporting their house's honour. In response to taunts about their own uncleanliness for example, they place a dead cat under the floorboards of a rival house. Moreover, Stalky and his friends might openly scorn the ethos of the school, but in fact they absorb all its values, turning out to be precisely the kind of army officer whom the school was designed to produce. Kipling represents this inevitable internalisation of ethos clearly in the final story in the collection, 'Slaves of the Lamp Part II'. It recounts the adventures of a grown-up Stalky on the North-West Frontier of India, employing the same tricks to defeat the Khye-Kheen and Malôt tribesmen as he had used to revenge himself on his Latin master. He is still not the gentlemanly, manly hero of *Tom Brown's Schooldays*, always playing fair, but certainly the rebellious boy has been transformed into the willing and devoted agent of empire. Ideological co-option has succeeded where physical coercion had failed.

Fighting at the furthest frontier of empire, if not beyond, Stalky at least remains as unconventional in his tactics as he had been at school. He has formed a strong bond with his Sikh soldiers, who revere him as an almost divine leader, and his old school friends rely on rumour to hear of his exploits. He has much in common with Kurtz in Joseph Conrad's *Heart of Darkness*, published in 1902, three years after the first edition of *Stalky & Co*. The similarity only emphasises the immersion of the classic boys' school story in the discourse of empire. *Tom Brown's Schooldays* can be understood as a preparation for imperial administrators, showing how such schools taught the values necessary for the Empire to be maintained. Tom's father is clear upon this point, admitting that he sends his son to school not 'to make himself a good scholar' but only so he might 'turn out a brave, helpful, truth-telling Englishman, and a gentleman, and a Christian.'[37] Don Randall has argued that Kipling went further. Stalky's school is 'not merely a training ground', but is itself an 'imperial space, a "combat zone" characterised by factional conflicts and territorial struggles.' He is referring to the war Stalky and the other schoolboys wage on the 'natives' of Devonshire, and the way in which 'boys and masters compete for control of various out-of-bounds spaces.' Much the same might be said of many other school stories. The boys of Frank Richards' Greyfriars College, for example, are at war with the local landowner, Sir Hilton Popper. It is not only in Kipling, then, that the school world is presented 'as a valid, and viable space for imperial endeavour'.[38]

It was the enduring popular stories about Greyfriars College by Frank Richards (the favourite pseudonym of Charles Hamilton) that provided the focus for George Orwell's stinging attack on school stories in 1940. Richards' narratives, featuring in weekly magazines like *The Magnet* (1908–40), Orwell thought deeply conservative. They possessed only two 'basic political assumptions', he wrote: 'nothing ever changes, and foreigners are funny.' 'Everything is safe, solid and unquestionable', he continued. 'Everything will be the same for ever and ever.' Orwell also insisted that these stories were read preponderantly by children from the lower-middle and working classes, rather than those who might actually be sent to the sort of expensive boarding school which they featured (attended, after all, by only three per cent of the population). This meant that the stories were 'a perfectly deliberate incitement to wealth-fantasy'. Above, all, they were a product of the English educational system, based more than anything else on status. It was a system, Orwell argued, in which people were segregated according to their schooling: the working classes did not pay for education; their social superiors were divided between those educated at minor private schools, and those who had attended the major public schools.[39] The shadow this demarcation could cast on the later life of a status-conscious adult is indicated by Charles Hamilton's own equivocation about whether or not he had attended a public school. 'He would not say that he had, but he more or less dared me ever to say that he had not', reported one interviewer, adding that 'I came away with the impression that, like so many of his boyish admirers, he had never been to a public school, but he wished that he had.'[40]

Against Orwell, it might be argued that the school story, perhaps particularly the girls' school story, was more often driven by an egalitarian impulse. As already noted, Brazil's *For the School Colours* and Brent-Dyer's *Exploits of the Chalet Girls*, amongst many similar texts, dealt with the successful integration into one school of girls from different social classes. The same might be said of Rowling's Harry Potter books, in which Ron Weasley, from a poor background, mixes on equal terms with Hermione Granger, from a squarely middle-class family (her parent are dentists) and Harry, who is descended from wizarding aristocracy. But what is important is that Orwell's analysis was widely held to be correct, so that after the Second World War school stories began to appear which deliberately challenged the genre's perceived elitism. Geoffrey Trease's *No Boats on Bannermere* (1949) and its sequels were very deliberately set in an average school. Its origin, Trease claimed, was a request from two girls he met when invited to speak at their school, that he should 'write true-to-life stories, about real boys and girls, going to day-schools as nearly everybody did'. In fact, their claim that 'No one seemed to write that sort' was not quite true.[41] Winifred Darch, for one, had written about ordinary schools in the 1920s and '30s.[42] But in any case, the idea of writing school stories which would not be set in exclusive, fee-paying and boarding establishments suited Trease's ideological agenda. He was a communist, and a firm believer that children's books must reflect real social realities. He had corresponded with Orwell, planning the establishment of 'some Leftish juvenile publishing scheme, pink in shade, perhaps backed by the T.U.C. [Trades Union Council] or the Liberal *News Chronicle*'.[43] The scheme never got off the ground, but *No Boats at Bannermere* was not the only book that might have been used as a prototype. *The Old Gang* (1947) by Laurence Maynell (writing as A. Stephen Tring) had already depicted the conflict between the pupils of two neighbouring schools, one a high-status 'grammar school', the other a lowly 'secondary modern'. It was an illustration of the divisions and jealousies established by the Education Act of 1944, which separated British children into three types of school depending on their performance in an examination taken when aged eleven.

Some of the post-War stories set in more realistic school settings have been judged to be just as formulaic as their boarding-school forerunners. E. W. Hildick's *Jim Starling* (1958) and its sequels, for example, are usually discussed in histories of the genre only because of their depiction of the grim Cement Street Secondary Modern School. Mabel Esther Allan's *The School on Cloud-Ridge* (1952) and *Lucia Comes to School* (1953), likewise, are most noteworthy because they are set in progressive schools, where the children impose discipline on themselves (not very different, in fact, from the lawlessness depicted in *Stalky & Co.*, and a theme exploited for its comic value by Gene Kemp in *Dog Days and Cat Naps* (1980) in which a class tries to discipline itself to demonstrate that they should be allowed on a school trip). William Mayne's school stories are also remarkable for their unconventional setting – in a cathedral choir school (presumably based on Canterbury, where Mayne had been a pupil). In some ways they are highly original, full of very subtle expression of the boys' mystification at the school's systems, and depicting a very close relationship between pupils and teachers. This intimacy is emphasised when, at one point in *A Swarm in May* (1955), the first novel in the series, the boys slowly bury their teacher in the sand. Probably because they have never lived outside a institution which provides for all their needs, Mayne's teachers are as dependent and ingenuous as the boys they teach. In other ways, the books are more conventional. Relationships between pupils are a major focus. Owen, the most junior chorister in *A Swarm in*

May, is infatuated with the oldest boy, Trevithic. Mayne also provides some of the standard moral lessons of the school story. The choir should not think of itself as a collection of individuals, but should work together. And the moral of *A Swarm in May* is apparently that 'we must all do our respective duties without argument'.[44] It is a lesson Owen has learned by finally accepting his role as 'Beekeeper', part of a cathedral ritual traditionally undertaken by the youngest pupil. Ultimately, for all its intricate patterning and emotional intelligence, *A Swarm in May* is as optimistic a novel as *Tom Brown's Schooldays*, dealing with a boy's discovery of his own true nature and his proper place in the community.

Mayne's school stories provide a detour from the main road taken by the genre in the post-War years – the gradual inclusion of a greater degree of social realism. Gene Kemp's *Cricklepit Combined School* (1977), set in a run-down school full of rowdy children, was one important contribution to this trend, but it was to reach its zenith in Britain not in books, but in a television programme: *Grange Hill*. This series, devised by Phil Redmond and running from 1978, was part soap opera but still fundamentally a school story. Indeed, it quickly produced a number of spin-off books, some based on the television plotlines, others original, the series beginning with the Marxist writer Robert Leeson's *Grange Hill Rules OK?* (1980). *Grange Hill* was immersed in the school story tradition, but also redefined it. Its attempt at realism was what impressed most early viewers, both positively and negatively. Some critics complained, for instance, about the improbable laxity of the teachers at Grange Hill School. In truth, these ineffective, solipsistic teachers are direct descendants of the masters in *Stalky & Co.*, while Grange Hill's long-time headmistress, Bridget McClusky, stands in a long line of stern but fair headteachers stretching back to Edgeworth's Dr. Middleton. *Grange Hill* was not realistic in its verisimilitude then, but because of its objective depiction of ordinary lives, following in the tradition of realist writers like Henry James. Indeed, it was almost Dickensian, often focusing on lower-class characters. In doing so, it was clearly different from American counterparts like Francine Pascal's *Sweet Valley High* books (from 1984), set in a far more glamorous school world and starring identical twins each of whom the narrator happily describes as 'about the most adorable, most dazzling sixteen-year-old girl imaginable'.[45] *Grange Hill*'s insistence of character development also marks a divergence from the classic British tradition, although again, it built on some recent developments. In earlier school stories the characters had often lived in a state of suspended animation. Frank Richards' Greyfriars stories, for instance, followed the academic calendar. But each September, the pupils returned to school no older than they had been a year before. But Geoffrey Trease's *Bannermere* series had already shown its protagonists advancing through their school years, until they ended up at university. *Grange Hill* imitated this (though the aging of the actors perhaps forced the issue). That there was seldom any prospect of the *Grange Hill* pupils graduating to university shows how far Phil Redmond had advanced Trease's attempt to write about real-life working-class schoolchildren.

Overall then, *Grange Hill* was not absolutely innovative, but the ideas Redmond took from contemporary children's books were accentuated so heavily and given such wide currency on television that they did change the direction of the school story. The two areas in which this is particularly true are his depiction of 'problems' and of the relationships between male and female characters. For most of the history of the British school story, schools had been single-sex. Only in the 1970s did fiction begin to catch up with reality of co-education. The moment at the very end of Gene Kemp's *The Turbulent Term of Tyke Tiler* (1977) when Tyke is revealed to be a girl, Theodora, might be taken as symbolic of the full admittance of co-education and its surrounding issues into the school story tradition. Certainly from the 1970s, single-sex establishments have become the exception in fiction. As for sex, it had been almost entirely absent from the British school story, except for some controversial references to homosexuality, in Alec Waugh's *The Loom of Youth* (1916) for example. This had not been the case in American texts. Much of Susan Coolidge's *What Katy Did At School* (1873) focused on the infatuation of Kate's school-girl friends with the boys at a neighbouring school. The same theme runs through the *Sweet Valley High* books, which star the flirtatious Jessica and the serially monogamous Elizabeth, although they remain essentially chaste. In Britain, the influence of books like

Judy Blume's *Forever* (1975) and Aidan Chamber's *Breaktime* (1978) was soon felt in school narrative, and sex, or at least relationships, became central.

The issue was treated in a number of contrasting ways. Anne Digby's *Boy Trouble at Trebizon* (1980) remained rather genteel, seeing relationships as an obstacle to be overcome if girls were to achieve academic or sporting success. More graphic are Robert Westall's *Falling into Glory* (1993) and *Doing It* (2003) by Melvyn Burgess, both involving a sexual relationship between a pupil and a teacher. Both these authors, in the manner of *Grange Hill*, did not seek to confine the action of their novels to school, but nevertheless revolved much of the plot around it. Both attempted to capture the authentic feelings of seventeen-year-old schoolboys. In *Doing It*, Dino is so desperate to lose his virginity that he betrays the girl-friend he has for years pursued for someone he thinks 'a bit of a slapper'; Jonathan is confused because the girl he desires is his best friend, and anyway, he 'can't bear the social humiliation of being seen out regularly with a fat girl'; and Ben has to deal with the devastating consequences of 'every schoolboy's dream . . . an affair with an attractive young teacher.'[46] Other important sexualised school stories include the Australian Jenny Pausacker's *What Are Ya?* (1987), which introduced lesbian sexuality into school, a theme already explored less graphically in the American Deborah Hautzig's *Hey, Dollface* (1979). Adèle Geras returned to the traditional boarding-school setting of the British school story for her fairy tale-inspired *Egerton Hall* trilogy (1990–92). In each of these, a girl is traumatised by her sexual encounters. In *The Tower Room* and *Pictures of the Night* the girl has to choose between a boyfriend and college; in *Watching the Roses* she is raped. All these texts demonstrate how radically sex has changed the previously stable patterns of school story life.

But ultimately it is probably the continuities which are more striking than the changes. A comparison of *Doing It* with *Stalky & Co.*, for instance, might at first seem absurd. Immediately highlighted would be the implausibility of Kipling's teenagers who are, apparently, entirely unconcerned with sex (although others have been dubious about Burgess's portrait of boys who are able to think about nothing else: 'God help the publishers and their grubby little lives if they think this tosh is realistic', wrote Anne Fine in one scathing review).[47] Yet Dino, Jonathan and Ben do fit nicely into the roles of Kipling's Stalky, M'Turk and Beetle. The close relationship and separation from the main body of the school are the same for both triumvirates. So too is the sense that school is a preparation for conquests and conflicts to come – at the ends of Empire for Stalky, and for Burgess's characters, in a 'world . . . full of good-looking girls'.[48] Above all, what reading the two books in parallel suggests is that the braggadocio of both sets of boys masks their vulnerability. The sexual swagger of Burgess's characters dissolves when faced with the possibility of actual sexual contact. Their ritualised bragging, it becomes clear, is chiefly intended to bolster their own self-esteem. It is an expression of their anxiety about how they are regarded within the school. So too, we cannot help but suspect, is Stalky's endless need to challenge prefects and teachers, to skip out of school to smoke, and to receive the homage of other boys, even M'Turk and Beetle ('Isn't your Uncle Stalky a great man?' he asks, having Beetle kicked until he concurs).[49] In this sense, both books are about boys desiring to be adults but confined by an environment which regards them as children.

Relationships and sex are not the only 'problem issues' to have featured in recent school stories. *Grange Hill* was celebrated for its plot lines involving, amongst other things, shoplifting, teenage pregnancy, suicide, Asperger's syndrome, child abuse, truancy, racism, disability, AIDS, playground knifings, rape, alcoholism, homophobia, drug-abuse and bereavement. Amongst this procession of problems, the one issue to feature most constantly was that consistent theme of the school story, bullying. Flashman, in *Tom Brown's Schooldays*, is perhaps the archetype, tyrannising smaller boys, stood up to by Tom, and then expelled, in this case for drunkenness. The key elements here are Flashman's confinement of his bullying to general harassment of younger boys, his only tangential relationship to the main plot, and his final punishment by the proper authorities. Each of these elements has been revised. In *Grange Hill*, the most notorious of its succession of bullies, Norman 'Gripper' Stebson (in the programme from 1981–85), excelled Flashman by demanding money with menaces, and then adding racism, to his campaigns of persecution. Likewise, in Aidan

Chambers' *The Present Takers* (1983), one of the first school stories to focus exclusively on bullying, Melanie Prosser used racism to cement her powers of extortion: '*She called me bootpolish and made her gang try to wash me off in the toilet and made some others write stuff on the walls about me which said Go Home*', one victim recalled.[50]

The way to deal with bullies had been re-assessed earlier. In a chapter of *Stalky & Co.*, ironically called 'The Moral Reformers', it was the boys themselves who ended the bullies' careers by luring them into positions of weakness and contriving for them to receive the same physical abuse as they had been inflicting. Again, comparisons with more recent school narratives are illuminating. In *Grange Hill*, 'Gripper' Stebson's career was ended when the pupils he had been terrorising ganged up to inflict retribution. But in a move which confirmed the programme's fundamental conservatism, a teacher stepped in at the last moment to prevent such vigilantism. Instead of being lynched 'Gripper' was expelled: a morally sound message for the audience, but, after *Stalky & Co.*, a re-investment of power, and both real and moral authority, in the adults. On the other hand, Chambers, like Kipling, was apparently convinced that bullying could be defeated only by pupils. Lucy, a victim of Melanie's harassment and extortion, knows that her teachers are 'hopeless', and that if she was to tell them about events in the playground, the teachers would 'make a fuss, but nothing will happen' except that the bullying would get worse. Even when Lucy's parents find out and confront Melanie's mother, they admit that they are powerless. The victims' own ingenious solution is to combine to expose Melanie's cruelty in the class newspaper, a rejection of the violence employed by Stalky and friends, though perhaps reminiscent of Beetle's journalistic attacks on his teachers. Finding herself exposed to ridicule, Melanie is forced to capitulate. It is apparently an optimistic resolution, endorsing the power of pupils but also of print: flattering for all those involved in the production and dissemination of children's literature. But in fact, this utopianism is subtly undermined by Chambers's complicated plot which has Melanie removed from school, ultimately, because of her father's physical abuse, a new kind of bullying that has been exacerbated, Chambers hints, by Lucy's mother's telling Melanie's mother that Melanie was a bully.[51]

The Present Takers was also groundbreaking because of its quiet determination to communicate some of the reasons why Melanie bullies. She is dyslexic, as is revealed by her notes demanding 'PENS REST' (rather than 'PRESENTS'), and she comes from what Chambers means his readers to understand as an uncaring, hostile home. Lucy's father attempts to explain this: 'maybe she's taking out on you something that other people have done to her'. In fact Lucy's insights into the situation are more astute: 'She gets worse if anybody tells. Like it was a competition between her and the grown-ups.'[52] Louis Sachar's *There's a Boy in the Girls' Bathroom* (1987), though designed for younger readers, takes this theme further, exploring the complicated mindset of Bradley Chalkers, a boy with severe behavioural problems (his favourite threat is 'Give me a dollar or I'll spit on you.'). His self-destructive attitudes are patiently unravelled by Carla, a compassionate and unconventional counsellor. Bradley's problem, like several children in the book, is that he is not clear exactly who he is, a confusion symbolically enacted when boys accidentally wander into girls' lavatories and vice versa ('I don't believe in accidents', Carla says). Neither Bradley's teachers, who have given up on him, nor his parents, who at one point want him transferred to military school, realise this. Indeed, it is the Concerned Parents Organization which gets Carla transferred ('Kids have enough *counselling*. What they need is more discipline. If they're bad, they should be punished'). But Carla insists that children must resolve their own difficulties by discovering their own identity and place within the community: 'I never tell them what to do', she says, 'I try to help them to learn to think for themselves.' 'But isn't that what school is for', one parent responds, 'To tell kids what to think?' On the contrary though, the school story schools are most often a neutral site, almost free from prescription and any imposition of identity, in which the process of individuation can work itself out. Carla, a teacher who herself breaks the school rules, is essentially an embodiment of this.[53]

The most compelling representation of school bullying remains, however, Robert Cormier's *The Chocolate War* (1974). Whereas in most school stories, it is the bully who is increasingly isolated, in Cormier's bleak novel it is Jerry Renault, the boy who stands up to bullying, who becomes an outcast. He cannot even turn to his teachers, for they connive in the persecution. At the end of the book, for his refusal to sell chocolates for a fund-raising scheme and for his defiance of the 'Vigils', the school's dominant gang, Jerry is beaten senseless. Even more shocking than the physical violence is what he had gained: the knowledge that that there is no alternative but 'to play ball, to play football, to run, to make the team, to sell the chocolates, to sell whatever they wanted you to, to do whatever they wanted you to do. They tell you to do your thing but they don't mean it. . . . Don't disturb the universe. . . . It's important. Otherwise, they murder you.'[54] It is a brutal, almost Orwellian, education in conformity that contains much wider social relevance. It wholly upsets the reader's expectations, for there is to be no vindication of the stance Jerry took against the bullies. It also overturns the whole school story tradition, of allowing the child to find his or her own identity, and to live independently within the community. It is for all these reasons that Cormier, in *The Chocolate War*, seems to be 'demolishing the school story', as Peter Hunt put it.[55]

But despite Cormier's nihilism, the school story still flourishes. Some remain serious and realistic; many others are more comic, perhaps especially in America. Louis Sachar's whimsical *Wayside School* series (from 1978) and Bruce Coville's *My Teacher is an Alien* (1989) are good examples. Comic school stories are not a new phenomenon. 'The funniest school story ever written', at least according to advertisements appearing in *The Nelson Lee Library* in 1915, was 'Charlie Chaplin's Schooldays', serialised in the weekly *Boy's Realm* magazine.[56] Its existence is testimony to the long-standing cross-media potential of the school story, and of its ability to merge successfully with other genres. Nelson Lee himself, the hero of innumerable magazine adventures, gives further proof of this. He was a second Sherlock Holmes who, forced to seek refuge from a gang of thieves, took up a teaching post at a public school, thereafter combining the roles of schoolmaster and detective. But if one is seeking evidence of the school story's ability to adapt, and to fuse with other genres, the classic example is now J. K. Rowling's *Harry Potter* novels. Like so many authors before her, Rowling has continued the traditions of the British school story while skilfully blending them with fantasy and adventure.[57] This ability to adapt has kept the school story alive for many centuries. The form shows no sign of obsolescence.

SUMMARY OF KEY POINTS

- In the classic school story, the school is not merely a setting for adventure but functions almost as a character itself. Narratives revolve around incidents and attitudes which are implicit in, not extrinsic to, school life.
- School stories tend to focus on socialisation: characters learn how to integrate successfully into a community and to reconcile the demands of self and society.
- A central theme of many school stories is the balance between submission and defiance, authority and autonomy. Pupils are often at war with teachers, but beyond this, a more enduring complicity often exists.
- The British school story can seem a repressive genre since it often endorses the individual's internalisation of school discipline and ethos.
- The great longevity of the school story is largely due to its adaptability: it has successfully combined with other genres, appeared in a range of different media, and has absorbed and responded to changing social conditions.

NOTES

1. George Orwell, 'Boys' Weeklies', in *The Collected Essays, Journalism and Letters of George Orwell*, ed. Sonia Orwell and Ian Angus (London: Penguin, [1968] 1970), vol.1, pp. 505–31 (p. 511).
2. Debbie Pinfold, *The Child's View of the Third Reich in German Literature* (Oxford: Clarendon Press, 2001), p. 46; Ben Hellman, 'Russia', in *International Companion Encylopedia of Children's Literature*, ed. Peter Hunt, 2nd edn, 2 vols (London: Routledge, 2004), vol. 2, pp. 1174–83 (p. 1180).
3. See Gillian Adams, 'Ancient and medieval children's texts', *International Companion Encyclopedia of Children's Literature*, Hunt (ed.), vol. 1, pp. 225–38 (p. 227).
4. See Jozef Ijsewijn, *Companion to Neo-Latin Studies Part II* (Leuven: Leuven University Press, 1998), pp. 229–31.

5. Evaldus Gallus, trans. John Brinsley, *Pueriles Confabula-tiunculae: or Childrens Dialogues, Little Conferences, or Talkings Together* (London: Thomas Man, 1617), pp. 15–16, 17–18, 4 and 29–32.

6. Geoffrey Trease, *Laughter at the Door: A Continued Autobiography* (London: Macmillan, 1974), p. 153; Isabel Quigly, *The Heirs of Tom Brown: The English School Story* (London: Chatto and Windus, 1982).

7. Roald Dahl, *Danny the Champion of the World* (Harmondsworth: Puffin, [1975] 1982), pp. 17, 103, 92–3 and 97.

8. Humphrey Carpenter and Mari Prichard, *The Oxford Companion to Children's Literature* (Oxford: Oxford University Press, [1984] 1995), p. 532.

9. For more on the eighteenth-century school story see Samuel F. Pickering, *Moral Instruction and Fiction for Children 1749–1820* (Athens, GA: University of Georgia Press, 1993), pp. 31–57.

10. L. T. Meade, *The School Favourite* (London: Chambers, 1908), pp. 79 and 99–102.

11. Maria Edgeworth, *The Parent's Assistant Part I*, 2nd edn, 3 vols (London: J. Johnson, 1796), vol. 1, p. 165.

12. Quoted in Quigly, *The Heirs of Tom Brown*, p. 210.

13. Louis Sachar, *Sideways Stories from Wayside School* (London: Bloomsbury, [1978] 2004), pp. 11–15.

14. Gillian Avery, *Nineteenth Century Children* (London: Hodder and Stoughton, 1965), pp. 167–9.

15. Thomas Hughes, *Tom Brown's Schooldays* (London: Parragon Classics, [1857] 1994), p. 139.

16. See Quigly, *The Heirs of Tom Brown*, pp. 208–10.

17. Edgeworth, *The Parent's Assistant*, vol. 1, pp. 220–1.

18. Kipling, *The Complete Stalky & Co.*, ed. Isabel Quigly (Oxford: Oxford World's Classics, [1899] 1999), pp. 52–3 and 196.

19. Hughes, *Tom Brown's Schooldays*, p. 244.

20. Ibid., p. 213.

21. Sarah Fielding, *The Governess; or, the Little Female Academy*, ed. Candace Ward (Peterborough, Ontario: Broadview Press, [1749] 1995), pp. 89–90. See Judith Burdan, 'Girls *Must* Be Seen *and* Heard: Domestic Surveillance in Sarah Fielding's

The Governess', *Children's Literature Association Quarterly*, 19 (1994), 8–14.

22. Beverly Lyon Clark, *Regendering the School Story: Sassy Sissies and Tattling Tomboys* (New York: Garland, 1996), p. 84.
23. J. K. Rowling, *Harry Potter and the Chamber of Secrets* (London: Bloomsbury, 1998), pp. 20–1.
24. Fielding, *The Governess*, p. 123.
25. Ibid., pp. 175–6.
26. Meade, *School Favourite*, p. 103.
27. Quoted in Pat Pinsent, 'Theories of Genre and Gender: Changes and Continuity in the School Story', in *Modern Children's Literature: An Introduction*, ed. Kimberley Reynolds (Basingstoke: Palgrave Macmillan, 2005), pp. 8–22 (p. 11).
28. Pinfold, *The Child's View of the Third Reich*, p. 46.
29. W. H. Auden, 'Honour' from *The Old School* (1934), quoted in *The Oxford Book of School Days*, ed. Patricia Craig (Oxford: Oxford University Press, 1994), p. 317.
30. J. M. Barrie, *Peter and Wendy*, ed. Jack Zipes (London: Penguin, [1911] 2004), pp. 131–2.
31. Geraldine McCaughrean, *Peter Pan in Scarlet* (Oxford: Oxford University Press, 2006), pp. 186–7.
32. Robert Cormier, *The Chocolate War* (London: Penguin, [1974] 2001), p. 36.
33. Gillian Cross, *The Demon Headmaster* (London: Puffin, [1982] 1998), pp. 132–3, 135, 18 and 90.
34. Elinor Brent-Dyer, *The Chalet School Goes To It* (London: Chambers, 1941), later re-titled *The Chalet School at War*, pp. 192 and 142; *The Chalet School and the Lintons* (London: Chambers, 1934), p. 200.
35. C. S. Lewis, *The Last Battle* (London: Grafton, [1956] 2002), p. 128.
36. See Robin Gilmour's *'Stalky & Co.*: Revising the Code', in *Kipling Considered*, ed. Phillip Mallet (Basingstoke: Macmillan, 1989), pp. 19–32.
37. Hughes, *Tom Brown's Schooldays*, p. 47.
38. Don Randall, *Kipling's Imperial Boy: Adolescence and Cultural Hybridity* (Basingstoke: Palgrave, 2000), pp. 91–2.
39. Orwell, 'Boys' Weeklies', in *Collected Essays*, pp. 518 and 511.

40. John Arlott, quoted in Carpenter and Prichard (eds), *Oxford Companion to Children's Literature*, p. 235. In fact, Richards attended private day schools in west London: Mary Cadogan, *Frank Richards: the Chap Behind the Chums* (London: Viking, 1988), p. 12.

41. Trease, *Laughter at the Door*, p. 149.

42. Sheila Ray, 'School Stories', in *The Routledge International Encyclopedia of Children's Literature*, ed. Hunt, vol. 1, p. 472.

43. Trease, *Laughter at the Door*, p. 26.

44. William Mayne, *A Swarm in May* (Haslemere: Jade Publishers, [1955] 1990), pp. 89–90 and 183.

45. Francine Pascal, *Sweet Valley High. Double Love* (London: Bantam Books, [1984] 1995), p. 2.

46. Melvyn Burgess, *Doing It* (London: Penguin Books, [2003] 2004), pp. 134, 153 and 317.

47. *The Guardian*, Saturday 29 March 2003.

48. Burgess, *Doing It*, p. 330.

49. Kipling, *Stalky & Co.*, p. 31.

50. Aidan Chambers, *The Present Takers* (1983), in *The Norton Anthology of Children's Literature*, ed. Jack Zipes *et al.* (New York: Norton, 2005), pp. 1919–87 (p. 1982).

51. Chambers, *Present Takers*, pp. 1969, 1975 and 1986.

52. Ibid., pp. 1940, 1976 and 1970.

53. Louis Sachar, *There's a Boy in the Girls' Bathroom* (London: Bloomsbury, [1987] 2001), pp. 5, 37, 152 and 149.

54. Cormier, *The Chocolate War*, pp. 205–6.

55. Peter Hunt, *An Introduction to Children's Literature* (Oxford: Oxford University Press, 1994), p. 152.

56. *The Nelson Lee Library*, 23 (13 November 1915).

57. See Karen Manners Smith, 'Harry Potter's schooldays: J. K. Rowling and the British Boarding-School Novel', in *Reading Harry Potter: Critical Essays*, ed. Giselle Liza Anatol (Westport, CT: Praeger, 2003), pp. 69–87 and David K. Steege, 'Harry Potter, Tom Brown, and the British School Story: Lost in Transit?' in *The Ivory Tower and Harry Potter: Perspectives on a Literary Phenomenon*, ed. Lana A. Whited (Columbia, MO: Missouri University Press, 2002), pp. 140–56.

CHAPTER 5

The Family Story

Naturally, given the place that children have occupied in society, probably the majority of children's fiction has been set within the family. It could be argued that all these texts are family stories. In James Janeway's *A Token for Children* (1672), for instance, the pious child protagonists typically expire surrounded by a close and supportive unit of siblings, parents and relatives. The eight-year-old Sarah Howley dies 'full of natural affection to her Parents', counselling them how to bear her death so soon after her brother's, and much of the text captures her warnings to her siblings to 'remember the words of a dying Sister'.[1] Even fantasy has frequently been familial. Much of the appeal of C. S. Lewis's *The Lion, the Witch and the Wardrobe* (1950) derives from the relationships between the four siblings. Philip Pullman's *His Dark Materials* trilogy (1995–2000) revolves to a surprisingly large extent around parent–child relationships. Will's bond with his mother and search for his father underlies much of his story. Lyra's gradual discovery that Lord Asriel and Mrs Coulter are her parents forms another important strand, as does the belated realisation of their responsibilities towards her. Even more dominated by ideas of inclusion and exclusion from families is J. M. Barrie's *Peter and Wendy* (1911), though few have called it a family story. The relationships within the Darling family – Wendy, John and Michael, and their parents – are central. The meaning of family, and of its absence, is even more intensely explored with the Lost Boys. They are children who have fallen out of their perambulators in the park who, not having been claimed within a week, have gone to live in the Neverland. Peter himself is another outcast from family. His perpetual boyhood stems from his escape from home on the day he was born, and from his mother barring the nursery window against his return and replacing him with another little boy (so he thinks).[2]

But are these all family stories? Many would favour a narrower definition, admitting only those texts which have been deliberately designed to depict family life and which focus on family relationships. Charlotte Yonge's *The Daisy Chain* (1856) is a good example, describing how the eleven children of the May family cope after a coaching accident kills their mother and injures their father. The remaining siblings constitute the 'daisy-chain' of the title. If this kind of Victorian family story tended to demonstrate the strength and stability of individual families, and of the institution as a whole, more recent variations have explored its weaknesses and collapse. Morris Gleitzman and Anne Fine, to take just two well-known examples, specialise in tragi-comic stories of family rivalries and commotions. Fine's *Madame Doubtfire* (1987; *Alias Madame Doubtfire* in the US) recounts how a divorced father dresses up as a nanny in order to gain access to the children he no longer sees. Gleitzman's *Two Weeks with the Queen* (1989) describes Colin's anger at his parents' favouritism towards his younger brother. Only later does Colin learn that his brother has leukaemia.[3] Yet such stories of family disintegration and reconstruction are not new. A hundred years earlier, Mrs Molesworth's *Sheila's Mystery* (1895) was exploring similar territory. The novel is about two sisters: pretty, sweet and serene Honor, and plain, jealous, querulous Sheila. Sheila thinks she has found the source of her unhappiness when she overhears her parents saying that she had been adopted. She runs away, slowly learns how to be happy, and eventually returns to her family. Only then does she learn that it is Honor, not her, who had been adopted. Sheila's mother's rhetorical question, 'I wonder if parents have often trouble like this', could stand almost as the epigraph for the entire genre, from the eighteenth to the twenty-first century.[4]

As these examples suggest, the paradox of the family story genre is that it probably includes more accounts of family disordering than family coherence. All the texts mentioned so far present families which have been disrupted, removing parents or children from one another by death, divorce, evacuation, flight, abandonment or some other mechanism – Mr March's military service in Louisa May Alcott's *Little Women* (1868), say, or Father's unjust incarceration in E. Nesbit's *The Railway Children* (1906).[5] Jan Mark suggests that the absence of complete families from nineteenth- and twentieth-century family stories is because authors realised 'that children with two harmonious parents were likely to have little to unsettle them'.[6] Gillian Avery agrees, noting that mothers, in particular, 'have a constricting effect on the plot and on the children's activities; their love is so embarrassingly obvious that it can't be overlooked, it stands in the way of that independence that children like to imagine.'[7] But the absence of whole and happy families from family stories is not merely a device to give children freer rein or to allow pathos and adventure into the narrative. Rather, the absence of one or more parents serves to endorse the importance of family. Very many family stories begin with a sundering but proceed to show how the protagonists continually strive to regenerate their family in revised forms. Frederick Marryat's *Children of the New Forest* (1847), for instance, begins when the four Beverley children are orphaned during the English Civil War, and follows their adventures as they learn to live hidden deep in the forest. Having been deprived of their family, the children almost immediately seek to recreate it. The eldest boy and girl, Edward and Alice, become the father and mother, while Humphrey and Edith play the roles of their children, gradually growing to maturity by following their elders' example. They even pretend that their old servant, Jacob, is the grandfather, ostensibly to give them a credible identity when they go to town, but clearly demonstrating their desire to reconstruct a family. Cynthia Voigt's *Homecoming* (1981) is similar. The Tillerman children have already been deserted by their father when they are abandoned by their mother. The novel recounts their long journey to find a new home, from Connecticut to Maryland, led by the thirteen-year-old Dicey. Eventually they arrive at their grandmother's house. But in fact, they have been able to reconstitute themselves as a family before this by themselves, each taking on distinct family roles.

For another author and critic, John Rowe Townsend, it was not so much the physical break-up of the family that was necessary for the family story to flourish, but rather for parents to have their authority diminished. *Little Women*, he argues, could become 'the first great example' of the family story only because it 'marks a relaxation of the stiff and authoritarian stereotype of family life'. 'The family story could not work in an atmosphere of repression or of chilly grandeur', he wrote, for its 'key characteristic is always warmth.'[8] This observation might be challenged on two counts. First, there is no particular reason why all family stories should necessarily be characterised by their warmth. Few would describe the thirteen Lemony Snicket books (1999–2006) as 'warm', but the adventures of Violet, Klaus and Sunny Baudelaire, as their wicked uncle Count Olaf attempts to destroy them, constitute the most popular children's family saga of recent times. Second, it is certainly possible to argue that many children's books featuring families which were published before *Little Women* are less disciplinarian and more affectionate than Townsend allows. Many of the stories comprising *The Children's Friend*, freely translated from the French of Arnaud Berquin in 1786, show this very well. In 'The Little Brother', for example, a young girl called Fanny Warrington is shown her new-born brother for the first time. She is disappointed because he cannot play or talk and seems so weak, and she doubts that she was ever so incapable. Her father carefully explains how tenderly Fanny's mother had cared for her:

If you did but know, my dearest Fanny, how much trouble you occasion'd her, you'd be astonish'd; for at first, you were so weak, you could not swallow any thing, and every day, we apprehended you would die. . . . and after she had once found means to make you suck, you soon became quite fat, and were the merriest little creature in the world. For two whole years, 'twas necessary every day and every minute of the day, she should attend you with the same degree of care and caution. Often, after she had dropt asleep thro' absolute fatigue, your crying would awake her. She would then get out of bed and hasten to your cradle. Fanny! my sweet Fanny! would she say, no doubt my pretty babe is dry; and put you to the breast.

The account of Fanny's early life is intended to show how devoted parents are to their children, giving up all their own pleasure. The aim of this is didactic, for having learned how good her parents have been to her, Fanny promises 'I will never grieve or disobey you for the time to come'.[9] But it is also as forceful an endorsement of family life as Jo March's much more famous exultation in the second part of *Little Women* (1869; known as *Good Wives* in Britain): 'I do think that families are the most beautiful things in all the world!'[10]

Although it might seem fairly normal today, the kind of family that Berquin depicted in 'The Little Brother' would have been understood as progressive in the late eighteenth century. Many affluent women did not breast-feed but employed wet-nurses for their children. The kind of affectionate, hands-on didacticism shown by Fanny's father might also have been regarded as unusual. Parents inspired to take this kind of direct role in raising their children were probably the primary consumers of the new children's literature that was emerging in the later eighteenth century. Naturally, as well as writing for this kind of family, authors usually wrote about them. John Aikin and Anna Laetitia Barbauld's *Evenings at Home* (1792–96) opens with a description of the happy Fairbourne family, a father and mother and their 'numerous progeny' of children. The reader is told that they all meet together in the evenings, when the boys are home from their boarding schools, to read to one another instructive stories, and it is these stories, in this frame, which fill the book's four volumes. A little less explicitly didactic, and more of a family story in the modern sense, is Dorothy Kilner's *The Holyday Present: Containing Anecdotes of Mr & Mrs Jennett, and Their Little Family* (c.1781). The action of this novel is comprised entirely of the interactions of six siblings and their parents. A typical episode involves Harriet and Charlotte arguing about whether they should keep their feet in the stocks (used to correct their posture) when their mother is out of the room. Charlotte does not, but in her haste to reinsert her feet when her mother returns, she knocks over a table and covers herself in ink. As a result, until 'papa and mamma told them that it was not *good natured*', her brothers tease her by calling her 'sister *Tawney* and *Charlotte Blacky*.'[11]

There is no doubt that these texts were designed primarily to be instructive but they are clearly also family tales. Indeed, they are actually about the institution of family itself as much as anything that would be written by Anne Fine or Morris Gleitzman. Sarah Trimmer's *Fabulous Histories* (1786) is another good example. It presents two interlinked families, one of humans and the other of robins (hence its later and more usual title, *The History of the Robins*). She domesticates her avian family to the very furthest extent of anthropomorphism, making Robin, Dicky, Flapsy, Pecksy, and their mother and father, thoroughly 'human' even if they live in a nest and eat worms. Pecksy is docile and considerate while Robin is rash and conceited. But it is after Dicky has eaten four worms himself without sharing them amongst his siblings that the principal lesson is given: 'In a family every individual ought to consult the welfare of the whole, instead of his own private satisfaction. It is his own truest interest to do so.'[12] Meanwhile, Trimmer has offered advice to parents too. The mother must be the core of the family, nurturing her children, while the father, though also working for its benefit, is allowed a wider ambit. Thus the human Mr Benson is largely absent from the story, leaving his loving if somewhat stern wife to dominate the household. And thus the mother robin, although she looks for food for her brood, confines herself to the immediate vicinity of the nest while her 'husband' scours a much wider area. This kind of moral tale was deliberately reconstructing the family as a close-knit and symbiotic group of two parents and their children, excluding other relatives, shutting out other members of the household such as servants, and increasingly centred around the nurturing mother. 'I view a mother as mistress of the revels among her little people', wrote Ellinor Fenn, the author of many instructive children's books in the late eighteenth-century, often under the pseudonym 'Mrs Lovechild'.[13]

These dedicated and capable women were increasingly cast as the 'mothers of the nation', as one recent study has called them. Their dutiful, nurturing, pious ethos shaped society's self-image, as well as being 'used to justify Britain's colonial imperialism'.[14] This is clearly to be seen in Barbara Hofland's *The Panorama of Europe* (1813), in which the mother of the family plays the role of England in a geographical pageant. She is, says her husband, 'a just representative of a country, which, like her, not only spreads her matronly arms over her own children, to rear them to virtue, and refine them to elegance, but extends the blessings to strangers also, and bids the children of many a distant land rejoice in her protection.'[15] Johann David Wyss's *The Family Robinson Crusoe*, translated from German into English in 1814 and better-known as *The Swiss Family Robinson*, also presents the family as both the practical and moral foundation of empire. Having been wrecked on an uninhabited peninsular, the family, like Daniel Defoe's castaway before them, make a successful life for themselves. It is the family, working together, that tames the wilderness. 'The ten years we have passed', says the father reviewing the progress of what he calls their 'colony', were 'years of conquest and establishment.' It is difficult to imagine a more vigorous endorsement of the family as the most proper and profitable social and political unit.[16]

In another sense too, many of the family stories of the nineteenth century are in the mould of *Robinson Crusoe*. The death of parents leaves the children like castaways, exiled from the world they have known and forced to make a new life on the rocky shore on which they have washed up. Charlotte Yonge's books are the most characteristic of the mid-Victorian family story. *The Pillars of the House* (1873), for example, begins with the death of the father, proceeds to the death of the mother, and then charts how the thirteen children rebuild their family life, with the oldest boy learning to be their new father. Although set firmly in the context of Victorian middle-class society, these children have to fend for themselves, and learn to renounce their childhoods, as much as any desert island castaway. Other good examples of this sort of story include *The Wide, Wide World* (1850) by Susan Warner (writing as Elizabeth Wetherell), with an orphaned girl brought up by a heart-hearted aunt, and Susan Coolidge's *What Katy Did* (1872), with a widowed father left to bring up a large family.

It is Alcott's *Little Women* (1868), however, which has become known as the milestone text in the history of the family story. This is no doubt largely because of its status as the first 'classic' of American children's literature as well as its enduring popularity. But many critics have also seen it as breaking the mould of its genre. Beverly Lyon Clark has claimed that *Little Women* 'marked a departure from the previous moralizing in children's literature'.[17] Ruth K. MacDonald acclaims Alcott's depiction of characters with 'flaws that no writer had previously dared to attribute to fictional characters for children', such as selfishness, vanity, temper.[18] For Shirley Foster and Judy Simons, *Little Women* is 'one of the first fictional texts for children to convey the difficulties and the anxieties of girlhood, and which suggests that becoming a "little woman" is a learned and often fraught process'.[19] All this may be true, but it is perhaps in the ways that Alcott refined the family story as it already existed that the book's success lies, rather than in the ways she transformed it. Most early reviewers commended Alcott not for any great originality, but for 'the thorough reality of her characters'.[20] And Alison Lurie is probably correct to suggest that *Little Women* remains popular fundamentally because 'it is the story of a united and affectionate family living in a small New England town' featuring 'kind, wise, and loving parents, always ready with a warm hug and a moral lesson, and four charming teenage daughters who', she adds, hinting at the book's nostalgic appeal, 'have never heard of punk rock or crack cocaine.'[21] Nikki Gamble agrees, noting that at least at first, *Little Women* provides 'a comforting and warm picture of family life; a celebration of love, duty and loyalty'.[22] The book is, as Gillian Avery has succinctly put it, 'the supreme celebration of family affection'.[23]

And yet Alcott's work can also be read as a much more pessimistic dissection of family life and its limitations. Elizabeth Lennox Keyser has proposed that Alcott's 'view of families in *Little Women* is complex and disturbing'. She notes that the book 'abounds in images of constriction, concealment, and pain'. For instance, having dirtied her own glove, through too close and unladylike an involvement with the real world we infer, Jo must force her hand into her sister's smaller glove if she is to appear like 'a real lady' at a Christmas party.[24] Such episodes are symbolic, says Keyser, of Alcott's interpretation of the family as an institution which enforces strict gender codes and which prevents Jo, and others like her, from achieving independence and fulfilment. Jo's literary instincts have to be curbed so that she learns to write what will serve the family best. And when she has a chance of achieving a kind of personal and artistic freedom with the sympathetic and supportive Laurie, Alcott deliberately destroyed the dream by refusing to allow Jo to marry him, the outcome her narrative had encouraged readers to expect. Professor Bhaer, the man Jo eventually marries at the end of *Good Wives*, is far more overbearing than Laurie, and, says Keyser, he perpetuates the patriarchally centred family from which Jo has been trying to escape and in which, ultimately, she is re-incarcerated.[25] Even if one does not accept that Jo is quite so crushed as all this, it is surely true that in most nineteenth-century children's literature, although families might be 'the most beautiful things in all the world', they are also usually founded on self-abnegation. Both girls and boys give up their individuality in order to support and sustain the family unit.

As we have seen with Voigt's *Homecoming*, stories in which children have been prematurely forced to take on adult roles because of parental absence were still being published in the late twentieth century. However, a century earlier there had been a reaction against narratives in which children were forced to grow up early. Kate Douglas Wiggin's *Rebecca of Sunnybrook Farm* (1903), L. M. Montgomery's *Anne of Green Gables* (1908) and Eleanor Hodgman Porter's *Pollyanna* (1913) are all novels about girls who have lost at least one parent, but these heroines appeal to the reader by virtue of their childishness, not their early-onset adultness. Wiggin's Rebecca does become nurse to her ailing mother; Montgomery's Anne does end the first novel in the series as a carer for Marilla, who had adopted her; and Porter's Pollyanna does learn to cope maturely with the injuries she sustains in a car accident. But even if these girls become exemplary paragons, it is their youthful candour, imagination and *joie de vivre* which are most celebrated, and which have an enormous impact on those around them. Pollyanna brings a new cheerfulness to the dour community into which she has been transplanted, and especially her severe aunt, encouraging them all to play the childish 'glad game' which makes them overlook their problems and focus on their blessings. Anne transforms Matthew and Marilla Cuthbert after they adopt her, bringing love and laughter into their previously strait-laced lives. And even more than the others, Rebecca is carefully constructed as an embodiment of the Romantic child, able to change lives because of a childlike innocence and ingenuousness which Wiggin characterises as semi-divine. The twelve-year-old Rebecca is first introduced in a chapter called 'We Are Seven', after William Wordsworth's poem, and her description makes clear that she is as transcendental and numinous a child as any Wordsworth wrote about:

> Rebecca's eyes were like faith . . . Their glance was eager and full of interest, yet never satisfied; their steadfast gaze was brilliant and mysterious, and had the effect of looking directly through the obvious to something beyond . . . a pair of eyes carrying such messages, such suggestions, such hints of sleeping power and insight, that one never tired of looking into their shining depths . . .[26]

The fascination of Rebecca's childishness is complicated by the obsessive relationship that Wiggin depicts between her and Adam Ladd (nicknamed 'Mr Aladdin'), eighteen years her senior. The novel ends when Rebecca is seventeen and Wiggin was careful to keep Rebecca as a non-sexual being, but Jerry Griswold has offered a convincing Oedipal reading of the text and has gone so far as to call Rebecca 'a *Lolita* without sex'.[27] From the point of view of the development of the family story, though, the important point is that *Rebecca of Sunnybrook Farm*, like other children's books of its time, celebrates not the bridging of the gap between childhood and adulthood but rather the gap itself.

Indeed, it is in family stories that the late nineteenth-century conviction that adults and children were entirely different kinds of creature, living in their own separate worlds, is perhaps most clearly visible. Mary Louisa Molesworth's children's novels were firmly located in middle-class families, generally with both parents alive, but they are set in what Gillian Avery calls the 'nursery world', 'where only the children have any real existence, where adults are kindly, ministering shadows, lacking substance and rarely playing an important part in the action of the story.'[28] *Carrots: Just a Little Boy* (1876) is the classic example, detailing the way that Fabian, always called 'Carrots' because of his red hair, is mothered by his sister Floss, only four years older, even though the children have what Kenneth Grahame called in *The Golden Age* (1895) 'a proper equipment of parents'. Indeed, *The Golden Age* contains the most vigorous deliberation on the gulf between children and adults who live side-by-side in the same house yet do not know each other. It is an account of the games and adventures of five siblings who despair at the dullness of grown-ups. These adults, the 'Olympians', have the freedom to do what they like, marvels the narrator, but inexplicably they spend their time in work, going to church, starting love affairs and other such tedious activities when they could be climbing trees, hunting chickens, pretending to be lions, exploding imaginary mines on the lawn and so on. Worse, the Olympians 'were unaware of Indians, nor recked they anything of bisons or of pirates (with pistols!) though the whole place swarmed with such portents.'[29] While J. M. Barrie, a few years later in *Peter Pan* (1904), would employ such representations of childhood innocence and imagination to entertain children, the effect Grahame hoped to achieve was probably more sentimental, and satirical. *The Golden Age* was intended for adults, designed to instil a nostalgia for vanished childhoods. But by pointing out to adult readers how trivial their concerns must seem to the innocent and open minds of children, Grahame was demanding a reassessment of adult priorities. In this, as in the fact that it was a book for adults that was quickly taken up by children, it is similar to Jonathan Swift's *Gulliver's Travels* (1726) in which the customs and attitudes of both the Lilliputians and Brobdingnagians seem preposterous to Gulliver when he views them from his different perspective.

The same mix of comedy, nostalgia and powerful satire is to be found in another celebrated set of family stories which focused on the unbridgeable gap between adults and children, E. Nesbit's *The Story of the Treasure Seekers* (1899) and its continuations *The Wouldbegoods* (1901) and *The New Treasure Seekers* (1904). These provide an episodic account of the adventures of the six Bastable children. As *The Treasure Seekers* opens, the Bastables' mother has died, and their father is absorbed in his precarious business concerns. It is his poverty which provides the theme for *The Treasure Seekers* as the children try all sorts of strategies to restore the family fortunes. After many miscarrying schemes, they are finally successful when their naivety and good intentions soften the heart of their 'Indian Uncle', whom they wrongly assume to be poor and in need of their charity, and he takes the family under his protection. The

Wouldbegoods begins with the children in disgrace for ruining his garden by acting out Rudyard Kipling's *Jungle Book*. The rest of the book details their attempts to be virtuous, like the children in the moral tales which they have read. Their good intentions almost always backfire.

Nesbit is often seen as another pivotal author in the history of children's literature. This is because her child characters seem free and autonomous. Nesbit clearly advocated the kind of upbringing that allows children to run free of adult supervision, and she derides the sort of coddling child-rearing that has afflicted Denny and Daisy, friends of the Bastables, who have turned out 'little pinky, frightened things, like white mice'.[30] In fact, the 'ideal' adults in Nesbit's books are generally not parents but avuncular older men, with no children of their own, characters like the 'Old Gentlemen' in *The Railway Children* (1906), the 'Indian Uncle' in *The Treasure Seekers* or 'Albert's Uncle', the recluse at whose house the children spend the summer in *The Wouldbegoods*. They are themselves child-like. When given the choice, the 'Indian Uncle' prefers 'play-dinner' to 'grown-up dinner': he lustily joins in with the children in 'hunting' their meal before eating it, and he 'slew the pudding in the dish in the good old-fashioned way.'[31] The same kind of ideal adult had featured in Grahame's *Golden Age*: the curate, 'who would receive, unblenching, the information that the meadow beyond the orchard was a prairie studded with herds of buffalo' and 'was always ready to constitute himself a hostile army or a band of marauding Indians on the shortest possible notice'.[32] It was to reach its apogee with Barrie himself, and his *alter ego*, Peter Pan, both, in different ways, grown-ups who had remained children. What this amounts to is a shifting of the balance in the family story. The relationship between parents and children had become marginal, and those adults who did intrude on the children's lives were no longer the bringers of discipline or wisdom, but themselves learned from, and were liberated by, the children. In a strange way, these novels constructing the child as wiser than the adult are similar to some of the family problem novels of the late twentieth century. In Morris Gleitzman's *Bumface* (1998) for example, Angus looks after his siblings as well as his television star mother. At its close, in order to force his mother to confront her responsibilities,

Angus deliberately spoils his own birthday party by behaving immaturely. It is his attempt to re-impose the breach that Nesbit, Grahame and Barrie had set up between children and their parents.

Much of Nesbit's writing for children is very political. In *The Wouldbegoods*, for instance, the Bastables attempt to force their benevolence on people, and so their plans always fail. Better to investigate the real needs of the poor rather than impose welfare, the book suggests: an endorsement of the position of the Fabian Society, of which Nesbit and her husband were founder members. Equally political, and equally focused on the workings of a single family, are Laura Ingalls Wilder's *Little House* books (1932–71). Each of the seven books is loosely based on the author's own experiences of a late nineteenth-century childhood on the American frontier, but they are not exactly autobiography. Wilder was too young to remember either the home in Wisconsin where *Little House in the Big Woods* (1932), the first novel, takes place, or the year her family spent on the prairie, later part of Kansas but then 'Indian Territory', which features in the second book, *Little House on the Prairie* (1935). Indeed, some of the alterations and absences in the books reveal much about Wilder's purposes in writing these fictionalised memoirs. For instance, she almost entirely omitted from her account the year her family spent in Burr Oak, Iowa, a town far removed from the frontier, where her insolvent parents managed an hotel and Laura and her sister Mary helped out as chamber-maids and waitresses. Omitting this from the books maintained the image that Wilder wanted to project, of a pioneer family living on the edge of the wilderness and always independent and free.

In the *Little House* books, freedom is made possible only by isolation, and isolation necessitates self-sufficiency. These are key themes of the books, and they underpin the idea of family that Wilder endorses. At the beginning of *Little House on the Prairie* Pa decides to move the family into the uncultivated 'Indian Territory', not even part of the United States at that time, because 'there were too many people in the Big Woods now.' They build their new cabin in as remote a spot as they can find. The nearest town, appropriately called Independence, is two days' journey away. Their nearest white neighbour, Mr Edwards, lives two miles away. Having built their cabin, the family faces the challenges of wolves, fire, fever and the native Americans who were already living in the vicinity. Perhaps unsurprisingly the family, and especially Ma, develops something of a bunker mentality, and the book can seem rather claustrophobic. Ma even tries to shut out the other white pioneers from her family. Edwards has helped them build their cabin, but Ma is reluctant to let Pa borrow nails from him. 'I don't like to be beholden, not even to the best of neighbours', she says. Above all, Ma loathes the 'Indians' who intrude (as she sees it) into her house. Pa is less insular, respecting the 'Indians' and cooperating with Edwards, but he is dismayed by the arrival of other colonists in the area and he makes a lock for the stable. 'When neighbours began to come into a country,' Laura recounts, 'it was best to lock up your horses at night, because, where there are deer there will be wolves, and where they are horses, there will be horse-thieves.'[33] The family is constructed as an entirely self-sufficient unit, and as the only social institution in which virtue can thrive. Any larger community – even the handful of settlers who follow the Ingalls family onto the prairie – is understood as necessarily ridden with corruption.

All of the *Little House* books explore the way that the family has, regrettably, to sully itself by a relationship with the larger community. It comes to a head in the fifth book in the series, *The Long Winter* (1942), when severe weather lays siege to the Ingalls. It is the family's self-sufficiency which enables them to survive the shortages, as they resourcefully eke out what little food they have. But it is when grain finally arrives in the local shop, brought by Laura's future husband Almanzo, that Wilder spells out her social credo. The storekeeper says he has the right to sell the grain at a huge profit. Pa, leading a deputation of angry townspeople, just manages to prevent violence but warns that they can boycott the shop. 'If you've got a right to do as you please, we've got a right to do as we please', he says. 'Don't forget every one of us is free and independent.'[34] The idea that the individual and the family is the only virtuous social unit is, of course, a very political point, and Wilder can seem a prophet of the socio-political views that came to dominate Britain and America in the 1980s. One of Margaret Thatcher's most famous pronouncements sums up Wilder's views perfectly: 'there is no such thing as society. There are individual men and women, and there are families. And no government can do anything except through people, and people must look to themselves first.'[35]

The politics of the *Little House* books is linked with the recent controversy about their authorship. Wilder, already 65 when the first book was published, was certainly encouraged in her writing of the books by her daughter Rose Wilder Lane, a professional novelist and journalist. However, in a book called *The Ghost in the Little House* (1993), William Holtz suggested that Rose substantially rewrote her mother's drafts. This conclusion is open to substantial doubt, but it is nonetheless interesting to note Rose's politics and the context in which the first *Little House* books were first published.[36] They appeared during the Great Depression of the 1930s and while Franklin D. Roosevelt was rolling out his New Deal policies of unprecedented social and economic intervention by the federal government. Rose has been described as a 'political crank, with a deep dislike of Roosevelt and the New Deal'.[37] Whether or not she should be considered as a co-author, the *Little House* books can easily be read as a critique of federal government. The Ingalls leave their cabin on the prairie (in Laura's narration at least) not because of their settlement's failure, but because 'some blasted politicians in Washington', in Pa's furious words, have reneged on their promise to 'make the Indians move on again' and open up the land for white settlement.[38] With anti-federal rhetoric like this, it is no wonder that the *Little House* books have become 'an icon of conservative political and family values in America'.[39]

Read more carefully, though, the *Little House* books can begin to seem less confident in their celebration of the independent, self-sufficient and virtuous nuclear family. Laura's narration does idealise her father and mother, and their devotion to their three daughters, but it also subtly reveals surprising tensions between them. Francis Spufford maintains that it is 'one of the quiet excellences of the whole series that they tactfully register, and offer to readers who are able to notice them, far more complication in the picture of the family than they ever comment on explicitly.'[40] The most obvious 'complication' of the happy family is Laura's resentment of her older sister Mary. Occasionally, this bubbles to the surface, as when they find Indian beads and, rather than keep some for herself, Mary gives them to her baby sister, Carrie:

Ma waited to hear what Laura would say. Laura didn't want to say anything. She wanted to keep those pretty beads. Her chest felt all hot inside, and she wished with all her might that Mary wouldn't always be such a good little girl. But she couldn't let Mary be better than she was.

So she said slowly, 'Carrie can have mine, too.' . . .

Perhaps Mary felt sweet and good inside, but Laura didn't. When she looked at Mary she wanted to slap her. So she dared not look at Mary again.[41]

But more deeply buried in the folds of the narration is conflict between Ma and Pa. They never argue, but Wilder allows Laura's narration to reveal Ma's frustration with Pa's wandering spirit. 'This is a country I'll be contented to stay in the rest of my life', Pa says when he has built his cabin on the prairie. But Ma knows him better than he knows himself, asking 'Even when it's settled up?'[42] Such veiled accusations are the only hints of Ma's resentment, but they destabilise the notion of the perfectly unified and contented family.

As for Laura herself, although her childhood is apparently idyllic, she is in a constant state of resistance to the role that has been assigned to her within the family, principally by Ma. She is not an obvious tomboy like Jo in *Little Women*, nor is her discontent ever very loud or explicit. But her mysterious longing to see an Indian baby is suggestive of a desire to escape the confines of her family and the kind of domestic femininity enjoined by her mother. When she actually meets Indian children, her restlessness finds its only open expression:

She had a naughty wish to be a little Indian girl. Of course she did not really mean it. She only wanted to be bare naked in the wind and the sunshine, and riding one of those gay little ponies.

But even before this, Laura's narration has quietly recorded the tension between her and Ma. 'What do you want to see an Indian baby for?' Ma scolds, adding 'Put on your sun-bonnet, now, and forget such nonsense.' It is the sun-bonnet that works as the most powerful symbol of Laura's incarceration within her mother's values. It stands for the circumscribed role that Ma's family values enforce on women, for 'its sides came past her cheeks' and 'she could see only what was in front of her'.[43] We realise too that it is designed to keep the sun from tanning Laura's face, preventing her from becoming like either the Indians or Pa, both of whom live freer and more natural lives on the prairie. The book, in fact, is suffused by Laura's simmering, though unspoken, desire to escape her internment within Ma's family values.

The *Little House* books compare interestingly with a British family story from the same period, Eve Garnett's *The Family from One End Street* (1937). Like Wilder, Garnett set her novel beyond a frontier, not among the 'Indians' but among the working classes, a setting very seldom previously used for family stories. Mr Ruggles is a dustman; Mrs Ruggles is a washerwoman. They have seven children, each of whom has a separate adventure. This marks a departure from most family stories, in which the siblings tend to stick together. Indeed, *The Family from One End Street* is in some ways not a very convincing family story. Until a final chapter when they are all together, the family can seem more literary 'ballast' than the main focus of the book, providing a context for the children's separate adventures. On the other hand, like the Ingalls, the Ruggles have a strong sense of the family identity and of the differences between them and the other inhabitants of Otwell. They know very well that they are not like the richer people they sometimes meet. More surprisingly, they are just as keen to separate themselves from their neighbours in One End Street as the Ingalls had been on the prairie. They are outraged, for example, at the interference in their affairs by 'Mrs. "Nosey Parker" Smith'.[44]

The Ruggles' attitude to interference in their lives by the state is more complicated. As in the *Little House* books, it is a major theme. It is clear that the 'welfare state' plays a substantial role in the Ruggles' lives. We learn in passing that when Mr Ruggles had broken his leg, national insurance money had supported the family. It is the state which provides a scholarship for Kate, the cleverest of the Ruggles children, to attend a secondary school. After a misunderstanding, the state even pays for Kate's school uniform. The Ruggles often invoke the power of the state to take over responsibility for the children, even if they do so for comic effect. When Mrs Ruggles is being pestered by one of her daughters, for instance, she vows that 'she would support no Government in future that did not promise immediate erection of Nursery Schools to accommodate under-school-age offspring, and relieve harassed mothers.' Garnett subtly indicates that Mrs Ruggles is perilously close to needing the state's childcare help too. In one chapter, young Jo Ruggles positions himself outside a tea shop, hoping to appear so hungry that people will give him money. He plans to spend his gains on seeing the new film at the cinema, and is annoyed when a kind lady buys him buns instead of giving him cash. But Garnett allows the reader to hear the woman wondering 'if she ought to see the Head Teacher about their getting a free meal at school'. Evidently, the local people's perception is that Mr and Mrs Ruggles are on the verge of needing state support. Elsewhere, Garnett seems to express a decided hostility to the welfare state. Mr Ruggles finds a substantial sum of money on his rounds, and honestly hands it in to the police. His friend doubts that he will receive any recompense, telling him of a man who found a pearl necklace worth thousands of pounds, but was rewarded with only a paltry sum of money by its owner. The necklace's owner justified her niggardliness by saying that 'nowadays people was so well-educated by the State they'd no excuse *not* to give back things they found'. The implication is that the institutional charity of the welfare state has caused the decline of genuine, personal gratitude and benevolence. In fact, because of the consistent endorsement of private charity over state support, the Ruggles' world can seem almost feudal. When they deferentially name their son after the vicar they are repaid with a pound note. Then when Mr Ruggles is eventually rewarded with two pounds for handing in the money he has found, tears come to his eyes, and the benefactor is left wondering whether to pity or envy the Ruggles for the simplicity of their lives.[45]

Garnett's preference for private, even feudal, support seems to be based on a conviction that state maintenance is really a challenge to the family. Whereas personal charity, being less comprehensive, simply sustains existing social structures, the welfare state has the potential to replace them. Kimberley Reynolds has made this point with particular reference to the chapter called 'The Baby Show', in which Mrs Ruggles enters her youngest child, William, in the contest to find 'Otwell's Best Baby'. The judges are doctors and nurses, and Mrs Ruggles seems to distrust their scientific talk and secretive ways. Their hospital training and modern techniques are an affront to the role of the mother, and to traditional methods. Reynolds concludes that Garnett recognised 'that many parents resented heavy-handed state intervention, seeing it as questioning their ability to look after their families properly.'[46] It was a theme that would surface more frequently after 1945, when state intervention became more firmly entrenched in Britain and America. The danger that the welfare state posed to the family was powerfully dramatised in John Rowe Townsend's *Gumble's Yard* (1961), for instance, in which four children are so worried that they will be separated from one another and forced into children's homes that they run away to live in a derelict warehouse.

With its concern with the impact of poverty and of the welfare state on families, *The Family from One End Street* should be regarded as an attempt at social realism, even if it is also comic and cute. After the Second World War, the family story would be increasingly dominated by the attempt to depict the sort of lives that children really led, perhaps especially working–class children, and the problems which afflicted real families and the emergence of different patterns of family life. The effects of parental abandonment and of fostering, for example, have been explored in a number of impressive novels including Betsy Byars' *The Pinballs* (1977), Katherine Paterson's *The Great Gilly Hopkins* (1979) and Jacqueline Wilson's *The Story of Tracy Beaker* (1991). Lesbian and gay families have been depicted in Susanne Bösche's *Jenny Lives with Eric and Martin* (translated into English, from Danish, in 1983) and Leslea Newman's *Heather Has Two Mommies* (1989). Divorce and its aftermath are investigated in Anne Fine's *Madame Doubtfire* (1987) and *Goggle-Eyes* (1989). And families in which parents, and especially fathers, are detrimental to their children's well-being include Louise Fitzhugh's *Nobody's Family is Going to Change* (1974) and Gary Kilworth's *The Brontë Girls* (1995). These are both complex family stories. In Fitzhugh's novel, the father is not physically abusive, but tyrannically insists that his son should find a respectable and lucrative profession rather than becoming the dancer that he himself wants to be, and that his daughter should not become a lawyer, but should find fulfilment in 'womanly' domestic duties. Fitzhugh explains his reasons. He has himself worked hard to establish himself as a member of the black middle class, and does not want his children to undo this work. Willie's wish to dance, his father fears, will only reinforce stereotypes of black people. Emma's desire to be a lawyer is interpreted by her father as a challenge to his authority and as a rebellion against the bourgeois family unit which he has striven so hard to create. *The Brontë Girls*, meanwhile, describes a father's attempts to bring up his family as if they were living in the mid-nineteenth century, 'a time when decent and moral behaviour was considered admirable.'[47] Kilworth's book is a satire on those who claim to want a return to traditional family values, for in fact, James Craster, the father, is a sanctimonious, hypocritical bully, and the family disintegrates. Faced with paternal oppression, one of Mr Craster's daughter contemplates suicide, just as Emma in *Nobody's Family is Going to Change* had been pushed into bulimia. Both novels raise the question of children's rights within the family, and whether children should obey their parents even if their authority has been undermined by cruelty or foolishness.

From a partial survey like this it certainly seems that in post-1960 family fiction 'the greatest shift is that the nuclear family itself has come under scrutiny', as Nikki Gamble has put it.[48] In a paradoxical way, though, these accounts of familial diversity and dysfunction do a great deal to reinforce the attractiveness of the kind of 'normal', nuclear family. Gay and lesbian family stories generally simply replicate standard family structures but with two parents of the same sex, their authors understandably seeking to downplay the difference. As we have already seen, in many accounts of absent parents, the children struggle to create a surrogate family out of their siblings or fellow foster-children (as in Byars' *The Pinballs*). Paterson's *The Great Gilly Hopkins* and Wilson's *The Story of Tracy Beaker* may depict girls made angry by their exclusion from traditional families, but both heroines idolise their absent mothers and are convinced that one day they will return. Even if these dreams do not come true, the nuclear family remains in place as the ideal to which they aspire.

Anne Fine's novels are similarly about broken families and derive their narrative momentum from the process of their reconstruction. *Goggle-Eyes* is about a divorced mother Rosie, her two children Kitty and Jude, and her new lover, Gerald. Kitty calls him 'Goggle-Eyes' because of the way she thinks he ogles her mother, and despises him because he disrupts their comfortable lives. For instance, Gerald is amazed that Rosie pays Kitty for gardening, asking whether Kitty pays her mother for her cooking and cleaning. 'I'm her *mother*', protests Rosie, to which Gerald replies 'You are her *family* . . .. You shouldn't be paying her for cooperation. No one should have to bribe their close relations to pull their weight. It is *disgusting*.' Cooperation is the book's central theme. Each family member might have their own talents and roles, but the family succeeds only by working for each other. What is surprising is that Kitty gradually comes to appreciate Gerald for, of all things, his role as the family's authoritarian patriarch. 'Bossing's no problem for Goggle-Eyes', she reluctantly admits, and she admires his 'Because I say so' attitude to problems like her sister's bedtime, especially when compared with Rosie's equivocation. There is a political subtext to all this too, for Gerald is a Thatcherite small businessman while Rosie is a left-wing peace protestor, two hostile positions in 1989 when *Goggle-Eyes* was published. To admire Gerald's authoritarianism and his strict economy is Fine's endorsement of Thatcherism, while her suggestion that split families can, with due care, be reconstructed in a new but still nuclear configuration is a way of reconciling social realities with the Thatcherite belief in family values. It is, therefore, a neat irony, though perhaps not a deliberate pun, that the most amusing parts of the novel depict anti-nuclear protests – not against nuclear families, but nuclear weapons. At these demonstrations, the police and the protestors collaborate, the former helping the latter to make symbolic cuts in a wire fence so that a point can be made but serious damage and violence avoided. This cooperation does not blur their different roles, but it does serve everyone's interest. What is true of politics, Fine argues, is true for families too.[49]

Not all family stories written since the 1960s are accounts of dysfunction and its repair. One of the most remarkable is Alan Garner's *The Stone Book Quartet* (1976–78), a very different kind of family story to the others discussed here but offering a profound analysis of the meaning of family. With the first of its constituent parts, *The Stone Book*, set in 1864, and the last (though the second to be published), *Tom Fobble's Day*, in 1941, the quartet is a vertical rather than horizontal family story, a sort of family saga. Garner has called it 'the emotional history of one rural family', and the family is clearly his own, although it is as untrustworthy an autobiography as Wilder's *Little House* books or Alcott's *Little Women*.[50] Each of the four books describes the events of a single day. In *The Stone Book*, Mary is shown a deep cave by her father, a stonemason. There she sees a cave painting depicting the hunt of a bison-like creature. Part of the design, an arrow head, is now her father's mason's mark, she realises. As she looks around, she sees on the cave floor innumerable footprints, of 'boots and shoes and clogs, heels, toes, shallow ones and deep ones, clear and sharp as if made altogether, trampling each other, hundreds pressed in the clay where only a dozen could stand.'[51] When her father tells her that each generation of their family has been taken to see this, just once, while they are small enough to fit through the underground passage, we realise that these footprints belong to her ancestors. The idea of ancestral inheritance sets the theme for the series. The second book, *Granny Reardun*, is about Mary's illegitimate son Joseph realising that he does not want to follow in his grandfather's footsteps as a stonemason, but would rather become a blacksmith. The third, *The Aimer Gate* shows him grown up during the First World War, trying to engage his own son in his interests. And the final book is set on the day Joseph dies, but celebrates his last work, an exceptional sledge made for his grandson William.

It is when exultingly flying down the snow-covered hill on his sledge that William comes to terms with the presence of his ancestors, just as Mary had done in the cave. 'He was not alone', he realises. 'There was a line, and he could feel it. It was a line through hand and eye, block, forge and loom to the hill. He owned them all: and they owned him.'[52] Being owned by one's ancestors is not necessarily oppressive, for the books have shown several deliberate breakings from the past, such as Joseph's joyful decision not to become a stonemason. Neil Philip has even gone so far as to say that *Granny Reardun*, and perhaps the quartet as a whole, speaks 'of the need of each generation to escape the shadow of the last'.[53] But the influence of family is inescapable. Indeed, much of the delight of the quartet is to trace the ways in which Garner dramatises this. His characters, though in different generations, behave the same way and do the same things (eat onions, say). They use the same phrases too. Thus the stonemason, Robert, prophesies that his grandson will say of him that 'he was a bazzil-arsed old devil' but a good builder, and, thirty years later, is the very phrase that Joseph uses to describe him. Even things that one character puts down, another will pick up decades later, like a pipe dropped in *The Stone Book* that resurfaces in *Tom Fobble's Day*, where Joseph finds it and blows through it, as if resuscitating the past.[54] In Garner's world, family is as enduring as the landscape in which the saga is set. Just as each generation of children play on the same hills and live in and about the same buildings, they also steer their own way through a cultural landscape slowly shaped by their forebears. In many ways Garner's understanding of the family is quite unique. But in the way that he presents family as a landscape through which the individual has to plot his or her own course, his work fits snugly into the longer tradition of children's family stories that this chapter has considered.

SUMMARY OF KEY POINTS

- The nuclear family has been the standard setting for children's fiction since the seventeenth century, although from the nineteenth century, family stories have just as often been about sibling-to-sibling as parent-child relationships.
- Most classic family stories are about family fracture, disorder or dysfunction, but generally focus on the reconstruction of the family.
- Even the books about non-traditional families that began to appear in the later twentieth century generally take the nuclear family as the ideal to which children should and do aspire.
- Family stories have often been political, exhibiting the family as the best foundation of empire, for instance, or defending the family against attack from the growing power of the state.

- Families have sometimes been represented as constrictive, especially for girls. But the majority of children's literature has endorsed the relationships between siblings, parents and children, and ancestors and descendents, as more liberating than limiting.

NOTES

1. *From Instruction to Delight: An Anthology of Children's Literature to 1850*, ed. Patricia Demers, 2nd edn (Don Mills, Ontario: Oxford University Press, 2004), pp. 56 and 58.
2. J. M. Barrie, *Peter and Wendy*, ed. Jack Zipes (Harmondsworth: Penguin, [1911] 2004), pp. 29, 27 and 98.
3. See *Family Fictions. Anne Fine, Morris Gleitzman, Jacqueline Wilson and others*, ed. Nicholas Tucker and Nikki Gamble (London: Continuum, 2001).
4. Mary Louisa Molesworth, *Sheila's Mystery* (London: Macmillan, [1895] 1896), pp. 75–6.
5. See Chamutal Noimann, ' "Poke Your Finger into the Soft Round Dough": The Absent Father and Political Reform in Edith Nesbit's *The Railway Children*', *Children's Literature Association Quarterly*, 30 (2005), 368–85.
6. Jan Mark, 'Family Stories', *The Cambridge Guide to Children's Books in English*, ed. Victor Watson (Cambridge: Cambridge University Press, 2001), p. 250.
7. Gillian Avery, *Childhood's Pattern: A Study of the Heroes and Heroines of Children's Fiction 1770–1950* (London: Hodder and Stoughton, 1975), p. 224.
8. John Rowe Townsend, *Written for Children* (London: Pelican, [1965] 1976), pp. 79–80.
9. Arnaud Berquin, trans. Rev. Anthony Meilan, *The Children's Friend*, 8 vols (London: 'Printed for the translator', 1786), vol. 1, pp. 38–40 and 45.
10. Louisa M. Alcott, *Good Wives* (London: Puffin, [1869] 1994), p. 339.
11. Dorothy Kilner, *The Holyday Present* (London: J. Marshall and Co., [1781?] c.1783), pp. 38–42.

12. Sarah Trimmer, *Fabulous Histories* (London: T. Longman and G. G. and J. Robinson, [1786] 1798), p. 69.
13. [Ellinor Fenn], *The Art of Teaching in Sport* (London: John Marshall, [1785?] c.1792), p. 6.
14. Anne K. Mellor, *Mothers of the Nation: Women's Political Writing in England, 1780–1830* (Bloomington, IN: Indiana University Press, [2000] 2002), p. 144.
15. Barbara Hofland, *The Panorama of Europe; or, a New Game of Geography* (London: Minerva Press, 1813), pp. 20–1.
16. Johann Wyss, *The Swiss Family Robinson*, ed. John Seelye (Oxford: Oxford University Press, [1814] 1991), pp. 451–2.
17. Beverley Lyon Clark, *Kiddie Lit. The Cultural Construction of Children's Literature in America* (Baltimore, MD: Johns Hopkins University Press, 2003), p. 105.
18. Ruth K. MacDonald, 'Louisa May Alcott', in *Writers for Children*, ed. Jane M. Bingham (New York: Scribners, 1988), p. 3.
19. Shirley Foster and Judy Simons, *What Katy Read: Feminist Re-Readings of 'Classic' Stories for Girls* (Iowa City, IA: University of Iowa Press, 1995), p. 87.
20. See Janet S. Zehr, 'The Response of Nineteenth-Century Audiences to Louisa May Alcott's Fiction', *American Transcendental Quarterly*, n.s. 1 (1987), 323–42 (p. 325).
21. Alison Lurie, *Boys and Girls Forever: Children's Classics from Cinderella to Harry Potter* (Harmondsworth: Penguin, 2003), p. 13.
22. Gamble, 'Introduction', *Family Fictions*, ed. Tucker and Gamble, p. 13.
23. Gillian Avery, 'The family story', *International Companion Encyclopedia of Children's Literature*, ed. Peter Hunt, 2 vols, 2nd edn (London: Routledge, 2004), vol. 1, pp. 454–66 (pp. 460–1).
24. Louisa M. Alcott, *Little Women* (London: Puffin, [1868] 1994), pp. 33 and 36.
25. Elizabeth Lennox Keyser, ' "The Most Beautiful Things in All the World"? Families in *Little Women*', in *Stories and Society. Children's Literature in its Social Context*, ed. Dennis Butts (Basingstoke: Macmillan, 1992), pp. 50–64 (pp. 53 and 62).

26. Kate Douglas Wiggin, *Rebecca of Sunnybrook Farm* (London: Wordsworth, [1903] 1994), p. 13.
27. Jerry Griswold, *Audacious Kids: Coming of Age in America's Classic Children's Books* (Oxford: Oxford University Press, 1992), p. 73.
28. Gillian Avery, *Nineteenth Century Children: Heroes and Heroines in English Children's Stories 1780–1900* (London: Hodder and Stoughton, 1965), p. 160.
29. Kenneth Grahame, *The Golden Age* (Ware: Wordsworth, [1895] 1995), pp. 1 and 2–3.
30. E. Nesbit, *The Wouldbegoods* (Ware: Wordsworth, [1901] 1995), p. 12.
31. E. Nesbit, *The Story of the Treasure Seekers* (London: Puffin, [1899] 1994), p. 222.
32. Grahame, *The Golden Age*, pp. 3–4.
33. Laura Ingalls Wilder, *Little House on the Prairie* (London: Egmont, [1935] 2000), pp. 1, 80 and 66.
34. Laura Ingalls Wilder, *The Long Winter* (New York: Harper Collins, [1940] 1971), p. 304.
35. Margaret Thatcher, in *Woman's Own* (31 October 1987).
36. William Holtz, *The Ghost in the Little House: A Life of Rose Wilder Lane* (Columbia, MO: University of Missouri Press, 1993).
37. Caroline Fraser, 'The Prairie Queen', *New York Review of Books*, 41 (22 December 1994), pp. 38–44 (p. 44).
38. Wilder, *Little House on the Prairie*, pp. 198 and 169.
39. Suzanne Rhan, 'What Really Happens in the Little Town on the Prairie', *Children's Literature*, 24 (1996), 117–26 (p. 125).
40. Francis Spufford, *The Child that Books Built* (London: Faber and Faber, 2002), p. 135.
41. Wilder, *Little House on the Prairie*, p. 112.
42. Ibid., p. 46.
43. Ibid., pp. 192 and 78.
44. Eve Garnett, *The Family from One End Street* (London: Puffin, [1937] 2004), p. 235.
45. Ibid., pp. 215, 170–1, 194, 222, 20 and 242.
46. Garnett, *Family from One End Street*, pp. 176; Kimberley Reynolds, 'Sociology, Politics, the Family: Children and

Families in Anglo-American Children's Fiction, 1920–60', *Modern Children's Literature: An Introduction*, ed. Kimberley Reynolds (Basingstoke: Palgrave Macmillan, 2005), pp. 23–41 (p. 36).

47. Gary Kilworth, *The Brontë Girls* (London: Methuen, 1995), p. 153.
48. Gamble, 'Introduction', *Family Fictions*, p. 26.
49. Anne Fine, *Google-Eyes* (London: Puffin, [1989] 1990), pp. 59, 105, 79–80 and 90–1.
50. Aidan Chambers, 'An interview with Alan Garner' in *The Signal Approach to Children's Literature* (Harmondsworth: Kestrel, 1980), pp. 276–328 (p. 290). See Charles Butler, *Four British Fantasists: Place and Culture in the Children's Fantasies of Penelope Lively, Alan Garner, Diana Wynne Jones, and Susan Cooper* (Lanham, MD: Scarecrow Press, 2006), pp. 205–6.
51. Alan Garner, *The Stone Book Quartet* (London: Harper, [1976–78] 2006), p. 31.
52. Garner, *Stone Book Quartet*, p. 166.
53. Neil Philip, *A Fine Anger: A Critical Introduction to the work of Alan Garner* (London: Collins, 1981), p. 137.
54. Garner, *Stone Book Quartet*, pp. 63, 102, 20 and 152.

CHAPTER 6

Fantasy

Fantasy is an extensive, amorphous and ambiguous genre, resistant to attempts at quick definition. It can incorporate the serious and the comic, the scary and the whimsical, the moral and the anarchic. It can be 'high' – taking place in alternative worlds – or 'low' – set in the world we know. Or it can combine the two. Besides texts set in other worlds, fantasy includes stories of magic, ghosts, talking animals and superhuman heroes, of time travel, hallucinations and dreams. It overlaps with other major genres, notably the fairy tale and the adventure story, but it intersects also with almost any other kind of children's book: the moral tale in the case of Charles Kingsley's *The Water-Babies* (1863), say, or the school story in the case of J. K. Rowling's *Harry Potter* books (1997–2007). The various forms of fantasy are, as Brian Attebery has put it, 'fuzzy sets, meaning that they are defined not by boundaries but by a center' and 'there may be no single quality that links an entire set'.[1]

But as a concept, fantasy is clearly central to any understanding of children's literature. Some have argued that fantasy is the very core of children's literature, and that children's literature did not properly exist until the imagination had been given an entirely free rein to entertain children in unreservedly fantastical books like Lewis Carroll's *Alice's Adventures in Wonderland* (1865) or Edward Lear's *Nonsense Songs, Stories, Botany, and Alphabets* (1870). Indeed, Wonderland, like Neverland, Narnia, Oz or *Tom's Midnight Garden* in Philippa Pearce's 1958 novel, can be regarded as spatial – or perhaps psychological – representations of child-hood, places from which one is exiled as soon as one grows up. But it has also been argued that all children's literature is necessarily a fantasy. In the same way that an author writing about Narnia or Neverland is creating a fantasy world which they imagine but cannot actually inhabit, so all adults writing about childhood are describing a world that they can no longer directly experience. According to this view, influentially set out by Jacqueline Rose in *The Case of Peter Pan or The Impossibility of Children's Fiction* (1984), even the most realistic children's story – an eighteenth-century moral tale, say, or a 'problem novel' in the twentieth – is actually an adult's fantasy of what childhood is, or should be.[2] And then in another sense, it might even be claimed that, because it relates that which has not taken place, all fiction should be under-stood as fantasy – although most critics have preferred to limit the genre to those texts depicting what *could not* (rather than *did not*) happen. Colin Manlove, for instance, argues that fantasy is 'fiction involving the supernatural or impossible'.[3] This is a workable definition that will serve well for this chapter (although it will be possible to consider only a small proportion of children's fantasy literature), but, like a number of common assumptions about fantasy it is far from unproblematic.

For one thing, the supernatural, the impossible and the unreal are not fixed. Is the bible to be regarded as fantasy fiction because it includes miracles? Is *The Divine Comedy* a fantasy because Hell, Purgatory and Heaven do not exist, or because Dante imagined them in a particular way? Are books about witchcraft fantasy? Certainly the two wicked witches in L. Frank Baum's *The Wonderful Wizard of Oz* (1900), or the schools for spells in Jill Murphy's *The Worst Witch* (1974) or J. K. Rowling's *Harry Potter* series, are improbable. But in early modern Europe and America witchcraft was regarded as a reality, so sixteenth- and seventeenth-century books such as Reginald Scott's *Discoverie of Witchcraft* (1584), or Cotton Mather's *The Wonders of the Invisible World* (1693) about the Salem witch trials, surely cannot be considered as fantasy. In the same way, a Victorian author writing about a human walking on the moon would be a fantasist, but a post-1969 writer would not. In other words, fantasy literature depicts things which are contrary to prevailing ideas of reality, rather than which are incontestably supernatural or impossible. But this is only the first of many complications. What of stories which purport to recount dreams, such as Lewis Carroll's *Alice's Adventures in Wonderland* (1865), John Masefield's *The Box of Delights* (1935), or perhaps Maurice Sendak's *Where the Wild Things Are* (1963)? These may be full of impossible things, but it is not defying reality to describe even the most unrealistic dream. Are such texts fantasy any more than, say, the stream-of-consciousness narratives of James Joyce or Virginia Woolf, which tried to show as realistically as possible a character's waking thoughts? Books about children's imaginary friends are curiously placed too. The eponymous heroine of Helen Cresswell's *Lizzie Dripping* stories (1972–75) imagines that she has a witch for a friend, but it is never quite clear whether the witch is simply a product of Lizzie's notorious mendacity, invented to rile her parents. Are the *Lizzie Dripping* books fantasy fiction, or accounts of a teenager's mischief, or insecurity? It is often very unclear where fantasy and realism begin and end. Rather than being a weakness, this ambiguity is one of the strengths of much good fantasy writing.

What seems particularly misguided is to regard fantasy and realism as mutually exclusive categories. It is surely not the case that all literature can be placed somewhere on a scale with pure fantasy at one end, and pure mimesis (the representation of reality) at the other, so that to increase the level of fantasy is to diminish the level of reality (or vice versa). This interpretation can make sense with texts like the *Alice* books, in which the gradual disintegration of the normal life of a genteel Victorian girl is marked by her encounters with progressively curiouser and curiouser creatures and situations. But it does not take sufficient account of fantasy novels which are just as remarkable for their representation of reality as for their supernatural dimension. One good example, already discussed in Chapters 1 and 5, is Sarah Trimmer's *Fabulous Histories* (1786), an account of a human family and a neighbouring brood of polite, thinking, talking robins. This is an anthropomorphic fantasy, not very dissimilar in some ways from Kenneth Grahame's *The Wind in the Willows* (1908) or E. B. White's *Stuart Little* (1945) or *The Trumpet of the Swan* (1970). But *Fabulous Histories* is also determinedly – some would say dispiritingly

– mundane. The robins do not drive motorcars like Grahame's Toad, nor become celebrity musicians like White's swan. Rather, they live in a nest, eat worms and learn to fly. The human characteristics that they do have are prosaic: a childish impetuousness, say, which they can be educated to overcome. This combination of fantasy and reality was not only popular in the early history of fantasy writing. Richard Adams published *Watership Down* in 1972, and its rabbits, like Trimmer's robins, can think and talk, but never wear clothes, go to market, or lose their identity cards – as Beatrix Potter's Peter Rabbit or Pigling Bland have a tendency to do. Fred Inglis has succinctly characterised this form of fantasy by noting that Adams 'gives rabbits consciousness, which they do not have, but keeps them as rabbits.'[4]

Another, rather different example of a text in which reality overwhelms the fantasy is William Mayne's *Earthfasts* (1966). This begins with the emergence from the ground, in the later twentieth century, of a boy called Nellie Jack John who had entered a cave in search of legendary treasure in 1742. He is befriended by the two heroes of the book, David and Keith. The 'explanation' for this time travel is that while underground, Nellie Jack John had picked up one of the candles burning around the sleeping King Arthur and his knights. Awakening Arthur has brought much disruption: standing stones become marauding giants, ancient boggarts (or house ghosts) revive, and finally, terribly, David disappears. Keith eventually realises that he must replace the candle in order to return Arthur to suspended animation and rescue his friends. Clearly *Earthfasts* is, in some respects, a classic time-slip fantasy. But as unlikely as it may seem from this synopsis, the novel is remarkable more for its depiction of life in a quiet Yorkshire village, and of the relationship between the boys, than for its fantastic elements. David and Keith's friendship is the central theme, Mayne subtly suggesting the affection, but also dependence and jealousy, that exists between them. Like Nellie Jack John, they are stolidly realistic in their view of events. Indeed, Mayne uses their practicality to demonstrate how unimportant he thinks it is to make the book's fantastical elements entirely credible. 'It was not possible by ordinary standards of thought, for a boy to walk for two hundred years underground, and then come out', David thinks. 'Nor was it possible for two more boys to meet him and talk to him, even fight with him for a moment.' But if 'the only explanation was the impossible one' then there are more important things to worry about:

> 'We've had supper and breakfast,' said David. 'But he hasn't. We'd better find him and take him some.'
> 'It's unreal,' said Keith.
> 'Unreal but actual,' said David. 'It was just like it was. If a thing's happened it's happened.'
> 'It isn't reasonable,' said Keith. 'It's an effect without a cause.'
> 'There's plenty of them,' said David. 'But he's the most orphanist person there ever was, and nobody else knows him. So if he exists, whether he's a cause or an effect, we've still got to do something about him.'[5]

Cradlefasts, a sequel published in 1995, continued to subordinate the fantasy to the representation of David's emotional development, using the time-slip mechanism to allow David to come to terms with the death of his mother and baby sister. What one comes to realise with Mayne's novels is that genre can be very unimportant. His fantasy writing focuses on character far more than either plot or the supernatural apparatus. If this is true for Mayne, it is also true, to a greater or lesser extent, of many of the most well-regarded authors of fantasy fiction such as Joan Aiken, Alan Garner, Susan Cooper, Ursula Le Guin and Philip Pullman.

Mayne's somewhat cavalier attitude to sustaining the integrity of his fantasy settings flies in the face of J. R. R. Tolkien's famous dictum that the author should strive to imagine a fully-formed 'Secondary World' into which the reader can enter:

> Inside it, what he [the author] relates is 'true': it accords with the laws of that world. You therefore believe it, while you are, as it were, inside. The moment disbelief arises, the spell is broken; the magic, or rather art, has failed.[6]

There is no doubt that Tolkien's strategy has worked. The phenomenal success of *The Hobbit* (1937) and *The Lord of the Rings* (1954–55), and the sincere flattery of dozens of imitative secondary-world fantasies, amply prove this. This is success achieved even though some critics have found Tolkien's writing so pompous that it is laughable. 'Very seldom does one encounter emotion this fraudulent and writing this bad in any genre', writes John Goldthwaite.[7] But this is perhaps missing the point. The important thing is that even passages of preposterously high-flown heroics do not break the spell that Tolkien has cast. That readers tolerate, and even approve, such overblown writing is the proof of Tolkien's skill in creating the 'truth' of his world.

But Tolkien was surely not quite right about when and why fantasy fails, at least not for all fantasy writing. In his extremely successful 'Discworld' series (from 1983) Terry Pratchett deliberately destabilises the feasibility of his creation. The world is flat and travels through space on the backs of four elephants, who themselves stand on a giant turtle. Although drawing on Indian mythology, this is a cosmology intended to be risible. Similarly, most of his characters and places have absurd names, designed to amuse rather than convince, and he delights in building plots by comically twisting well-known stories. In *The Amazing Maurice and His Educated Rodents* (2001) a troupe of rats works a scam based on the traditional story of the Pied Piper of Hamelin, and it is a rat called 'Dangerous Beans' who eventually saves the town of Bad Blintz from the real danger they uncover. Pratchett's kind of comic, self-ironising and referential fantasy is part of a long tradition. 'Uncle David's Nonsensical Story about Giants and Fairies' in Catherine Sinclair's *Holiday House* (1839) is similar, with the giant Snap-'em-up described as so tall that he 'was obliged to climb up a ladder to comb his own hair', boiling his kettle on Mount Vesuvius, and making tea in a large lake.[8] Just as deliberately absurd is W. M. Thackeray's *The Rose and the Ring* (1854), beginning with Valoroso xxIV, King of Paflagonia, becoming so engrossed in a letter from Prince Bulbo, heir to the throne of Crim Tartary, that he allows his 'eggs to get cold, and leaves his august muffins untasted.'[9] In late twentieth-century children's books, this whimsicality is understood as postmodern irony. Diana Wynne Jones' *Howl's Moving Castle* (1986) is archly set in a land 'where such things as seven-league boots and cloaks of invisibility really exist'. It takes for its heroine Sophie, who complains that she is the eldest of three children because 'Everyone knows you are the one who will fail first, and worst, if the three of you set out to seek your fortunes.'[10] Tolkien's dictum applies even less to what has been called 'low fantasy', in which the magic intrudes into normal life. P. L. Travers, for example, did little to maintain the credibility of *Mary Poppins* (1934), creating a world in which statues and characters from books can come alive, where children can grow and shrink, where the animals in the zoo mysteriously find themselves free and the visitors caged, where gingerbread stars are pasted into the sky. The magic is almost entirely random and, annoyingly to some critics, inconsistent in scale, sometimes affecting only the children, sometimes changing the entire world.

What all these examples suggest is that the supernatural and the normal exist together in fantasy texts, in various proportions and combinations, but that there is no ratio which governs their relationship. To increase one is not to diminish the other. Alison Lurie has noted that William Mayne's writing is often 'in the tradition of [Jorge Luis] Borges or [Gabriel] Garcia Marquez', and their kind of magic realist writing is a case in point, depicting events which are beyond belief but also doggedly realistic.[11] Science fiction operates on a similar principle, but almost exactly the other way around. If magic realists revel in the impossibility of the things they show, goading readers into accepting them in spite of their better judgment, science fiction writers delight in the plausibility of their fantasies, daring their readers to disbelieve things which have been made to seem almost true. Thus, Jules Verne's stories, such as *Journey to the Centre of the Earth* (1864) or *From Earth to the Moon Direct* (1873), are often utterly fantastical, at least in their original nineteenth-century context, but rely for their effect on an underlying viability. Preparations for the journey into the earth are meticulously specified. The voyage to the moon is described in great technical detail (remarkably similar to the actual landings of the late twentieth century). *Twenty Thousand Leagues Under the Sea* (1873) was based on voyages really being undertaken by a French experimental submarine – just as Richard Adams closely based *Watership Down* on R. M. Lockley's scientific study *The Private Life of the Rabbit* (1964). These works offer an endorsement of Tolkien's view, that the reader's conviction must be maintained. The critic Tzvetan Todorov agreed, using the issue of credibility to distinguish between fantasy and the literature of the 'marvellous'. In the latter, he argued, the reader simply accepts that supernatural events are taking place and does nothing to try to explain them. In successful fantasy, Todorov argued, there is almost always some attempt to understand and explain the strangeness and, right up until its conclusion, the reader often cannot quite decide whether the events being described are natural or supernatural.[12]

In children's fantasy writing this uncertainty is often personified in the text by a leading character, who represents the readers and their responses to the strangeness. In Penelope Lively's *The Ghost of Thomas Kempe* (1973), for example, ten-year-old James Harrison only gradually comes to realise and accept that the mysterious occurrences taking place in his new home are caused by a poltergeist. We readers are also initially unsure, despite the book's giveaway title, and we sympathise with James as he tries to find rational explanations for the ghost's interventions in his life. Similarly, in secondary world fantasies, even if child protagonists often display a surprising *sang-froid* when they suddenly arrive in the new world, their willingness to suspend disbelief helps to bridge the gap between misgiving and conviction for the reader too. In C. S. Lewis' *The Lion, the Witch and the Wardrobe* (1950), Lucy Pevensie, then later her other siblings, act as the reader's representatives in Narnia, vicariously exploring and interpreting. They conduct us through this world, mediating our encounters with the fantastic until we become acclimatised to the weirdness. (Lewis's concern that readers would be mystified or shocked by his fantasy world explains his insistence, against all advice, that the recognisable, benign figure of Father Christmas should feature in *The Lion, the Witch and the Wardrobe*.[13]) Tolkien used the same strategy in *The Hobbit*, carefully mediating the reader's reactions to dwarfs, elves, goblins, a wizard and a dragon through the responses of an equally surprised, safe and familiar pseudo-child, Bilbo Baggins. Equally, in his two *Alice* books (1865 and 1871), Lewis Carroll relied on the normality and common sense of Alice to give the reader some kind of perspective on the bizarre creatures he had invented. Without her, Wonderland would surely be not intriguing and amusing, but absurd and tiresome. Her curiosity, concern or impatience, and her struggle to make sense of what she finds, makes what would otherwise be baffling twaddle into captivating nonsense.

However, in some of the best fantasy fiction the protagonist exploring the fantasy world on our behalf is not wholly to be trusted. Alice gives a very partial impression of the people she meets in Wonderland, mediated by her social prejudices and her rather prim and pretentious character. Likewise, it is one of the successes of *The Hobbit* that Bilbo, and through him the reader, is gradually forced to reassess initial character judgments. The dwarfs, for example, begin as jolly scamps in coloured hoods who might have wandered in from Walt Disney's *Snow White and the Seven Dwarfs*, released in the same year as *The Hobbit*. But it is Bilbo's gradual reassessment of their character and motives that transforms them into the much grimmer, almost Wagnerian desperadoes of the novel's close. Those who guide the protagonists can be untrustworthy too. The Cheshire Cat is famously unfathomable, but Peter Pan is actually deliberately misleading as an explainer of the customs of Neverland and the ways of the world. Trying to persuade Wendy about the faithlessness of adults, he lies, unforgivably, about having been forgotten and replaced by his mother.[14] Farah Mendlesohn has commended the work of Dianna Wynne Jones because it 'continually asks us to consider the reliability of whoever is offering to guide us through the dark woods'.[15] This is disorientating for the reader – as if Gandalf, Hagrid or Mrs Doasyouwouldbedoneby had turned out to be self-serving and deceitful impostors.

Some fantasy novels turn all this on its head. In Mayne's *Earthfasts*, or Lively's *Ghost of Thomas Kempe*, it is boys from 'our world' (although still fictional of course) who have to help visitors from the past adapt to their new surroundings. Similarly, in Philip Pullman's *His Dark Materials* trilogy, the 'real' world is introduced only in the second volume, *The Subtle Knife* (1997). When Lyra, the self-assured heroine of the first volume, enters 'our' Oxford she suddenly loses all her savvy and confidence and has to be guided by Will. The first thing that happens to her is that she is knocked down by a car. She finds herself 'a lost little girl in a strange world' and is mystified by all that she sees: 'What could those red and green lights mean at the corner of the road? It was all much harder to read than the alethiometer.'[16] This kind of de-familiarisation can be comic. It is also part of a long tradition of satirical texts (the most famous of which is Montesquieu's *Persian Letters* of 1721) which purport to describe the travels of a foreigner, describing his bemusement at customs and habits which the reader takes for granted, and thus bringing them into question. Transferring this technique to fantasy fiction can be just as comical and just as satirical, but it also helps to draw attention to the arbitrariness of a distinction between fantasy and reality. An excellent example is *Howl's Moving Castle*, in which Diana Wynne Jones takes her characters from the magical land of Ingary to a contemporary, and rainy, Wales. Narrated from Sophie's Ingarrian point of view, Wales is a strange place. People wear tight blue clothes on their legs which force them to walk 'in a kind of tight strut'. In the house they visit, ironically called 'Rivendell' after the 'Last Homely House' in *The Hobbit*, people watch 'magic coloured pictures moving on the front of a big, square box' and can hardly be distracted from what only the reader recognises as computer games. The trip to Wales strengthens Jones' characterisation of the wizard Howl as an ordinary teenage boy. In Wales he is called Howell, a common name, and he is bullied by his sister, which explains his dread of confrontation even in Ingary where he is a powerful wizard. But when he gives his nephews a new computer game that is set 'in an enchanted castle with four doors' each opening on a different dimension – just like his own Moving Castle in Ingary – the reader is forced to consider that one person's fantasy is another's reality, that they are relative terms, not opposites, but different ways of looking at the same thing.[17]

Alan Garner's *Elidor* (1965) provides one of the best examples of a novel in which the divide between reality and fantasy is disintegrating. Four children, a little like the Pevensies, enter a fantasy world and take back with them four 'Treasures'. If these are kept safe, Elidor will be saved from the 'Darkness' that has cursed it. But the rest of the novel is concerned with the attempts of the enemies of Elidor to break through into the Watson children's world to take back the Treasures. Garner's success is in showing how the 'real' and fantasy world lie on top of each other, touching at certain points. The wasteland of Elidor maps precisely onto the derelict Manchester of the Watson children, with its bombed-out buildings and half-demolished slums. There are places where the two worlds touch, explains Malebron, their guide in Elidor, especially those which have been 'battered by war' and where 'the land around quakes with destruction': the slums of Manchester and the war-torn castles of Elidor.[18] In *The Lion, the Witch and the Wardrobe*, the touching point is more mundane: a wardrobe (although made from a Narnian tree, as Lewis explained in his 'prequel', *The Magician's Nephew*). But in another way, the parallelism of the two worlds is even more striking than in *Elidor*. The Pevensie children have been evacuated from London to avoid the air-raids of World War Two, but, as Maria Tatar has pointed out, they 'end up fighting the war by proxy against the armies of the White Witch', until, as Lewis gleefully puts it, 'all that foul brood was stamped out'. They then bring peace and prosperity to post-war Narnia through their wise and benign rule.[19] Five years after the end of the Second World War, Lewis's fantasy was celebrating a victory over tyranny and his hopes for reconstruction. He was also showing how impossible it is to exclude children from conflict, for the Pevensies find their own way to fight. Fantasy, we find, is not an escape from reality but, often, a rewriting of it.

Indeed, even if fantasy writing is, by definition, generally disengaged from reality, it is often easy to discern its entanglement in the ideological controversies of its day. This may be, of course, because fantasy so readily invites symbolic readings. Writing during the political crisis caused by the French Revolution in 1790s Britain, for instance, the radical Thomas Spence argued that 'the stories of enormous and tyrannical giants, dwelling in strong castles, which have been thought fabulous, may reasonably be looked upon as disguised truths, and to have been invented as just satires on great lords'.[20] Some modern critics' exercises in contextualisation can seem even more fanciful, notably attempts to read every detail of the *Alice* books as a comment on late-Victorian politics and society.[21] Yet there can be little doubt that Kingsley's *The Water-Babies* (1863) was a response to on *The Origin of Species* (1859) – an attack on those who unthinkingly denounced Darwin's theories.[22] Equally apparent are the political resonances of the many children's science fiction fantasies published during the Cold War. Robert O'Brien's *Z for Zachariah* (1975), set after a nuclear holocaust, and Jean Ure's *Plague 99* (1989), about an almost equally destructive pandemic, are clearly reflective of anxieties about an imminent apocalypse.

But it is not much more difficult to read the classic 'high fantasies' politically. Both Lewis's *Narniad* and Tolkien's *The Hobbit* advance a particular political economy, fundamentally that developed in the later nineteenth century by proto-socialist thinkers like John Ruskin and William Morris (themselves both authors of fantasy fiction). By the time Tolkien and Lewis were writing, this was a more paradoxical position, conservative in its contempt for the values of industrialised modernity, its casual snobbishness, its traditionalist pietism and its advocacy of autocratic leadership, but hostile to the gross inequalities of unfettered capitalism and concerned with the values of ordinary people, especially the artisan. These contradictions run through *The Hobbit*. The Trolls are mocked and derided for their plebeian names ('Bill Huggins'), Cockney slang ('lumme'), vulgar appetites (beer) and supposedly working-class attitudes (querulousness; an inability to look beyond the present). The Goblins are characterised as a brutal industrial proletariat making 'no beautiful things' but efficiently mass-producing 'Hammers, axes, swords, daggers, pickaxes, tongs' (some of these, one notes, featuring on the Soviet flag). Yet Tolkien equally attacks the rich: not only dragons' pointless and unproductive hoarding ('they hardly know a good bit of work from a bad, though they usually have a good notion of the current market value') but also those leaders who 'have a good head for business' but are 'no good when anything serious happens'. The men of Esgaroth depose these 'old men and the money-counters', crowning the belligerent Bard as their king in place of the non-monarchical 'Master'. In doing so they reveal a reactionary, authoritarian and perhaps even slightly fascistic tendency in Tolkien's fantasy.[23] With its simultaneously anti-socialist and anti-capitalist agenda, it might be said that Tolkien was trying to steer a middle way between the main clashing ideologies of the late 1930s, but it might be noted that the politics of *The Hobbit* are not, in some ways, so very far removed from the rhetoric of Nazism.

The politics of gender in *The Hobbit* are also extremely intriguing. It is very notable that *The Hobbit* contains no living female characters. This might, in itself, be indicative of a desire on the author's part to make Middle Earth a sort of pre-Lapsarian Eden, free, like Narnia, from the complications of sex. But it might also be part of what one critic calls Tolkien's 'subtle contempt and hostility towards women'.[24] Yet it must be clear to any reader with an eye for psychological detail that one of the most important characters in *The Hobbit* is Bilbo's dead mother, Belladonna Took, introduced right at the start of the novel. It is she who has bequeathed to Bilbo 'something not entirely hobbitlike': a thirst for adventure. Once we notice this, it is difficult not to conclude that Bilbo's real quest is to please his absent mother.[25] In any case, the novel is hardly a celebration of machismo. Some of the most influential characters exhibit what might be thought of as 'female' characteristics: Gandalf and Beorn are both nurturing, even maternal figures. And ultimately Bilbo does not triumph because of any 'manly' accomplishment, but because he relinquishes any pretensions to honour or soldierly loyalty, sacrificing his own interests rather than sticking to a destructive desire for profit or prestige. At the novel's close he is congratulated for domestic virtues: 'If more of us valued food and cheer and song above hoarded gold,' says Thorin Oakenshield with the wisdom of one on his deathbed, 'it would be a merrier world.'[26] Of course it would still be a stretch to regard *The Hobbit* as a feminist text, but Tolkien's decision to erase the feminine does raise some interesting questions about the role of gender in high fantasy more generally. Low fantasy fiction written for children in the nineteenth and early twentieth centuries had been written about girls as much as boys: Carroll's Alice, Barrie's Wendy and Baum's Dorothy amongst many others. Tolkien's decision to exile women from Middle Earth seems like a deliberate attempt to masculinise the genre, especially since the sorts of text that he took as a model had included female characters in important roles, the Anglo–Saxon epic *Beowulf* for example. High fantasy of the sort that Tolkien pioneered was cast as a masculine genre right from the start.

It has taken decades for this to change. Female protagonists may have become more common – like Sabriel and Lirael in Garth Nix's 'Old Kingdom' series ('Abhorsen' in the USA, 1995–2003). But what Ursula Le Guin calls 'the intense conservatism of traditional fantasy' based on 'the establishment or validation of manhood' has remained firmly in place. This can be seen from Le Guin's own work, and her reflections on it. In her early fantasy fiction, she came to realise, she 'was writing by the rules', employing an essentially masculinist paradigm. In the first three Earthsea novels (1968–72), she acknowledged, 'the fundamental power, magic, belongs to men; only to men; only to men who have no sexual contact with women.'[27] They follow the story of a male magician Ged, and were, by any standard, extremely successful (as well as being, in some ways, politically radical, for Ged was black). But when Le Guin came to add to the series with *Tehanu* in 1990, followed by *Tales from Earthsea* and *The Other Wind* in 2001, she used the opportunity to recreate her imagined world from a feminist perspective. Not only did she make her central characters female, but she 'reinvented the past', as Perry Nodelman has put it, to show that magic had once been practiced by women, that the forces of patriarchy had later combined to deny them this power, and that Ged's own magic derived from an 'unauthorised' female teacher.[28] Le Guin sought to show how males had appropriated magic in Earthsea, how this had caused social and spiritual corruption, and how the damage could be repaired by the less aggressive behaviour of Tehanu, whose magic aims at reconciliation rather than dominion. But of course this feminised, feminist revision provides another demonstration of the ways in which fantasy has been adapted to suit changing social and cultural values. As Le Guin put it, 'even in Fairyland there is no escape from politics.'[29]

If it is a misapprehension that fantasy is not political, so it is also wrong-headed to imagine that fantasy writing is always liberating in a way that other genres are not. Fantasy does, of course, allow the reader to enter worlds where normal laws and limits do not apply. Harry Potter is clearly liberated by removal from his dreary and disciplined life in Privet Drive to the magical world of Hogwarts. Readers enjoy Rowling's books, it is often said, precisely because they are not like humdrum life. In particular it has been suggested that they have been popular because they offer a change from realistic, issue-based fiction that, some say, is imposed on unwilling children by adults who think they know what is best. But fantasy is seldom actually very anarchic. Hogwarts, like most schools in children's literature, is a very regulated world: disciplined, rule-bound and hierarchically ordered. High fantasy too is generally very structured. It tends to abound in authority figures who impose order, the benign but dictatorial Aslan in the *Narniad* being a classic example. And most authors are careful to ensure that their protagonists (and thereby their readers) always know exactly what they are doing in the fantasy world. In *The Lion, the Witch and the Wardrobe* it is notable that the Pevensie children are not much disorientated by their arrival in Narnia. This is partly because of their trusting nature, but also because they so obviously have a purpose there. The prophesy explained to them by Mr Beaver, but alluded to by Mr Tumnus almost as soon as Lucy first steps into Narnia, leaves little room to doubt the children's trajectory:

> 'Down at Cair Paravel – that's the castle on the sea coast down at the mouth of this river which ought to be the capital of the whole country if all was as it should be – down at Cair Paravel there are four thrones and it's a saying in Narnia time out of mind that when two Sons of Adam and two Daughters of Eve sit in those four thrones, then it will be the end not only of the White Witch's reign but of her life, and that is why we had to be so cautious as we came along, for if she knew about you four, your lives wouldn't be worth a shake of my whiskers!'[30]

This use of a prophecy that must be fulfilled is a common motif in fantasy writing. In *Edidor* the Watsons are even shown a book by Malabron which contains a picture of them, as well as the usual prophetic verses.[31] It is, perhaps, a hangover from the medieval quest narratives which influenced much fantasy fiction. But it is also a means by which the fantasy world can be ordered. In Russell Hoban's *The Mouse and His Child* (1969) there is both a quest and a prophecy. The Child, welded to his father because together they form a clockwork toy, wants to find a home and a mother, as well as to become 'self-winding'. Hoban emphasises the quest element by introducing a frog toward the beginning who pretends to read the mice's fortune. He is as surprised as anyone when a true spirit of prophecy mysteriously overcomes him and he divines that 'The enemy you flee at the beginning awaits you at the end.' 'That isn't much to look forward to', says the Mouse, rightly, but his Child, and the reader, take a sense of direction from the prediction.[32] Prophecy and quest mean that readers are likely to be less bewildered by the weird fantasy world Hoban has created. Alice's progress along the chessboard, culminating in her inevitable coronation as a queen, imposes the same kind of order in Carroll's *Through the Looking Glass*. Some authors deliberately play with this prophesy motif. In *Howl's Moving Castle*, Diana Wynne Jones introduces a witch's curse in Ingary which orders the fate of the novel's lead characters, but turns out actually to be a photocopied homework exercise which has somehow been carried through from 'our' world. A prophesised narrative structure can be constricting. In *The Lion, the Witch and the Wardrobe* the Pevensies' destiny is set out for them, and the only anxiety is whether Edmund will be brought round to join his siblings on the four thrones. In *His Dark Materials*, Philip Pullman seems to be reacting against the lack of free-will in Narnia. Lyra and Will (his name is far from insignificant) are continually having to make their own choices. It is noticeable that, unlike the Pevensies, Harry Potter, or the return of the king in *The Lord of the Rings*, their coming is not foretold, although the fate of the world hangs on it.

We get the impression that Narnia has been waiting for the Pevensie children, as Sleeping Beauty's palace has been waiting for the Prince. If Narnia has not quite been in a state of suspended animation, then it has certainly been gripped by an endless winter, with all the unnatural stasis and sterility this implies, until the children's arrival brings renewal. Indeed, in the majority of parallel-world writing we find that the world revolves around the protagonists. This is not to say that they remain stationary while the world around them is transformed, although this does sometimes seem to be the case, as in Catherine Storr's *Marianne Dreams* (1958), an account of the adventures in a dream-world created by the heroine's doodles with a magic pencil while she is confined in a sick-bed. Rather, in books like *The Lion, the Witch and the Wardrobe*, we get the impression that the fantasy world lacks an independent existence, that it has only been created for the benefit of the central characters. Carroll's *Alice* books provide another example. The Mad Hatter's tea party might have been going on before Alice arrives, and the tarts might have been stolen out of her sight, but we nevertheless get the impression that Wonderland and the Looking-Glass world exist for Alice's benefit, and almost that the inhabitants are on standby until Alice appears to interview them. We might call this 'Ptolemaic' fantasy, the world revolving around the protagonist as Ptolemy thought the sun, stars and planets revolved around the

Earth. But some fantasies are more 'Copernican', with the protagonist often disoriented, travelling through a fixed universe, as Copernicus realised the Earth revolved around the sun.

Lucy Boston's *The Children of Green Knowe* (1954) is one such text. The past inhabitants of a house called Green Knowe blithely continue to live their unchanging lives, as ghosts of a sort, while the at first mystified protagonist, Tolly, slowly learns about their history and is occasionally able to see them and join in with their games. Kingsley's *The Water-Babies* is similar. Tom, a chimney-sweep, is transformed – into an 'Eft' – which means that he can begin a new, clean life in an aquatic world which was always there, but hidden (though what Kingsley does not make immediately clear is that Tom has in fact drowned, and that his existence as a Water-Baby is his afterlife). In this kind of 'Copernican' fantasy, the protagonists are generally powerless and shy in the fantasy world. In 'Ptolemaic' fantasies, child characters become powerful and important figures, although in their real worlds they have been weak. In Garner's *Elidor*, Roland is the youngest and feeblest of the siblings, but 'Here, in Elidor,' he is told by Malebron, 'you are stronger', and discovering this, he leads his siblings in their quest.[33] For Roland, as for Harry Potter, Lyra Silvertongue, Bilbo Baggins and the Pevensies (especially Lucy), all of whom are subordinate in their home worlds, no less than the fate of the world rests on their shoulders once they enter the fantasy.

Another common assumption about fantasy writing is that it represents the antithesis of the didactic tradition in children's literature. Many histories of children's books make this case, arguing that in the late eighteenth and early nineteenth centuries, delight and instruction were at war within children's texts, fantasy eventually, and inevitably, triumphing.[34] This paradigm can be collapsed in at least two ways. First, many early didactic texts were often couched as fantasies. Sarah Trimmer's *Fabulous Histories* (1786) and Dorothy Kilner's *The Life and Perambulations of a Mouse* (1784) are good examples. Eighteenth-century secondary world fantasies exist too, most famously Swift's *Gulliver's Travels* (1726), which came to be read by children soon after its publication. Alternative worlds are also to be found in some very early texts that were always intended for the young, such as *The Prettiest Book for Children; Being the*

History of the Enchanted Castle; Situated in One of the Fortunate Isles, and Governed by Giant Instruction (1770). The description provided by 'Don Stephen Bunyano' focuses almost entirely on the educational opportunities that the Giant Instruction wisely provides there, but the Fortunate Isles are part of the tradition that would lead to Charles Kingsley's St. Brendan's Isle in *The Water-Babies*, J. M. Barrie's Neverland or the archipelago of islands in Le Guin's Earthsea series.

Second, didacticism has consistently remained at the heart of children's fantasy writing. The ground-breaking fantasies of the 1860s and 1870s certainly had not lost their determination to teach. It is difficult to imagine a more preachy text than *The Water-Babies*, which uses the medium of fantasy to attack spiritual corruption as well as the more worldly scandal of child chimney-sweeps. Mrs Bedonebyasyoudid represents the spirit of the Old Testament, and Mrs Doasyouwouldbedoneby the New. Mother Carey and the little girl Ellie play other parts in this theological masquerade, allowing Tom, eventually, to find his way to Heaven by going to the Other-end-of-Nowhere – that is to say, Hell – to save his old master, Grimes. The novel reads rather like a medieval morality play. George MacDonald's novels expound similar social and spiritual teachings. *At the Back of the North Wind* (1871) combines accounts of the harsh lives of the poor, like Nanny, a destitute crossing-sweeper, with an allegorical representation of salvation. In *The Lion, the Witch and the Wardrobe* the didacticism is even clearer. Edmund transgresses, giving way to greed, selfishness and spite, and is punished by the cruelty of the White Witch and being denied a Christmas present. This, it has been pointed out, is the sort of morality that a child can easily understand and might wish for: no tedious moral lectures nor long drawn-out process of repentance, but clear punishment, quick confession, and a swift readmission to the good graces of those he has wronged. His sins are completely forgotten by the time he takes up his place as one of the monarchs of Narnia.[35]

Other fantasy novels teach more sophisticated lessons. In Anne Barrett's *Caterpillar Hall* (1950), for instance, a magic umbrella allows Penelope to see the moments from other people's childhoods when they wanted something as badly as she wanted the umbrella. Their frustrated desires explain why they have become the adults they are – strict, sad, wistful, angry – and Penelope cannot help but empathise. The didacticism of *The Hobbit* is less ostentatious but equally central to the story. Suddenly taking a more serious turn, the novel ends with Bilbo stealing the prized Arkenstone from his dwarf companions, or rather appropriating it as his share of the treasure, and passing it to the dwarfs' enemies so that it can be used as a bargaining chip in the brokering of a treaty. Read as a fable, the moral is about the importance of overcoming avarice and selfishness, perhaps even selfhood. This goes some way to answering the question archly raised by the narrator at the very start of the novel: Bilbo 'may have lost the neighbours' respect, but he gained – well, you will see'. He gains much from the adventure, including the ring that would feature so prominently in the Tolkien's further account of Middle Earth's history, but it is how he changes as a person that the narrator was surely referring to. 'You are not the hobbit that you once were', Gandalf tells him at the end of the novel.[36] What Bilbo has acquired is a stronger sense of his identity, the knowledge that he can survive outside the comfort of his home, and a life of creativity and fulfilment instead of timidity and torpor. Ultimately, *The Hobbit* is more a novel of personal development, or *Bildungsroman*, than a straightforward fantasy quest narrative. Even Carroll's *Alice* books, often regarded as the books in which unhampered fantasy finally triumphed over the instructive tendency, can be regarded as didactic in this way. There may be no religious allegory, nor social realism, and it would be reductive to suggest that Carroll had intended only to write a *Bildungsroman*, but Alice does return from Wonderland wiser, and more aware of her own identity, than she was. At the start of her adventure she is downright insensitive. Meeting a mouse, the first thing that comes into Alice's mind as a fit subject for conversation is her cat, Dinah, 'such a capital one for catching mice'. She repeats the same mistake several times, but slowly learns to be more empathetic. By the time she is being told by the Mock Turtle about whiting (a kind of fish), she has at least come to realise that she must watch what she says: 'I've often seen them at dinn—', she says, checking herself just in time (leaving the Mock Turtle to wonder where Dinn actually is).[37]

More obvious is Carroll's representation of his heroine's psychological development. From the fall down the rabbit-hole, which might easily be understood as a kind of birth, Alice grows steadily in Wonderland, her adventures paralleling a child's gradual maturation. Her first encounters are with small, cute creatures – rabbits and mice – but progressively she meets more frightening adults: the Duchess, the Hatter, the Queen. These are not the safe, pleasant interactions of the nursery. Nor do these new acquaintances help Alice much, but rather challenge her. They are competitive, capricious, selfish and deceitful. Increasingly, she is confronted with all sorts of 'adult' concerns too: anger, fear, nostalgia, death, judgment. These encounters shape Alice's sense of self, which she had wrongly thought of as set and stable. She comes to doubt herself, and to develop – in size, but also psychologically. Indeed, the books can be understood as a quest for identity. In *Through the Looking Glass*, Alice advances until she reaches psychic fulfilment as a queen. In Wonderland, she keeps growing and shrinking until she finds out what her right size is. The text is dominated by questions of identity. Having grown enormously, she loses the certainty that she and her body are one, considering sending a letter to 'Alice's Right Foot, Esq.' – a male form of address, we note. Later, she seriously wonders if she is actually Ada or Mabel. It is the Caterpillar who confronts her most bluntly about this. 'Who are *you*?' he quizzes. Alice cannot answer, saying that she was one thing when she got up, but 'I think I must have been changed several times since then'. For the caterpillar, presumably later to metamorphose into a moth or butterfly, such transformation is natural. For Alice it is a source of great anxiety, manifested when the Wood Pigeon asks why it should matter whether she is a little girl or a serpent: ' "It matters a good deal to me," said Alice hastily'.[38]

If Alice is gaining a sense of self, she is also learning other vital lessons about the rules of life, and more particularly, their dismaying inconstancy. The Queen's croquet game (or the Caucus Race, or Lobster Quadrille) is incomprehensible to Alice, apparently without rules. But everyone else seems to understand. As is often pointed out, this replicates the way that many aspects of the adult world might appear to a child encountering them for the first time. Alice longs for rules, but is constantly disappointed. She believes she knows how tea parties should be conducted, but the Mad Hatter shows she cannot be so sure. She is proud of knowing how judicial trials work, but the Wonderland court works on principles that she cannot fathom. Only the Cheshire Cat seems to acknowledge that there are no rules and one can never fully make sense of what is happening. The Alice books are not didactic in a conventional sense, but like other *Bildungsromans*, by dramatising some of the difficulties of interacting with the adult world, they do offer the reader an oblique education, and comment on, if they do not quite help with, the construction of a stable identity.

Fantasy is extremely well suited to consideration of questions of identity. The journey to another world, or another time, decontextualises the protagonists, removing them from the structures that locate and bind them into a particular role within the family, the school, or the larger society. They then have to discover afresh who they are, and, usually, can return to their reality at the end of the novel with a stronger sense of themselves. Perhaps this helps to explain why children's fantasy has become increasingly prevalent. Quite apart from the many satisfactions it offers to the readers, authors find the form eminently suitable for the transmission of lessons on selfhood, these being regarded now as the best kind of instruction that good children's literature can and should teach. Identity exchange fantasies, such as F. Anstey's *Vice Versa; or, A Lesson to Fathers* (1882) or Mary Rogers' *Freaky Friday* (1972), show this clearly. In the former a haughty businessman and his schoolboy son find themselves inhabiting one another's bodies; in the latter, a teenager is metamorphosed into her mother. By the end of the novels, the characters have gained a cross-generational empathy and a stronger sense of their own identity. The same questions of selfhood are explored more directly in Penelope Farmer's *Charlotte Sometimes* (1969), in which a 1960s schoolgirl is somehow transported back and forth between her own time and the period of the First World War, where everybody knows her as a girl called Clare. Unsurprisingly, Charlotte finds it increasingly difficult to cling to her own identity. She has to discover what it is that makes her Charlotte, and not Clare. Less schizophrenic, but no less disconcerting, is Jones's *Howl's Moving Castle*, in which the young heroine Sophie is magically aged. She prematurely learns a great deal about life as an old woman, but she also comes to accept that, even as a girl, she possesses many of the characteristics that she will have when old. The reader finds, from Sophie's experience, that the child is already the adult that he or she will become. The search for one's mature identity is central to Philip Pullman's *His Dark Materials* too. Children's demons change shape, but settle into a fixed form when they reach adulthood. The trilogy concludes when Lyra and Will's demons finally settle, symbolising the same realisation of identity that forms the denouement of many other children's fantasy novels.

The relationship between childhood and adulthood is a related theme, often central to fantasy fiction and particularly time-slip novels. Philippa Pearce wrote that she 'wanted to explore that almost unimaginable concept of adults having once been children', and to do so devised *Tom's Midnight Garden* (1958).[39] Its eponymous hero is a lonely child on the verge of adulthood who has been sent away to live with his strict aunt and uncle. He finds that, every night, he can visit a garden that no longer exists. There, he finds solace in the friendship of a Victorian girl called Hattie. Only right at the end of the novel does he discover that the old woman who lives upstairs from his aunt and uncle is in fact Hattie, now grown up. *Tom's Midnight Garden* is an entrancing and gripping novel and it would be quite unfair to call it a didactic text, but it was clearly constructed to tutor its readers. Each time Tom returns to the garden he finds Hattie at a different age. When, finally, he returns to find that Hattie has grown up, he is devastated, but slowly he learns to reconcile himself to the loss, or rather to accept that people develop and change. The lesson applies directly to Tom too, for we understand that his unhappiness was the result of an unwillingness to accept change in his own life. As well as showing that the old were once young, Pearce teaches young readers that they cannot hold onto childhood forever. The book serves equally well to teach adult readers that they cannot forever treat their sons and daughters as children. All things change, Pearce shows, but just as Hattie, however old, will always be Hattie, and just as the house to which Tom has moved will always retain traces of its former inhabitants, so identity remains secure despite external alteration.

Perry Nodelman has noted that 'children's literature is frequently about coming to terms with a world one does not understand – the world as defined and governed by grownups and not totally familiar or comprehensible to children'.[40] Good fantasy literature dramatises this experience, transporting its characters into a past time or new world where all is strange and perplexing. Perhaps this mirroring of their own daily experience helps to explain why children relish fantasy so much. Or perhaps it is because in a new world where nobody knows the rules, children are not placed at a competitive disadvantage, and consequently feel the equal of adults in a way that they do not in their real lives. In certain time-slip novels, when a figure from the past is propelled into their lives, these children become, relatively speaking, figures of knowledge and authority. This is certainly the case in Lively's *The Ghost of Thomas Kempe* or Mayne's *Earthfasts*. In other fantasies, where the children are sent into the past, or another dimension, they are equally significant, fêted because of their exoticism, or honoured and empowered because, like the Pevensies in Narnia, they find themselves to be somehow vital to the well-being of the world. This fantasy of empowerment is central to the appeal of fantasy writing to children. But the genre has appealed to the adults who write it surely at least in part because it can so easily be adapted to provide lessons of all kinds, moral, political, practical and psychological.

SUMMARY OF KEY POINTS

- No children's books are pure fantasy, but combine fanciful and realistic elements. To increase the amount of fantasy is not to diminish the reality, nor vice versa. Fantasy has often been used to satirise or rewrite reality.
- Most fantasy writing is not completely anarchic, but presents carefully structured alterative realities which are usually controlled by strict rules.
- Fantasy can be both empowering or disorientating for protagonists and readers.
- The process of self-discovery, and questions about how identity remains fixed despite external change, are central to much good fantasy writing.
- Fantasy has always included, and continues to include, didactic elements.

NOTES

1. Brian Attebery, *Strategies of Fantasy* (Bloomington, IN: Indiana University Press, 1992), pp. 12–13.
2. Jacqueline Rose, *The Case of Peter Pan or The Impossibility of Children's Fiction* (London: Macmillan, 1984).
3. Colin Manlove, *The Fantasy Literature of England* (Basingstoke: Macmillan, 1999), p. 3. For wider discussions see Eric S. Rabkin, *The Fantastic in Literature* (Princeton: Princeton University Press, 1976), Rosemary Jackson, *Fantasy: The Literature of Subversion* (London: Methuen, 1984), Kathryn Hume, *Fantasy and Mimesis: Responses to Reality in Western Literature* (New York: Methuen, 1984), Lucie Armitt, *Theorising the Fantastic* (London: Arnold, 1996) and Peter Hunt and Millicent Lenz, *Alternative Worlds in Fantasy Fiction* (London: Continuum, 2001), pp. 1–41.
4. Fred Inglis, *The Promise of Happiness: Value and Meaning in Children's Fiction* (Cambridge: Cambridge University Press, 1981), p. 208.
5. William Mayne, *Earthfasts* (London: Hodder, [1966] 1995), pp. 25 and 27–8.
6. J. R. R. Tolkien, 'On Fairy-stories', *The Tolkien Reader* (New York: Balantine, [1947] 1966), p. 37.
7. John Goldthwaite, *The Natural History of Make-Believe: A Guide to the Principal Works of Britain, Europe, and America* (New York: Oxford University Press, 1996), p. 218.
8. Catherine Sinclair, *Holiday House* (London: Hamish Hamilton, [1839] 1972), p. 127.
9. W. M. Thackeray, *The Rose and the Ring or the History of Prince Giglio and Prince Bulbo* (London: John Murray, [1854] 1909), p. 1.
10. Diana Wynne Jones, *Howl's Moving Castle* (London: Harper Collins, [1986] 2005), p. 9.
11. Alison Lurie, 'William Mayne', in *Children and their Books: A Celebration of the Work of Iona and Peter Opie*, ed. Gillian Avery and Julia Briggs (Oxford: Clarendon Press, 1989), pp. 368–79 (p. 375).
12. Tzvetan Todorov, *The Fantastic: A Structural Approach to a Literary Genre*, trans. Richard Howard (Ithaca, NY: Cornell University Press, [1970] 1975), pp. 41–2.

13. A. N. Wilson, *C. S. Lewis: A Biography* (London: Collins, 1990), p. 221.
14. J. M. Barrie, *Peter and Wendy*, ed. Jack Zipes (London: Penguin, [1911] 2004), p. 98.
15. Farah Mendlesohn, *Diana Wynne Jones: Children's Literature and the Fantastic Tradition* (New York: Routledge, 2005), p. 90.
16. Philip Pullman, *The Subtle Knife* (London: Scholastic, [1997] 1998), pp. 68, 73 and 77.
17. Jones, *Howl's Moving Castle*, pp. 146–7, 148–9 and 151; J. R. R. Tolkien, *The Hobbit* (London: Collins, [1937] 1998), p. 64.
18. Alan Garner, *Elidor* (London: HarperCollins, [1965] 2002), p. 54.
19. C. S. Lewis, *The Magician's Nephew* (London: Collins, [1955] 1980), p. 219, and *The Lion, the Witch and the Wardrobe* (London: Grafton, [1950] 2002), p. 166. Maria Tatar, ' "Appointed Journeys": Growing Up with War Stories', in *Under Fire: Childhood in the Shadow of War*, ed. Elizabeth Goodenough and Andrea Immel (Detroit, MI: Wayne State University Press, 2008), pp. 237–50 (p. 243).
20. Thomas Spence, *Pigs' Meat; or, Lessons for the Swinish Multitude*, 2 vols (London: T. Spence, c.1795), vol. 2, p. 209.
21. See Jo Elwyn Jones and J. Francis Gladstone, *The Red King's Dream, or Lewis Carroll in Wonderland* (London: Jonathan Cape, 1995).
22. See also Rose Lovell-Smith, 'Eggs and Serpents: Natural History Reference in Lewis Carroll's Scene of Alice and the Pigeon', *Children's Literature*, 35 (2007), 27–53.
23. Tolkien, *The Hobbit*, pp. 51–4, 84, 37–8 and 302–3.
24. In Tolkien's work, Catharine R. Stimpson argues, women 'are either beautiful and distant, simply distant, or simply simple' and in *The Lord of the Rings*, she adds, there is outright misogyny, as when a 'jubilant, exultant Tolkien tells how Sam forces Shelob [a monstrous spider that Stimpson identifies as a 'bitch-castrator'] . . . to impale herself, somewhere in the region of the womb, on his little knife.' *J. R. R. Tolkien* (New York: Columbia University Press, 1969), pp. 18–19.
25. Tolkien, *The Hobbit*, p. 13. See William H. Green, ' "Where's mama?" The construction of the feminine in *The Hobbit*', *The Lion and the Unicorn*, 22 (1998), 188–95.

26. Tolkien, *The Hobbit*, p. 346.
27. Le Guin, *Earthsea Revisioned* (Cambridge: Green Bay, 1993), pp. 8, 5, 7 and 9.
28. Perry Nodelman, 'Reinventing the Past: Gender in Ursula K. Le Guin's *Tehanu* and the Earthsea "Trilogy"', *Children's Literature in Education*, 23 (1995), 179–201. See also Laura B. Comoletti and Michael D. C. Prout, 'How They Do Things with Words: Language, Power, Gender, and the Priestly Wizards of Ursula K. Le Guin's Earthsea Books,' *Children's Literature*, 29 (2001), 113–41.
29. Le Guin, *Earthsea Revisioned*, p. 7.
30. Lewis, *The Lion, the Witch and the Wardrobe*, p. 77.
31. Garner, *Elidor*, p. 56.
32. Russell Hoban, *The Mouse and His Child* (London: Faber & Faber, [1969] 2005), p. 26.
33. Garner, *Elidor*, p. 48.
34. See Geoffrey Summerfield's *Fantasy and Reason: Children's Literature in the Eighteenth Century* (London: Methuen, 1984).
35. Doris T. Myers, *C. S. Lewis in Context* (Kent, OH: Kent State University Press, 1994), p. 132.
36. Tolkien, *The Hobbit*, pp. 12 and 361.
37. Lewis Carroll, *Alice in Wonderland*, ed. Donald J. Grey (New York: W. W. Norton, [1865 and 1871] 1992), pp. 18, 26 and 80.
38. Carroll, *Alice in Wonderland*, pp. 14, 15, 35 and 43.
39. Obituary of Phillipa Pearce, *The Daily Telegraph*, 27 December 2006.
40. Nodelman, 'Some Presumptuous Generalizations About Fantasy', in *Only Connect: Readings on Children's Literature*, ed. Sheila Egoff *et al.*, 3rd edn (Toronto: Oxford University Press, 1996), pp. 175–8 (p. 178).

CHAPTER 7

The Adventure Story

It is hard to pin down precisely what distinguishes the adventure story from other kinds of writing for children. There are many classic texts which seem straightforwardly to fit the description. Daniel Defoe's *Robinson Crusoe* (1719) and Jonathan Swift's *Gulliver's Travels* (1726) are often seen as forerunners. Historical novels in the vein of Sir Walter Scott became popular with children in the nineteenth century – Frederick Marryat's *Children of the New Forest* (1847), for instance, or, in America, the 'Leather-Stocking Tales' by James Fenimore Cooper, culminating in *The Last of the Mohicans* (1826). High Victorian tales of quests and hazards like Jules Verne's *Twenty Thousand Leagues Under the Sea* (1873) or Henry Rider Haggard's *King Solomon's Mines* (1885) might be regarded as characteristic of the genre. Or perhaps only those novels placing children, not adults, at the centre of events can be regarded as truly archetypical: Robert Louis Stevenson's *Treasure Island* (1883), say. Some adventures seem playful, other deadly serious. Arthur Ransome's *Swallows and Amazons* (1930), however exciting, is essentially an elaborate game. At around the same time the Hardy Boys (from 1927), Nancy Drew (from 1930) and Enid Blyton's Famous Five and Secret Seven (from 1942 and 1949) were unmasking hardened villains and solving serious crimes – although these are hardly 'hard-boiled' thrillers. In novels like Ian Serraillier's *The Silver Sword* (1956) or Anne Holm's *I Am David* (1963), with their protagonists on the run from persecution, the stakes are much higher and the tension much more taut. More recent adventure stories vary in tone in complex ways. Anthony Horowitz's *Stormbreaker* (2000) and Charlie Higson's *Silverfin* (2005) may be all-action thrillers set in the world of international espionage, but they are as fantastical, if not quite as comic or camp, as the James Bond films that inspired them. There is very little to joke about in Robert Cormier's *After the First Death* (1979) or Peter Dickinson's *The Seventh Raven* (1981), in which international terrorism provides the adventure. Often in children's books the narrators provide retrospective accounts of events, so the excitement does not come from knowing whether they live or die, but from discovering how they have coped with their traumatic experiences.

What even this short list demonstrates is that the boundaries of the children's adventure story are very blurred. Many of these books were first intended for an adult audience. Some deliberately sought a cross-over readership of adults and children: *King Solomon's Mines*, for example, was dedicated 'to all the big and little boys who read it'.[1] Others were abridged for younger readers. *Robinson Crusoe*, for instance, has been one of the most frequently rewritten of all books, pirated abridged editions appearing within the year of its first publication. Editions designed especially for children were being produced by the 1760s, although children had no doubt been reading chapbook versions much earlier. The thousand-plus pages of its three volumes were sometimes reduced to as few as eight pages.[2] As for *Gulliver's Travels*, the versions designed for children, whether by publishers or film-makers, have easily supplanted Swift's original: the cute and comical Lilliputians remain in the public imagination, sometimes with the gross and oafish Brobdingnagians, but the absurdism of book three, and the misanthropy of the Yahoo and Houyhnhnm section, together with the satirical intent of the whole, have routinely been discarded.[3] Another blurred boundary is the line between fiction and reality. If Defoe and Swift provided ersatz travellers' tales, other adventures stories were (more or less) true. In the nineteenth century, descriptions of the expeditions of James Cook and Mungo Park, and later David Livingstone and Henry Stanley, were marketed for children. These accounts could be extremely exciting, especially once they were abridged. Adventure novels like *King Solomon's Mines* and

Verne's *Journey to the Centre of the Earth* (1864), based around the fragmentary maps left by previous explorers and describing expeditions across *terra incognita*, clearly owed a great deal to these non-fictional texts. The line between adventure stories and history books is similarly indistinct. Even without any blatant fictionalisation, biographical accounts of Alexander the Great, William Tell, Dick Turpin, Admiral Nelson, Florence Nightingale or Anne Frank could provide as much adventure as any wholly imagined narrative. Biblical stories and classical myths were also doubtless read as adventures, and continue to be so: Hercules, Odysseus, Samson, David and Goliath.

In fact, it is open to question whether adventure is a distinct and demarcated literary genre at all. Few texts can be regarded as *only* adventure. The adventure in *Swallows and Amazons* animates a fairly traditional family story for instance. Likewise, Serraillier's *The Silver Sword*, Holm's *I Am David* and Beverley Naidoo's *The Other Side of Truth* (2000) are first and foremost refugee stories, dealing with the horror of war and repressive states and concomitant issues of fear, freedom and identity. The adventure, it might be said, simply provides the frame. Adventure enlivens most children's historical novels too, but in the best examples, it remains subordinate to the skilful recreation of the historical period, and the other concerns of the author. In early children's historical novels, authors used adventure to teach history, as is made clear by the title of Barbara Hofland's *Adelaide; or, the Intrepid Daughter: a Tale, Including Historical Anecdotes of Henry the Great and the Massacre of St. Bartholomew* (1822). Isaac Taylor's *Scenes in Africa* (1821) was more overtly didactic in intent, much of the text taking the form of conversations between a child and an instructor, just as if they are in the classroom. But the lessons are inserted in an exciting narrative in which the child and his teacher are captured by pirates, sold into slavery and then freed by the Emperor of Morocco to continue their educational journey around Africa.[4] This didactic dimension of children's adventure stories has never entirely faded. G. A. Henty claimed that 'any one who has read with care the story of *The Young Buglers*', his novel of 1880, 'could pass an examination as to the leading events of the Peninsular war.'[5] The historical accuracy of his novels was always promoted by his publishers as a major selling point.[6] In the twentieth century authors were making similar claims about the veracity, and therefore educational potential, of their novels. In a postscript to her novel describing the birth of printing in England, *The Load of Unicorn* (1959), Cynthia Harnett admitted her account was '*only* a story', but, pointing out her meticulous research, hoped that there was not 'too much "fiction"'.[7]

Historical fiction has also been tailored to fit other agendas. In Mark Twain's *The Prince and the Pauper* (1882), the young King Edward VI learns how the poor live when he is mistakenly driven from the royal court, although it is the story of how he reclaims the throne that probably interests the reader more. In *Bows Against the Barons* (1934), Geoffrey Trease used the Robin Hood stories to preach a sort of chivalric communism. 'We're comrades in Sherwood, all equal', Robin tells the sixteen-year-old hero, Dickon, recruiting him join a rebellion against the rich and powerful oppressors.[8] 'It is a constantly shifting and changing story that holds one all the way, with its adventures and strange peoples and places', the distinguished historical novelist Rosemary Sutcliff has noted, writing of Henry Treece's experimental novel of life in Neolithic Europe, *The Dream-Time* (1967). But the adventure is generally the vehicle for the novel's other concerns, in this case 'a plea for people to get to know each other and care about each other more; for peace instead of war, making instead of breaking.'[9] The adventure story, it might be argued, is not really a genre at all, but rather a sort of flavour or colouring, used to give an appealing taste or appearance to works with other agendas.

One other very blurred boundary is between adventure stories and fantasy fiction. J. R. R. Tolkien's *The Hobbit* (1937), C. S. Lewis's Narnia books (1950–56), Philip Pullman's *His Dark Materials* (1995–2000), not to mention many fairy stories, both traditional and modern, are all tales of adventure. But in another sense too, almost all adventure stories are fantasies. The children's adventure story typically takes for its protagonists figures who are unimportant in their normal lives. They are usually on the margins of the community, neglected and often victimised – like Cinderella, or the waif-like Lyra in *His Dark Materials*, or the fatherless boys of Stevenson's *Kidnapped* or *Treasure Island*. Even if it is only because they are children (or simply small, as in the case of Bilbo Baggins), these protagonists, before they begin their adventures, are identified as powerless and dependent. The narrative then suddenly places these characters right at the centre of important events. They have to encounter great dangers and to make momentous choices. A great deal often hinges on their success or failure, not only for them themselves, but for those around them, and sometimes society as a whole. Essentially, the adventure story is a fantasy of empowerment. It makes the marginal and insignificant character central and crucial. The reader vicariously shares this thrill of aggrandisement. Subordinate and dependent in their real lives, children reading these books are invited to imagine themselves as influential and important. The adventure story is the imaginary fulfilment of the wish to be significant.

A classic example of this is the widely popular child detective sub-genre, exemplified in the American *Nancy Drew* and *Hardy Boys* books, the *Tintin* comic strips by the Belgian 'Hergé' (from 1930) and Erich Kästner's *Emil and the Detectives*, published in Germany in 1929. In Britain, the most popular examples are probably the twenty-one novels of Enid Blyton's *Famous Five* series, although others, such as C. Day Lewis's *The Otterbury Incident* (1949), are much more critically well-regarded. Blyton's five – Julian, Dick, Anne and Georgina ('George'), and a dog, Timmy – are ordinary enough, and holiday in ordinary enough places. In each of the books, though, they are catapulted into importance by their discovery of sinister plots which only they can foil. In triumphing over the criminals they assert their equality with, or actually superiority to, adults. They often become the dominant figures in their own families, frequently rescuing Quentin (George's father, the uncle of the other children). This fantasy of empowerment takes on a national dimension too. The left-wing Erich Kästner had certainly understood the collaboration of righteous children against depraved adults as political. In his account of the formation of a gang of twenty-four Berlin children, some rich, some poor, to recover the money stolen from him, Kästner created an optimistic parable about the power of youth to regenerate a corrupt society. Due to its immense popularity the book was not burned by the Nazis, as were some others Kästner had written, but nor was it reprinted, and attentive readers in Germany and abroad might well have understood it as an anti-Nazi document.[10] For their part, just like Emil's 'detectives' or many a superhero, the Famous Five are also the defenders of society, engaged in a continual fight against injustice. More specifically, it should be noted that Blyton's series began in 1942, during the darkest days of the Second World War. With its chief character sharing the name of England's patron saint, it is easy to see how the series appealed to child readers by providing them with a fantasy of their own centrality to the fight against the nation's enemies. The books could give children a sense that, metaphorically, they too were joining the war effort.

The detective story is just one classification of adventure, but most others, in different ways, can also be said to appeal to the child's desire for consequentiality.[11] 'Hunted Man' adventures, such as Stevenson's *Kidnapped* and Holm's *I Am David*, or, for an older audience, John Buchan's *The Thirty-Nine Steps* (1915), dramatise this desire most clearly. The hunted children may often be unwitting and powerless victims, but the relentlessness of their pursuers shows just how significant these children actually are. Likewise, in children's historical novels, the young protagonists frequently find themselves playing pivotal roles in great events. In Susan Cooper's *Victory* (2006), the fictional Samuel Robbins is pressed into naval service as a ship's boy and finds himself being rescued by Admiral Nelson and later present at Nelson's death at the Battle of Trafalgar. In 'Wanderer' stories, such as Verne's novels, the central protagonists establish their significance by visiting places and witnessing events that few, if any, have seen before.

Similarly, in what are often called 'Robinsonnades', the species of adventure novels derived from *Robinson Crusoe*, the castaways are of necessity at the centre of all the action. In most early examples, like *The Swiss Family Robinson* (1812–13) begun by Johann David Wyss, or Marryat's *Masterman Ready* (1841–42), children were marooned along with their parents. But by the mid-nineteenth century, child characters found themselves alone on their desert islands. Here, through heroic acts and tremendous feats of endurance, they were able to assert their credentials as worthy and preternaturally mature heroes. R. M. Ballantyne's *The Coral Island* (1858), for instance, closes with a 'native' chief telling Jack Martin, 'Young friend, you have seen few years but your head is old. Your heart also is large and brave' – an affirmation of maturity and importance that Jack (and the reader) would have valued highly. Indeed, when the chief continues that 'We, who live in these islands of the sea, know that Christians always act thus' and 'we hope many more will come', Jack becomes not only a child capable of survival away from civilisation, and not merely a missionary (like the rather dull ones he encounters on the island), but a kind of apostle, personifying both the religion that will enlighten the world and the righteousness of empire.[12]

In some fantasy adventures this wish-fulfilment of significance is taken to even greater lengths. The child protagonist becomes not merely an evangelist, but a Messiah. At the beginning of C. S. Lewis's *The Lion, the Witch and the Wardrobe*, for example, the four Pevensie children are neglected and frequently admonished, but once through the wardrobe, they find that Narnia revolves around them. Four thrones wait for them there, and it is the success or failure of their actions which will determine the fate of the entire kingdom. Only they can end the eternal winter and redeem creation. Lyra and Will in Philip Pullman's *His Dark Materials* have equal cosmic significance, becoming the new Adam and new Eve. But what is fascinating is the way in which the imbalance between children's everyday powerlessness and the power that they obtain in these adventures is represented and resolved. In Susan Cooper's *The Dark is Rising* series, for instance, her heroes are young boys, but paradoxically they are also amongst the 'Old Ones', destined to lead the eternal fight against the forces of Darkness. Cooper's depiction of the impossible duality of their situation, having to behave like children in front of their parents but simultaneously defeat the rising Dark, can be almost comical. In *The Dark is Rising* (1973) the eleven-year-old Will Stanton knows he must get to the Manor, but his parents are unwilling to brave the blizzard to get there. Despite being the only one who can break the power of the Dark, Will is compelled to resort to childish pleading and sulking to persuade his father to let him go. Only when this fails does he reveal his power to the mysterious 'Walker' who is sheltering with the family, frightening him into convulsions so that Will's parents have to consent to taking him to the Manor for treatment.[13] At all costs, it seems, he must retain his childish powerlessness in front of his parents, while simultaneously fulfilling his Messianic destiny. From the reader's point of view, this two-facedness is important in maintaining their fantasy of empowerment. Like Will, they need to reconcile the comforts of childish dependence with the desire to imagine themselves more important and endangered than they seem. Cooper is very successful at depicting this tension. In the first novel in the series, *Over Sea, Under Stone* (1965), just as he is about to find the Grail which will help to keep the Dark at bay, Barney Drew hears voices inside his head:

> Who are you to intrude here, the voice seemed to whisper; one small boy, prying into something that is so much bigger than he can understand, that has remained undisturbed for so many years? Go away, go back where you are safe, leave such ancient things alone . . .[14]

Cooper is dramatising Barney's longing for the insignificance and childishness which he had formerly resented. She shows her protagonists coming to terms with unaccustomed power, caught between their longing to control events, and their doubts that, after all, they are only children. Tolkien's Frodo, Pullman's Lyra and Stevenson's Jim Hawkins experience the same doubts.

The preservation of the ordinary childishness of heroes and heroines engaged on really very remarkable adventures is important for another reason too: it helps to allow readers to envision themselves as possible participants in the adventure. Nina Bawden began her novel *On the Run* (1964) by trying to establish the ordinariness of the origins of her adventure, and in doing so provides what might be read as an adventure-writer's manifesto:

> There are two things to remember about adventures. They always happen when you are not expecting anything to happen and the beginning is usually quite unexciting and ordinary so that you seldom realize that something important has begun. Adventure always creeps up on you from behind.[15]

Many authors have gone to great lengths to establish the possibility, or even likelihood, of adventure. C. Day Lewis began *The*

Otterbury Incident, for example, by having George, the narrator, muse on the beginnings of the story that would end with him and his friends bringing a gang of crooks to justice. 'Suppose I say it all began when Nick broke the classroom window with his football', he starts, but quickly wonders if this only happened because they were fighting against another gang of boys, or because they had been playing at being soldiers before that. This discussion of the mundane origins of the adventure, and of the impossibility of saying when it started, is supposed to show that it might have happened to anyone. When he concludes that the adventure could not have happened 'if there hadn't been a real war and a stray bomb hadn't fallen in the middle of Otterbury' the intention is surely to universalise the events even further, to make George and his friends the representatives of any and all children who had lived through the Blitz, and to establish the War itself as the ultimate adventure, the Otterbury incident being merely an outcrop of something that had united the nation in one great escapade.[16] In a way, Peter Pan's announcement that 'To die would be an awfully big adventure' makes the same point: that adventure does not happen only to a few lucky characters in novels, but to all.[17] Peter has it the wrong way round though, for ultimately everyone is part of the same great adventure: life.

Children's authors and publishers had not always sought to give the impression that ordinary children could easily find themselves embroiled in adventure. Even if the popular literature that children sometimes read in the eighteenth century was full of daring deeds, the books published especially for them then seem designed to minimise the appeal and likelihood of adventure. Chapbook versions of *Robinson Crusoe* portrayed him as a lone figure active and armed against the perils of his hostile island, for instance, but versions especially for children focused much more on the domestic elements of his story. Their illustrations tend to show Crusoe sitting at his table, with his pots neatly arranged around him, his garden cleared and separated from the jungle, and his guns hung up unused on the wall of his hut. The ending of these children's editions was often rewritten so that Crusoe regretted deserting his parents and causing them grief.[18] Similarly, despite the fact that Britain was at war for much of the eighteenth century and that many children were actively engaged in these conflicts at home and even in the military, children's books dealing with warfare tended to emphasise its horrors, not its excitement. Even during the age of Nelson and Napoleon, books like William Francis Sullivan's *Pleasant Stories; or, The Histories of Ben, the Sailor, and Ned, the Soldier* (c.1818) were carefully designed to dampen boys' martial ardour. It begins with the return to his family of an ex-serviceman who warns his nephews not be to be so foolish as to enter the armed forces. They ignore his advice, but their own hardships, punishments and wounds soon convince them that he was right.[19]

By the nineteenth century, the age of the classic adventure story, any reluctance to embrace adventure was generally held to be cowardly, or 'muffish'. 'There are three distinct classes of boys', says Ralph, authoritatively, in Ballantyne's *The Gorilla Hunters* (1861), 'namely, muffs, sensible fellows, and boasters'. In order to become a 'sensible fellow', Ralph explains, it is important for boys to be 'inured from childhood to trifling risks and light dangers of every possible description, such as tumbling into ponds and off trees'. Boys 'ought never to hesitate to cross a stream on a narrow unsafe plank *for fear of a ducking*' nor 'to decline to climb up a tree to pull fruit merely because there is a *possibility* of their falling off and breaking their necks.' This reasoning 'applies to some extent to girls as well', Ralph concludes, for all children should 'encounter all kinds of risks, in order to prepare them to meet and grapple with the risks and dangers incident to man's career with cool, cautious self-possession', whether it be fighting off a furious leopard or 'being set on fire by means of crinoline'.[20] Ballantyne's philosophy of adventure stands in stark contrast to the ethos of the cautionary and moral tales of eighteenth and early nineteenth centuries. Many of these had been designed specifically to dissuade children from climbing trees or crossing streams on narrow, unsafe planks.

Yet the dominance of the moral tale form had never removed all adventure from children's literature. Despite being pilloried by some as the very antithesis of excitement, morality could certainly co-exist with adventure. A good example is the story of Thomas Two-Shoes. In *The History of Goody Two-Shoes* (1765), perhaps the most famous of the eighteenth-century moral tales, Margery (nicknamed 'Goody') is a poor orphan who learns to read, becomes a teacher, brings harmony to her village, and ends happy and rich having married the local magnate. Early on in the book Goody is separated from her brother Tommy who is sent off to sea. He returns at the end of the story, having made his fortune. Most eighteenth-century editions of *Goody Two-Shoes* contained a short appendix, outlining how Tommy had become so wealthy. His story had the tone of a chapbook tale. He was castaway 'on that part of the coast of *Africa* inhabited by the *Hottentots*', where he found a mysterious book 'which the *Hottentots* did not understand, and which gave him some Account of *Prester John's* Country'. He tames a lion and sets out to explore, ending up in the Land of Utopia. Here he finds a statue, with an inscription revealing that on May Day morning the statue's head will turn to gold. Finding it does not do so, he solves the riddle by digging where the shadow of the statue's head falls, and finds the hidden treasure of an ancient philosopher.[21]

Several writers took this rather scanty account as an invitation to write a fuller sequel, but in it is an 1818 version that most interestingly puts flesh on the bare bones of the original story. The author, Mary Belson Elliott, was concerned with the continuity of her sequel, taking pains to account for Thomas being called 'Two-Shoes' and scrupulously explaining why Goody and Tommy could not correspond during their adventures. She expanded the story substantially too, sending Tommy to the West Indies, where he becomes involved in a slave insurrection, and only then describing how Tommy himself becomes enslaved in Africa. Tommy earns his freedom by exposing a plot being hatched by other slaves to assassinate their owner. This echoes events in Jamaica earlier in the novel, when his life had been preserved only because a slave called 'Black George' had betrayed a plot to murder the island's white population. Both Black George and Tommy triumph over what Elliott suggests is their self-interest in wanting to be free, preferring at all costs to preserve peace and prevent bloodshed, and to trust in God for their delivery from slavery. The biggest change, though, is in the way Tommy acquires his fortune. For Elliott, solving a riddle and discovering hidden treasure was either too preposterous or insufficiently edifying. Her Tommy becomes rich by honest trade, as well as receiving a legacy from the friend whose life he had saved by betraying the conspiracy. Elliott, in a word, has moralised the tale. She even ends the book with 'a slight account of the places named in this history' for those readers who 'may not have studied Geography'. Yet this has by no means eliminated the adventure. Her 67-page narrative encompasses, amongst much else, the persecution of its hero by a cruel sea captain, a slave rebellion, a night of terror being held prisoner at gun-point, a ship-wreck, capture by Algerine pirates, six years in slavery in Tunis, and a comic interlude during which Thomas cures a canary's broken leg by attaching a prosthetic limb.[22] Predating all of James Fenimore Cooper's and Frederick Marryat's novels, Elliott's *Adventures of Thomas Two-Shoes* has a claim to be considered one of the very first modern children's adventure novels, even if it also clearly displays the author's didactic, Quaker impulses.

Certainly *The Adventures of Thomas Two-Shoes* fulfils many of the criteria of the genre as it was to develop during its nineteenth-century heyday. It has a characteristic setting, a characteristic hero, and a characteristic plot. These elements can be quite straightforwardly elaborated, even though the best adventure stories are generally those which interestingly and provocatively diverge from the usual formula. For one thing, most classic adventure stories share an exotic setting. Elliott's *The Adventures of Thomas Two-Shoes* took the reader from Britain to the Caribbean and Africa then back again. Desert islands and polar wastes would prove popular, as would subterranean and, later, extraterrestrial destinations. If set in Britain, the adventures often take place on the margins – Cornwall, Wales, the Highlands of Scotland. If set in America, the adventures most often occur just beyond the western frontier, as in Barbara Hofland's early Texan story *The Stolen Boy* (1830), or innumerable Westerns, or Laura Ingalls Wilder's *Little House* books (from 1932). Equally, the exoticism could be provided by historical remoteness. At first, Henty tended to set his adventures during the military campaigns of the eighteenth and early nineteenth centuries: *The Young Buglers: a Tale of the Peninsular War* (1880) or *The Cornet of Horse: a Tale of Marlborough's Wars* (1881). Increasingly he began to delve further into ancient history to find more alien locations: *The Young Carthaginian: a Story of the Times of Hannibal* (1887), *For the Temple: a Tale of the Fall of Jerusalem* (1888) and *The Cat of Bubastes: a Tale of Ancient Egypt* (1889). He exposed his readers to the exoticism of working-class life too in books such as *Facing Death: The Hero of the Vaughan Pit – A Tale of the Coal Mines* (1882) and *Through the Fray: A Tale of the Luddite Riots* (1886). The same 'historical remove' tactic has since been endlessly employed. In many cases it is fair to say, as Kirsten Drotner has alleged of S. Bracebridge Hemyng's 'Penny Dreadful' adventure stories about Jack Harkaway, that these changes of historical or geographical locations are simply changes of scenery, while the central characters, and the author's preoccupations, remain largely unchanged.[23] Henty for one is guilty as charged, his unpretentious, plucky, honourable boy heroes remaining very much alike wherever they are to be found, and his concern to advance a particular idea of Britishness consistently being in view. His preface to *Beric the Briton: a Story of the Roman Invasion* (1893), for instance, reminded his readers that they were descended from 'the valiant warriors who fought so bravely against Caesar' that he was depicting, and linked Boadicea's revolt against 'the oppressive rule of Rome' with Britain's nineteenth-century imperial mission.[24] Rosemary Sutcliff's more sophisticated historical adventure *Outcast* (1955) also features a boy called Beric, but Sutcliff took great pains to describe life in Roman Britain and fastidiously emphasised its differences from her own era. Her story is concerned primarily with Beric's ostracism. Born a Roman, but orphaned in a shipwreck, Beric is taken in by a Celtic tribe, but is later expelled and ends up as a slave on a Roman galley. His personal tragedy becomes an emblem of the destructiveness of tribal groupings, quite opposite from the happy story of ethnic assimilation and nation-building presented by Henty.

The most accomplished historical novelists are true to their period in another way too, developing a style which matches their subject. Leon Garfield's novels depicting the adventures of children in the mid-eighteenth century seem stylistically to be very like the picaresque novels first published then. The opening of Garfield's *Jack Holborn* (1964) clearly shows the debt to Tobias Smollett's *Roderick Random* (1748) or Henry Fielding's *The History of Tom Jones, A Foundling* (1749):

My story must begin when I boarded the *Charming Molly* at Bristol. Before that there's little to tell. My name is Jack, surnamed 'Holborn' after the parish where I was found: for I had neither father nor mother who'd cared enough to leave me a name of my own.[25]

Henry Treece's novel of the Neolithic era, *The Dream-Time* (1967), was more experimental, written in 'very short and simple words' since his characters 'were so near the beginning that they can have had only the fewest and simplest of words with which to talk to each other and share their thoughts and feelings and ideas'.[26] This was taking the exoticism of the adventure story to new heights, defamiliarising the language of the novel, as well as its location.

The characteristic plots of the adventure story are as conventional as the exoticism of its settings, and can be taxonomised in much the same way that Vladimir Propp set out the fundamental narrative units of fairy tales in *Morphology of the Folktale* (1928). Most stories start with a domestic crisis of some kind which means that the protagonists have to leave the security of their home. This is generally followed by a minor adventure, during which they prove their worth, and then the opening up of the quest which will provide the main excitement for the rest of the novel. This quest is generally structured as a series of more minor crises which culminate in the completion of the mission: finding the treasure, solving the crime, freeing the hostage, returning home, and so on. Protagonists are usually either born with, or come into possession of, a special asset which helps them: a special skill, a clever pet, a weapon. Sometimes it is this asset which establishes the quest, like Jim Hawkins' map in *Treasure Island*. Generally the protagonists are not quite alone, being accompanied by a faithful companion. This figure can be a surrogate parent, like Jacob Armitage in Marryat's *Children of the New Forest*, who helps the orphaned children to become self-sufficient once they have been 'marooned' in their secret hideaway deep in the forest. More interesting are ambiguous figures who both teach and terrorise the children at the centre of the adventure, guarding and threatening in equal measure. One classic example is J. M. Barrie's Peter Pan; another is Long John Silver in Robert Louis Stevenson's *Treasure Island*. According to the conventional adventure tale structure Silver should be the villain of the novel, whom Jim Hawkins must overcome if he is to succeed in his quest. Certainly Silver terrifies Jim, and is murderous, treacherous and selfish. But, in what Dennis Butts calls 'the greatest irony in the book' they also become like father and son, Silver looking after Jim, and Jim ardently admiring Silver.[27] In this respect *Treasure Island* causes readers more confusion, but is perhaps ultimately more satisfying, than another of Stevenson's split-personality novels, *The Strange Case of Dr Jekyll and Mr Hyde* (1886), for Silver is both Jekyll and Hyde at once, needing no potion to transform him. Jim recognises both sides to himself too, and as Stevenson's narrative shuttles him backwards and forwards between the mutineers and the loyalists, he finds himself wanting to remain faithful to his respectable friends Squire Trelawney and Captain Smollett but also strongly drawn to the pirate life.

In modern and contemporary adventure stories this classic plot structure has been amended in some interesting ways. Robert Cormier's *After the First Death* (1979), for instance, is a gripping and complex account of a terrorist hijacking of a bus full of school-children which pits its three focalising characters in conflict with one another. Sixteen-year-old Miro is elated with the prospect of making his first kill – the bus-driver – and thereby announcing his manhood to Artkin, the leader of the terrorist cell. The plan is con-fused when it turns out that the bus is being driven by Kate, a young woman, unexpectedly substituting for her uncle. She is taken hostage along with the children, and it is through her eyes that we view much of the 'operation'. Much the same age as Miro and, as he notices, 'almost a mirror to himself', is Ben, the son of the army officer in charge of the attempt to rescue the children. He enters the story when he is recruited to act as a go-between during nego-tiations with the terrorists. This is an adventure story then, but distinctively modern in its subject-matter and also in its rearrange-ment of the plot structure. Kate's quest, insofar as she has one, is to stay alive. She fails, for Miro eventually succeeds in the mission he had originally set himself: killing the bus-driver. Indeed, in one way at least Miro does succeed as any Henty hero might, sacrificing himself for the greater glory of his homeland's freedom: 'It does not matter whether or not I get away', he tells Kate before he murders her, 'Whether I live or die. Whether anyone else lives or dies. I have served my purpose.' Ben's adventure is more complicated still. When he delivers his message to the terrorists they torture him to reveal the time at which the army will launch their attack. He surrenders to the pain and divulges the plan, only to find out later that his father had deliberately fed him misinformation, knowing that Ben would be tortured and that he would 'betray' him. Unable to forgive his father's deception, but guilty also at his own weakness and credulity, Ben commits suicide. Miro, meanwhile, overcomes any doubt or remorse about murdering Kate, kills again, and ventures onwards 'into the world that was waiting for him.'[28]

Cormier's ending takes up elements of the classic adventure tale but distorts them horribly. Miro's resolution is a chilling reiteration of the rejection of 'sivilization' and decision to 'light out for the Territory' with which Mark Twain ended *The Adventures of Huckleberry Finn* (1884). *After the First Death* is also dominated by relationships between fathers and sons. Miro reverences Artkin as Jim Hawkins admires Long John Silver, always seeking to impress him. Just as Jim betrays Silver's plot, and Ben 'lets down' his father, Miro is responsible for Artkin's death, failing to warn him of the soldiers' attack in his own eagerness to escape. He is driven to shoot Kate only when she makes him realise that Artkin was probably his actual father, her murder a result of the self-loathing he feels at his probable patricide. This is the same self-loathing that drives Ben to suicide, and that torments Ben's father, whose haunted narration takes over from Ben's at the end of the novel. This is pessimism without hope of redemption, characteristic of Cormier's rejection of any need in children's literature for happy endings.[29] He is also apparently arguing that in the modern, post-Vietnam War world, the old, straightforward adventure is no longer possible. Ben's father seems to realise this, talking of his enlistment, with a friend called Jack Harkness, on the very day after the Pearl Harbour attack, and their ardent patriotism, 'pure and sweet and unquestioning'. Ben's generation, his father knows, is not so trusting. It 'looks at itself in a mirror as it performs its duties. And wonders Who are the good guys? Is it possible we are the bad guys?'[30] Only murderous terrorists have the old faith and desire for heroism. Jack Harkness (whose very name links him with an outdated literary tradition, reminding us of Jack Harkaway, the hero of S. Bracebridge

Hemyng's classic Victorian adventure tales) died at Iwo Jima, and with him died the age of adventure.

Yet, since Cormier, many writers have endeavoured to rehabilitate the children's adventure novel. For some, this has meant finding new contexts for adventures, and sometimes adding a political dimension. For instance, Beverley Naidoo's *Journey to Jo'burg*, published in 1985, was set in contemporary South Africa (where it was banned until 1991), and used the classic quest/journey theme to expose the injustice and cruelty of the apartheid regime. Others have more stubbornly attempted to reintroduce old adventures to new audiences. One American firm has republished all of G. A. Henty's books in paper and electronic format for a twenty-first century readership because, their advertisements assert, 'the examples set by Henty's heroes of honesty, integrity, hard work, courage, diligence, perseverance, personal honor, and strong Christian faith are unsurpassed.'[31] In Britain, two publishers announced in 2003 that they were 'so fed up with feminism and political correctness' that they would republish 'great buccaneering, derring-do, true-life adventures' under the 'Young Spitfire' imprint, since, they said, boys needed books demonstrating 'masculine principles and masculine emotions.'[32]

Authors such as Charlie Higson, with *Silverfin: A James Bond Adventure* (2005), and David Gilman, with *Danger Zone: The Devil's Breath* (2007), have also tried to lure boys into reading with exciting adventures, but they take themselves less seriously than Henty, writing with a degree of irony and much postmodern self-referentiality. These books are the equivalents of the *Star Wars* and *Indiana Jones* films (from 1977 and 1981 respectively) which revitalised the adventure film genre after its post-Vietnam fall from fashion. Like the films, the books delight in cliché, picking up familiar motifs from the classic adventure tradition and employing them with a knowing nod to the audience, or giving them a new twist. This tendency to pastiche, though not undermine, the classic adventure genre is immediately evident with Joshua Mowill's *Operation Red Jericho* (2005). It is set in 1920s Shanghai and follows Becca and Doug's investigation of their parents' sudden disappearance, leading to the discovery of an ancient secret society. The book purports to be the account of these adventures passed down by

Becca to her great-nephew, the author, and it includes her letters and diaries, her fold-out maps, sketches and photographs. The book even comes bound with an elastic cord, such as an adventurer might use to keep her book tight shut while she is being chased by ruthless, but slightly hapless, villains. The improbability of these adventures is emphasised. One might even think that the authors invite their readers to conclude that the adventures of Great-Aunt Becca, or Higson's young James Bond or Horowitz's Alex Rider, are actually taking place in these characters' imaginations.

Despite these rehabilitation strategies, the adventure genre remains tainted for many modern readers because of two things: its association with empire, and its perceived misogyny. These are certainly the two areas that most critical debate has focused on. In its representation of gender, for instance, the classic adventure story can seem extremely conservative. Kimberly Reynolds has suggested that by the late Victorian period, children's literature had bifurcated into separate canons for girls and for boys. 'Girls' stories' such as those appearing in *The Girl's Own Paper*, and by L. T. Meade and Evelyn Everett-Green, endorsed the values of domesticity. Meanwhile adventure tales by Henty, and those that appeared in *The Boy's Own Paper*, were designed to encourage what John Ruskin identified as the specifically male talent for 'speculation and invention . . . adventures . . . war . . . conquest.' These separate boys' and girls' literatures 'rejected modifications to attitudes towards sexual difference', Reynolds argued, while at the same time these same attitudes were being challenged in fiction for adults. Worse still, the values of the Victorian age stayed in place in children's literature long after the age that spawned them had passed. 'Today's juvenile fiction', Reynolds wrote in 1990, 'carries within it images, structures, attitudes and value systems which are at least partially shaped by their earlier counterparts.'[33] According to this analysis, the adventure story is almost irredeemably sexist.

The same might be said of the imperialism of the adventure story. The genre's genesis and apotheosis in the early and late nineteenth century respectively should be seen, Dennis Butts states, 'both as an expression and a result of popular interest in the rise of the British Empire'.[34] Henty is the classic example, the writer who, according to Kathryn Castle, 'exemplified the ethos of the new imperialism, and glorified its military successes.'[35] His novels exhibit a thoroughgoing racism. The 'natives' of the Empire, and especially sub-Saharan Africans, 'are just children', his characters are wont to proclaim:

> They are always laughing or quarreling. They are good-natured and passionate, indolent, but will work hard for a time; clever up to a certain point, densely stupid beyond. The intelligence of an average negro is about equal to that of a European child of ten years old.[36]

These people are not children in the same sense as his heroes are still children. For Henty's Europeans, childhood is a state of potentiality; for his Africans it is a state of incapacity. His heroes exhibit natural abilities but can also be schooled, both before and during their adventures, to make them civilised adults. The 'natives' cannot be educated. As Lord Kitchener observes in one novel, there may be 'a lot of good in these black fellows if one could but get at it.' The only means to 'get at it', of course, was to impose the yoke of Empire.[37]

But the encoding of imperialist ambition in the adventure story was not unique to the Victorian period. *Robinson Crusoe*, Edward Said pointed out, 'is about a European who creates a fiefdom for himself on a distant, non-European island'. This is important not only because it shows the colonial impulse was embedded in adventure fiction long before the idea of a British Empire had reached maturity, but also because Defoe's novel can be seen as the 'prototypical modern realistic novel'.[38] As such, Said argued, it reveals how almost all modern fiction is in some ways concerned with the imperial project. Certainly, the adventure novel in particular seems structurally imperialist, no matter where or when it is set, or indeed whether or not it emerged from a nation which had established or retained a formal empire. In the typical 'imperial romance', as Claudia Marquis calls it, a boy is thrown into a struggle for which his background has not specifically prepared him, but in which he triumphs, against lesser people, by virtue of the values that his society has imbued him with (resourcefulness, honour, perseverance, pluck). When he triumphs, he affirms his home culture, legitimising its dominion over inferior peoples and uncivilised lands.[39]

As Claudia Nelson puts it, 'The struggle between stereotypical hero and equally stereotypical villain becomes emblematic of Britain's noble quest to civilize non-Western societies.'[40] A similar point can be made for American children's literature. The United States may have lacked an empire on the European model, but its adventure stories generally affirmed 'civilised' America's right to dominate 'inferior peoples' – slaves, Native Americans, the poor – both within and beyond its borders. It can be argued that the recurrent descriptions in children's literature of white children's attainment of dominion over foreign lands and indigenous people is a sort of symbolic re-telling of the imperial enterprise. One might even go so far as to say that it represents a sort of fantasy of colonialism, and that the need constantly to re-stage the colonial act reveals a lack of confidence in its legitimacy and sustainability, rather than any self-assured sense of mission. Certainly, neither direct nor oblique representations of colonial adventure suddenly vanished from children's literature after the loss of Empire. As M. Daphne Kutzer puts it, 'the desire for empire does not go away' in British children's literature, or if it does, it is 'replaced by its close cousin, nostalgia for a lost and more powerful Britain and a more perfect British past.'[41]

Yet it is possible to dispute both the inherent anti-feminism and imperialism of the adventure story. Certainly girls happily read what we might think of as boys' books. Sally Mitchell draws on memoirs and surveys to show that many late Victorian and early Edwardian girls avidly consumed adventures stories and identified with their heroes.[42] Equally, even in the Victorian period, many adventure stories featured girls as central characters. *The Girl's Own Paper* feminised some adventure classics, serialising Elizabeth Whittaker's 'Robina Crusoe, and her Lonely Island Home' (1882–83) for example. Original adventure novels for and about girls were hardly unknown either. Bessie Marchant, sometimes called 'the female Henty', wrote many, including *Three Girls on a Ranch: A Tale of New Mexico* (1901) and *Molly Angel's Adventures* (1915), the story of a fourteen-year-old girl left to fend for herself on the Western Front of the First World War.[43] From here, it was only a short distance to Captain W. E. Johns' novels about 'Worrals of the WAAF' (1941–50). As a Flight Officer in the Women's Auxiliary Air Force, Joan Worralson's official job was to deliver aircraft to the men who would fly them into battle, but she often found herself drawn into actual combat, though always by chance rather than intention, becoming in effect the female 'Biggles'. This rather clumsy compromise between wanting to make the adventures of heroines as exciting as those of heroes, yet not being prepared entirely to efface the 'proper' divide between men's and women's lives, was commonplace. In *Little Miss Robinson Crusoe* (1898), by 'Mrs. George Corbett', the castaway's life is full of adventure. She fights with 'an awful enemy' (a giant crab) and 'a fearful-looking beast' (an octopus), and must confront a 'hideous-looking snake' and 'death-dealing flowers', not to mention overcoming all the usual problems attendant on being marooned on a desert island (hers is starkly called the 'Land of Death', because of its frequent earthquakes and eruptions). But Leona Robinson, though announced as a tomboy from the start, must also exhibit her feminine qualities: making her own clothes, describing herself as a 'born cook' who 'fairly revelled in the concoction of all sorts of wonderful things', thinking of her desperate search for food as a trip 'to market', and making herself a doll to mother, because, although she had a pet monkey, 'how much more comforting a baby would be'.[44]

However awkwardly achieved, this kind of merging of gender roles has become very significant for some critics. Martha Vicinus has found that Victorian biographies of eminent women often encouraged readers to emulate their more 'masculine' traits, such as courage, initiative and independence.[45] Claudia Nelson notes that supposedly 'feminine' virtues like patience, self-effacement and chastity, and the nurturing and domestic instinct, were at the heart of much Victorian children's literature, even the ostensibly masculine adventure story. At least before the last years of the nineteenth century, they exhibit a 'complex mythology', she argues, 'in which the desire to reject the feminine ethic combats the desire to embrace it.'[46] Megan Norcia has gone further, arguing that this hybridity was designed to enable girls to 'join and surpass their male counterparts in the imperial project.' Norcia notes that Isabel Fraser, the central character in L. T. Meade's 1892 novel *Four on an Island: A Story of Adventure*, is simultaneously a female Crusoe and an 'Angel of the House'. It is her domestic skills which keep her and her companions alive on their desert island, and which enable them to maintain their English identity in these most difficult and foreign of circumstances. '*Four on an Island* not only posits that girls be allowed to participate in adventure,' Norcia concludes, 'but it demonstrates that they are *more fit* than boys to do so, because they, like Crusoe, are the preservers of nation through the establishment and maintenance of the domestic space.'[47]

It is books like *Four on an Island* that show how deeply enmeshed so much Victorian adventure writing was in the colonial project. But just as Norcia, Nelson and other critics have detected a certain blurring of gender roles in the classic adventure story, so it is also sometimes possible to identify a more vexed relationship with empire. Most of the 'westerns' that proliferated in the dime novels and magazines of the late nineteenth century were clear that the white hero was manifestly destined to exert dominion over the entire continent, no matter how many 'Indians' he had to kill in the process. But some also endorsed, either directly or indirectly, the values of the American wilderness and its 'noble savage' inhabitants. It is possible to read James Fenimore Cooper's series of *Leather-Stocking Tales* (1823–41), John Cawelti has concluded, in two apparently contradictory ways: 'From one angle, it appears to be an affirmation of the benevolent progress of American civilisation; from another, it is an attack on the same civilization as measured against the natural nobility of a pastoral hero.'[48] The same duality persisted in many later Westerns, and is certainly to be found in Laura Ingalls Wilder's half-frightened, half-admiring treatment of the 'Indians' in her *Little House* novels (from 1932). Ma might be continually telling Laura to be more civilised and less like the 'Indians', but Laura's sense of adventure inspires her fascination with their lives, and she comes to share Pa's grudging respect for their dignity, self-sufficiency and oneness with nature.

Other kinds of frontier novel exhibit the same tensions. In Stevenson's *Kidnapped* (1885), for instance, the Scottish Lowlander David Balfour at first derides the more 'primitive' Highland culture represented by Alan Breck. By the end of the novel, though, David has come to respect the generosity, stubbornness and nobility of the Highlanders, and to forget what he had formerly thought their foolish devotion to a former king and their 'childish' vanity and rages (just as Alan has come to accept David's thrift, rationality and his status as one of colonisers of the still wild Highlands). A confused relationship between colonised and coloniser is also at the heart of much of Rudyard Kipling's writing. On one level, *Kim* (1901) validates the 'Great Game' of empire, its orphaned hero discovering his identity, and his duty, as a member of the white ruling class who can perform great deeds in the British secret service. But the novel is all about cultural hybridity. More fluent in vernacular languages than English, and more at home on the streets than in the institutions of the Raj, Kim is as much Indian as he is British (if British at all: his father was a Catholic Irishman). Don Randall's book *Kipling's Imperial Boy* (2000) has taken this case furthest, arguing that Kipling uses adolescent heroes wrestling with their own identities – Kim, Mowgli in *The Jungle Books* (1894–95) and Stalky in *Stalky & Co.* (1899) – to explore the possible futures of the Empire after the shock of the Indian Rebellion of 1857. Their amalgamation of cultures, and perhaps even races, and their reconciliation of imperial duty with respect for the civilisation of the colonised, might be Kipling's answer to the contradiction of Britain's position in India.[49]

Nevertheless, most critics continue to explore the ways in which the classic adventure story helped to recruit boys into the ranks of those who would support, administer or fight for the Empire.[50] One fictional boy deeply affected by the adventure stories to which he is devoted is Oswald Bastable in E. Nesbit's *The Wouldbegoods*, published in 1901, towards the end of the Second Boer War. 'I should like to be a soldier', 'to go to South Africa for a bugler', Oswald declares following his reading of S. R. Crockett's *The Surprising Adventures of Sir Toady Lion* (1897), in which two young boys play at being military heroes. When soldiers pass by his house, Oswald and the rest of the Bastable children cheer them lustily. 'It was glorious', Oswald comments. All this, though, is a prelude to the real subject of the chapter. News arrives from the South African war that a local man, Bill, has been killed. Trying to alleviate the grief of Bill's mother, the Bastables characteristically succeed only in making things worse when they construct a fake tombstone for the fallen hero. Although the chapter ends happily when Bill returns home, wounded rather than dead, what Nesbit provides is a sophisticated satire on the unthinking patriotism engendered by the sort of adventure books that the Bastables have been reading. There are hints of this right from the start. When the soldiers pass by, the Bastables deck themselves out with ancient swords and bayonets borrowed from the house in which they are staying. Oswald's offhand comment that 'They are very bright when you get them bright, but the sheaths are hard to polish' provides a metaphor for the easiness of militarism (the bright swords) and the difficulty of maintaining peace (the dull scabbards). Likewise, when the soldiers depart for the war, their officer's comment to the children that his troops will have to change out of their ceremonial uniforms and wear 'mud-colour' foretells their likely fate, to fall on the field of battle, without even a grave like that which the Bastables enthusiastically construct for Bill. The fiasco of the erroneous telegram bearing the news of Bill's death adds to the critique of war, a critique made more pathetic by the dismal comedy of the children's attempts to memorialise the soldier. After all this, Oswald's final ruminations must be read as deeply ironic. 'I am very glad *some* soldiers' mothers get their boys home again', he says, once Bill has returned:

> But if they have to die, it is a glorious death; and I hope mine will be that. And three cheers for the Queen, and the mothers who let their boys go, and the mother's son who fight and die for old England. Hip, hip, hurrah![51]

Nesbit, whose book appeared in the same year as the notorious 'Khaki election' of 1901, was evidently satirising the power of the adventure story to inspire thoughtless patriotism and militarism in young boys. What is extraordinary is that this closing passage of the chapter has routinely been omitted from modern editions of the novel. This must presumably be because the abridgers have missed Nesbit's irony, or because they deem readers likely to take Oswald's sentiments at face value – and such an enthusiastic endorsement of militarism (*if* taken at face value) would be unacceptable in children's books published after the World Wars. But whichever way we interpret it, the decision of later abridgers to omit the chapter's original ending is also testimony to the power of the adventure story to captivate, and even indoctrinate, by offering children a heroism that their routine real-life subordination makes especially appealing.

SUMMARY OF KEY POINTS

- Adventure stories provide a fantasy of empowerment for children, describing a heroism that their real-life powerlessness makes especially appealing.
- Many of the best adventure stories depict a conflict between children's yearning for consequentiality and their residual desire for protection and supervision.
- Early children's books often portrayed adventure as something to be avoided, but from the mid-nineteenth century adventure was represented as something that might happen to anyone and ought often to be welcomed.
- Classic nineteenth-century adventure stories were often less sexist, racist and imperialist that modern critics sometimes suggest, one of their common themes being an endorsement of ethnic, gender and generational empathy and hybridity.

NOTES

1. H. Rider Haggard, *King Solomon's Mines* (London: Puffin, [1885] 1994), p. i.
2. See Pat Rogers, 'Classics and Chapbooks', in *Books and their Readers in Eighteenth-Century England*, ed. Isabel Rivers (Leicester: Leicester University Press, 1982), pp. 27–45 and Martin Green, *The Robinson Crusoe Story* (University Park, PA: Pennsylvania State University Press, 1990).
3. See M. Sarah Smedman, 'Like Me, Like Me Not: *Gulliver's Travels* as Children's Book', in *The Genres of Gulliver's Travels*, ed. Frederick N. Smith (Newark, DE: University of Delaware Press, 1990), pp. 75–100.
4. Isaac Taylor, *Scenes in Africa, For the Amusement and Instruction of Little Tarry-at-Home Travellers* (London: Harris and Son, 1821), pp. 2–3.

5. G. A. Henty, *The Young Buglers, A Tale of the Peninsular War* (London: Blackie, [1880] 1887), p. iii.

6. See Leonard R. N. Ashley's *George Alfred Henty and the Victorian Mind* (San Francisco, CA: International Scholars, 1999).

7. Cynthia Harnett, *The Load of Unicorn* (London: Egmont Books, [1959] 2001), p. 244.

8. Geoffrey Trease, *Bows Against the Barons* (London: Elliott and Thompson, [1934] 2004), p. 27.

9. Rosemary Sutcliff, 'Postscript' to Henry Treece, *The Dream-Time* (London: Heinemann Educational Books, [1967] 1974), p. 96.

10. See Gerda Faerber, '*Emil and the Detectives*: a Publishing Story', *Signal*, 89 (1999), 100–14.

11. The classifications that follow are partly based on the taxonomy of adult adventure stories developed by Martin Green in *Seven Types of Adventure Tale: An Etiology of a Major Genre* (University Park, PA: Pennsylvania State University Press, 1991).

12. R. M. Ballantyne, *The Coral Island* (Ware: Wordsworth, [1858] 1993), p. 264.

13. Susan Cooper, *The Dark is Rising* (London: Puffin, [1973] 1976), pp. 185–8. See M. Daphne Kutzer, 'Thatchers and Thatcherites: Lost and Found Empires in Three British Fantasies', *The Lion and the Unicorn*, 22 (1998), 196–210 (p. 198).

14. Susan Cooper, *Over Sea, Under Stone* (London: Puffin, [1965] 1968), p. 194.

15. Nina Bawden, *On the Run* (London: Puffin, 1964), p. 7.

16. C. Day Lewis, *The Otterbury Incident* (London: Puffin, [1948] 1961), p. 11.

17. J. M. Barrie, *Peter and Wendy*, ed. Jack Zipes (London: Penguin, [1911] 2004), p. 84.

18. Andrew O'Malley, 'Crusoe at Home: Coding Domesticity in Children's Editions of *Robinson Crusoe*', *British Journal for Eighteenth-Century Studies*, 29 (2006), 337–52.

19. See M. O. Grenby ' "Surely there is no British boy or girl who has not heard of the battle of Waterloo!": War and Children's Literature in the Age of Napoleon', in *Under Fire: Childhood in the Shadow of War*, ed. Andrea Immel and Elizabeth

Goodenough (Detroit, MI: Wayne State University Press, 2008), pp. 39–57.

20. Crinolines were stiff petticoats worn under women's dresses. Ballantyne, *The Gorilla Hunters* (London: T. Nelson, [1861] 1874), pp. 64–5.

21. Anon., *The History of Little Goody Two-Shoes* (London: T. Carnan and F. Newbery, [1765] 1772), pp. 144–54.

22. Mary Belson Elliott, *The Adventures of Thomas Two-Shoes* (London: W. Darton, 1818), p. 63.

23. Kirsten Drotner, *English Children and their Magazines 1751–1945* (New Haven, CT and London: Yale University Press, 1998), p. 105.

24. G. A. Henty, *Beric the Briton: a Story of the Roman Invasion* (London: Blackie, [1893] no date), 'Preface', p. 6.

25. Leon Garfield, *Jack Holborn* (Harmondsworth: Kestrel, [1964] 1984), p. 7.

26. Sutcliff, 'Postscript', in Treece, *Dream-Time*, p. 95.

27. Dennis Butts, 'The Adventure Story', in *Stories and Society: Children's Literature in its Social Context*, ed. Butts (Basingstoke: Macmillan, 1992), pp. 65–83 (p. 75). See pp. 70–3 for a concise analysis of the formal characteristics of the children's adventure story.

28. Robert Cormier, *After the First Death* (London: Puffin, [1979] 1998), pp. 199, 217 and 233.

29. See Judith Elkin *et al.*, 'Cormier Talking', *Books for Keeps*, 54 (1989), 12–13 and Judith Plotz, 'The Disappearance of Childhood: Parent-Child Role Reversals in *After the First Death* and *A Solitary Blue*', *Children's Literature in Education*, 19 (1988), 67–79.

30. Cormier, *After the First Death*, p. 134.

31. Robinson Books website <http://www.robinsonbooks.com/> [accessed 26 November 2007].

32. Nigel Reynolds, 'Forget the namby-pamby girly stuff, here are ripping yarns for real chaps', *The Daily Telegraph*, 9 October 2003.

33. John Ruskin, *Sesame and Lillies* (1871), in Reynolds, *Girls Only? Gender and Popular Children's Fiction in Britain, 1880–1910* (Hemel Hempstead: Harvester Wheatsheaf, 1990), pp. 50 and 152–4.

34. Butts, 'The Adventure Story', p. 66.
35. Kathryn Castle, *Britannia's Children: Reading Colonialism Through Children's Books and Magazines* (Manchester: Manchester University Press, 1996), p. 55.
36. G. A. Henty, *By Sheer Pluck* (London: Blackie, 1884), p. 118.
37. G. A. Henty, *With Kitchener in the Soudan* (London: Blackie, 1903), p. 206.
38. Edward Said, *Culture and Imperialism* (London: Chatto and Windus, 1993), pp. xii–xiii.
39. Claudia Marquis, 'Romancing the Home: Gender, Empire, and the South Pacific', in *Girls, Boys, Books, Toys: Gender in Children's Literature and Culture*, ed. Beverley Lyon Clark and Margaret R. Higgonet (Baltimore, MD: Johns Hopkins University Press, 1999), pp. 53–67 (p. 54).
40. Claudia Nelson, *Boys Will Be Girls: The Feminine Ethic and British Children's Fiction, 1857–1917* (New Brunswick, NJ: Rutgers University Press, 1991), p. 119.
41. M. Daphne Kutzer, *Empire's Children: Empire and Imperialism in Classic British Children's Books* (New York: Garland, 2000), p. 129.
42. Sally Mitchell, *The New Girl: Girls' Culture in England, 1880–1915* (New York: Columbia University Press, 1995), especially pp. 111–13.
43. See Michael Paris, *Warrior Nation: Images of War in British Popular Culture, 1850–2000* (London: Reaktion, 2000), p. 23, and Krista Cowman, '"There are kind Germans as well as brutal ones": The Foreigner in Children's Literature of the First World War', *The Lion and the Unicorn*, 31 (2007), 103–15.
44. Mrs. George [Elizabeth Burgoyne] Corbett, *Little Miss Robinson Crusoe* (London: C. Arthur Pearson, 1898), pp. 78, 194, 150, 172, 221, 146, 125 and 127.
45. Martha Vicinus, 'Models for Public Life: Biographies of "Noble Women" for Girls', pp. 52–70 in *The Girl's Own: Cultural Histories of the Anglo-American Girl, 1830–1915*, ed. Claudia Nelson and Lynne Vallone (Athens, GA: University of Georgia Press, 1994).
46. Nelson, *Boys Will Be Girls*, p. 118.

47. Megan Norcia, 'Angel of the Island: L. T. Meade's New Girl as the Heir of a Nation-Making Robinson Crusoe', *The Lion and the Unicorn*, 28 (2004), 345–62 (pp. 358, 348).

48. John G. Cawelti, *Adventure, Mystery, and Romance: Formula Stories as Art and Popular Culture* (Chicago, IL: University of Chicago Press, 1976), p. 207.

49. Don Randall, *Kipling's Imperial Boy: Adolescence and Cultural Hybridity* (New York: Palgrave, 2000).

50. See J. A. Mangan, 'Noble Specimens of Manhood: schoolboy literature and the creation of a colonial chivalric code', in *Imperialism and Juvenile Literature*, ed. Jeffrey Richards (Manchester: Manchester University Press, 1989), pp. 173–94 and Christopher Parkes, '*Treasure Island* and the Romance of the British Civil Service', *Children's Literature Association Quarterly*, 31 (2006), 332–45.

51. E. Nesbit, *The Wouldbegoods* (Ware: Wordsworth, [1901] 1995), pp. 43–4, 48 and 57.

Conclusion

Several things make children's literature unique among the many branches of academic literary study. First, as is often pointed out, it is the only category of literature that is defined in terms of its intended readership. Canadian literature, for instance, does not consist of all, or only, books read by Canadians. And crime fiction, to take another example, is not defined as those novels read by criminals. But children's literature is not children's literature because it is written *by* children, nor because it is *about* children, but only because of who it was ostensibly written *for*. This is connected with a second peculiar characteristic of children's books: that the intended audience is seldom actively involved in studying it academically. If we attempt to view books through children's eyes, or try to analyse texts on their behalf, we must remain aware that this is at best a kind of ventriloquism. Perhaps, as some critics suggest, we should acknowledge that children's books never really become the cultural property of children at all: they are written by adults, to suit adult purposes, and for kinds of children that adults construct to be the perfect readers of their books. If this is the case, there is no inconsistency whatsoever in adult critics discussing children's books, on their own terms, and without the least reference to any real children.

Another important difference between children's literature and the main body of literary studies is the condescension, even disdain, with which it has sometimes been greeted. Sustained study of children's literature in universities began only in the 1960s, a product of political shifts that led to distrust of the traditional canon and perhaps to a less formalist approach to literature that laid more stress on texts in context, rather than studying books simply for the sake of their stand-alone literary accomplishment. Nevertheless, this first entry of children's literature into the academy was often met with suspicion. Teaching, studying and researching children's literature could be characterised as beneath the dignity of serious students and academics. It was regarded as being too easy or, perhaps worse, too much fun. Or the whole undertaking could be presented as regrettable since it shattered the fondly remembered 'magic' of children's books, or even the 'innocence' of childhood. In 1992, Beverly Lyon Clark taxonomised 'Thirteen Ways of Thumbing Your Nose at Children's Literature' and other critics, both before and since, have also tried to pinpoint exactly why and how children's literature had been marginalised.[1] Was it due to turf wars between departments of education and departments of literature? Was sexism at its root, because children's literature had become associated predominantly with female teachers and students? Was it due to an unshakeable perception that studying children's literature was undemanding? When I was appointed to a job in children's literature in the School of English at Newcastle University in 2005, the *Guardian* newspaper, generally supportive of educational innovation, reported 'That's not going to be very hard, is it? The writing's big and there are lots of pictures.'[2]

But such condescension is on the wane, both generally and in almost all academic establishments. This might be for a variety of reasons. An increase in the attention paid to children's literature is probably tied up with its new-found centrality in culture: the *Harry Potter* effect as it might succinctly be called. Children's books – and not only J.K. Rowling's – have become the bestsellers of the late twentieth and early twenty-first century. They have crossed over into the reading lives of adults, and into cinema, theatre, computer games and many other media. This phenomenon demands scholarly attention. Meanwhile, trends within universities have also continued to advance the study of children's literature. For one thing, undermining literary canons, in some cases as soon as they begin to form, has become almost *de rigueur*. For another, new critical work on children's literature, perhaps especially theoretical and historical, has shown that teaching and research in children's literature cannot reasonably be regarded as in any way less sophisticated than work in more established fields. Indeed, many teachers have now recognised that one of the most effective ways to introduce recondite subjects and concepts to students – eighteenth-century cultural history, say, or the idea of the postcolonial – is through children's literature. After all, children's books often seem to invite readings that focus on historical context or that expose theoretical problems. And then the sheer popularity with students of courses in children's literature has been difficult to ignore. With British students now joining their North American counterparts in paying tuition fees, and so being increasingly regarded as the paying customers of universities, academics are becoming aware that their curricula must reflect what students want as well as what they are supposed to need. The commissioning of books like this *Edinburgh Critical Guide to Children's Literature* is testament to both the increased respectability and a new perceived saleability of children's literature studies.

What all this means is that children's literature studies, having achieved a certain maturity as a discipline, now stands at a fork in the road. One path leads towards the full integration of the study of children's books into the wider study of literature in general. The other option is to protect its separateness. Both alternatives have their rewards and their hazards. The erasure of the divide between the study of adult and children's literature might be taken as an indication that an equality, long sought and long resisted, has finally been reached. It could also open up new ways of exploring children's books. If academic books on Canadian literature, or crime fiction, or poetry (to take some arbitrary examples) were to include books designed for children alongside books for adults, not even hiving them off to a separate chapter, then a new kind of analysis would have to evolve, based perhaps more on formal qualities and generic continuities than issues of readership and reception. But the risks of such an approach are obvious. Writing for children has its own distinct genres, and although fantasy novels, say, or school stories, have sometimes been written for adults, it might be argued that these specialised forms of children's literature require independent consideration. Similarly, it might be argued that the more frequent presence of illustration in children's books, or the need to write for consumers with certain reading and comprehension competencies, or certain age-related needs, boundaries and desires, demands special teaching strategies and critical machinery. One might go further, arguing that the integration of the study of children's books into the study of literature in general risks institutionalisation. We might remember that one of Beverly Lyon Clark's 'Thirteen Ways of Thumbing Your Nose at Children's Literature' was for critics to refuse to acknowledge a divide between literature for children and for adults, thus, she worried, keeping the idea of a literature especially for children out of the intellectual limelight. Perhaps what makes children's literature studies so vital is its position on the outside, its practitioners imagining themselves as a sort of guerrilla force fighting against outdated, repressive literary orthodoxies. And some critics and teachers might be anxious to retain their position outside mainstream literary studies for more pragmatic reasons. Complete integration would mean renouncing a separate infrastructure for children's literature studies – its separate sub-departments within literature or education programmes, its discrete conferences, societies, awards and publishing outlets.

Yet the loss of a discrete academic community and identity is surely not to be regretted when weighed against a higher esteem for the subject and the practical advantages of integration. Certainly, it would be ludicrous to suggest that it should become a point of principle that children's literature should never be considered as a separate entity. And it would be very regrettable if the student, teacher or critic ever lost sight of the age of the intended (and actual) readership when discussing children's books. But to investigate writing for children and adults together must benefit both. Any appreciation of postcolonial children's literature, for example, will be impoverished if it is not placed in its wider literary and cultural contexts, and this will require it to be read collectively, not even only in parallel, with works originally intended for adults. Equally, any understanding of the postcolonial will be diminished if books produced for children are not evaluated as an important part of that discourse. To ignore children's literature in thinking about cultural responses to the Enlightenment, for instance, or to Darwinism, or to the Cold War, would not only render the research incomplete, but would be missing out on some crucial and immensely revealing data.

Of course much admirable work that considers adult and children's writing together has already been done, both by those who would consider themselves specialists in children's literature and those who would not. Now that the study of children's literature has become securely established, this work can provide the foundation for a new, less circumscribed approach to children's books, with writing for adults and writing for children read together and within the same contexts. Such criticism should blur the boundaries of children's literature, not define and police them. If this is how the future of children's literature studies does develop, then a critical guide to children's books might soon become obsolete. But one of the advantages of working in an area of literary studies that is still rapidly developing is that the directions it will take are entirely unpredictable. However much academic sense it might make to see the borders of children's literature studies overrun, from both sides, perhaps its students, teachers and researchers will respond to their subject's hard-won acceptance by protecting their gains and defending their territory. Academic protectionism or free-trade: it will be fascinating to find out which approach, if either, prevails.

NOTES

1. Beverly Lyon Clark, 'Thirteen Ways of Thumbing Your Nose at Children's Literature', *The Lion and the Unicorn*, 16 (1992), 240–44.
2. Alice Wignall, 'Harry Potter studies', *Guardian Education Supplement*, February 15 2005. The article did add 'Oh, don't be facile. It's a perfectly respectable academic discipline.'

Student Resources

Abridgement

A shortened version of a text, often produced in the belief that it will make an adult book more suitable for children. Cuts may be made to reduce the length of the work, to make its style more accessible, or to exclude material that is perceived to be unsuitable. Books designed originally for children are also sometimes abridged for new generations of readers, often without any acknowledgment that cuts have been made. See also **adaptation** and **bowdlerisation**.

Adaptation

A text not simply **abridged** but largely or wholly re-written. This may be for presentation to a different audience (children rather than adults; very young children rather than older children) or for presentation in a different format (children's poem rather than folk ballad; film rather than book). See **recontextualisation** and **remediation**.

Annual

A publication appearing at the same time each year, often at the end of the year for the Christmas market. Annuals became established in the early nineteenth century, and were increasingly compilations of pre-existing weekly or monthly publications bound together in new covers.

Anthropomorphism

Attribution of human attributes or personality to non-human things – often animals, but also inanimate objects such as dolls. Stories about them, and even narrated by them, have formed a staple of children's literature since the eighteenth century.

Ballad

A poem that recounts a story, often set out in 'ballad stanzas' of four lines rhyming *abcb*, and, strictly speaking, designed to be sung.

Battledore

Originally, a **hornbook** but lacking the horn covering. From the mid-eighteenth century, the term usually refers to the hornbook's replacement, an oblong card, folded into three, on which the alphabet and other text and images were cheaply printed.

Bibliotherapy

The production and use of books representing specific social, psychological or physiological problems as therapy for readers concerned by, or suffering from, these same dilemmas or conditions.

Bowdlerisation

The editing of a text to omit any material considered offensive or unsuitable, usually used in a pejorative sense. The term is derived from Thomas Bowdler's *Family Shakespeare*, published in 1818 for use by children with their parents.

Catechism

A series of questions and answers designed originally to educate and enforce religious orthodoxy. At first an oral process, catechisms were printed for children from the sixteenth century, and by the eighteenth century were being used for secular education, particularly mathematics and geography.

Chapbook

Although strictly speaking texts sold by travelling pedlars called 'chapmen', the term is often used loosely to describe various forms of short and cheap pamphlets common from the sixteenth to the nineteenth centuries. Usually containing popular and plebeian material, they were designed for a cross-generational audience, but in the early 1800s chapbooks designed especially for children were produced in large numbers.

Chromolithography

See **Lithography**.

Copperplate engraving

An illustration technique adopted for some children's books from the mid-eighteenth to the early nineteenth centuries. Lines are cut into the smooth metal plate which is then inked. The ink is wiped from the plate so that it remains only in the grooves. When printed this can produce precise, high-quality images, and engraved text and image can be combined on a single plate.

Counter-factual history

An account of a course of events which has not, but might have, happened. Such 'virtual histories' are not uncommon in children's literature, for instance Michael Cronin's *Against the Day* (2003) about Britain under Nazi occupation or Joan Aiken's *The Wolves of Willoughby Chase* sequence (from 1962), in which the Hanoverian

Succession of 1714 did not take place. Philip Pullman presents a similar alternative reality in the **secondary world** of his *His Dark Materials* (1995–2005), in which the Protestant Reformation, and certain key inventions, have not occurred.

Crossover literature

Texts originally marketed for either children or adults but adopted, without **abridgement** or **adaptation**, by a mixed-aged readership. J.K. Rowling's *Harry Potter* novels provide a good example, but the phenomenon has existed for many years, as for instance with Rudyard Kipling's *Kim* (1901).

Dime novel

Cheaply produced **series fiction** produced in America from the 1860s for a mixed-aged readership, often containing sensationalist material and similar to the British **penny dreadful**.

Disneyfication

A usually pejorative term for the ways in which children's literature and world folklore have been adapted, and commodified, by the films, theme parks and other products of the Walt Disney Company.

Emblem

A picture with a symbolic meaning, accompanied by text that explains the symbolism and sometimes adds a moral. Religious emblem-books were produced for children from the seventeenth century.

Engraving

See **Copperplate engraving**, **Process engraving** and **Wood engraving**.

Evangelical literature

Writing that stresses the literal truth of the Christian Scriptures, the personal responsibility of all individuals for their own salvation (even children) and the need for social reform on religious principles. Evangelical children's literature was common in the later seventeenth century (see **Puritan literature**), and was revived in the early nineteenth century.

Filmsetting or photocomposition

A printing process, in use for children's books since the 1950s, that involves projecting the material to be printed onto photographic film and then making printing plates from the film.

Folktale

Stories of great antiquity, with no known author and originating in an oral tradition, and told by, or about, ordinary working people. Many **adaptations**, both direct or indirect, have been produced for children. See **Legend** and **Myth**.

Frontispiece

An illustration facing the title-page of a book, common in eighteenth- and nineteenth-century children's literature.

Gesta Romanorum

'Acts of the Romans': a compendium of legends, biographies and stories popular with children in Latin and English, and in manuscript and print forms, from the fourteenth to the eighteenth century.

Golden Age

A term sometimes applied to the period from the publication of *Alice's Adventures in Wonderland* (1865) to the 1910s or 1920s during which much innovative, successful and enduring children's literature was published in Britain. The existence of a second Golden Age in the 1950s and 1960s is sometimes posited.

Harlequinade

Picturebooks originally based on pantomime performances, allowing the reader to reproduce stage effects by lifting flaps to reveal new scenes underneath. Produced from 1770 until the early nineteenth century, these represent an early example of **remediation**.

Hornbook

The alphabet and other simple educational and devotional material printed on paper attached to a piece of wood shaped like a small paddle or bat, and often covered with a protective translucent sheet of horn. Used throughout the early modern period and evolving into the **battledore**.

Imprint

Details of a book's publisher, place of publication and date, usually printed on the title-page or elsewhere in the book's front-matter. By extension, also used for the series brand names used by publishers (for example, **Ladybird**).

Intertextuality

The incorporation or referencing of other already existing writing in a text, a common phenomenon in children's literature. This can be explicit, as when E. Nesbit's Bastable children in *The Treasure Seekers* (1899) deliberately model their own lives on the characters they have read about in nineteenth-century fiction, or more allusive, as when Will Parry in Philip Pullman's *Northern Lights* (1995) almost gives up his quest so that he can return to help his ailing mother, just as Digory had almost broken an oath for his sick mother in C.S. Lewis' *The Magician's Nephew* (1955).

Jest book

Collections of comic anecdotes, stories, jokes and verses, cheaply published for a mixed-age audience, often in the form of a **chapbook**, from the sixteenth to the early nineteenth century.

Ladybird books

A publisher's **imprint** in use from 1915 (and surviving a takeover of the original company by Penguin Books in 1999). The books adopted their distinctive standard size and use of full colour on every page in the 1940s, and were organised into a Key Words Reading Scheme from 1964.

Legend

Like the **folktale**, legends have no known author and derive from an oral tradition, but they usually concern great heroes and (less often) heroines, possibly actual historical figures, and may originally have been told by specialised story-tellers. See also **Myth**.

Letterpress

Printed text, as opposed to illustration. Also used to distinguish material printed from raised type or blocks from that printed from **lithographic** plates.

Limerick

Five-line comic verse form, with rhyme structure **aabba**, used for children's poetry since the early nineteenth century. Edward Lear used the form extensively in his nonsense verse, but the term itself was not current until the 1890s.

Lithography and Chromolithography

A process of printing in which the artist draws directly onto a stone or metal plate with a crayon that repels water. When the plate is wetted and then inked, the ink adheres only to those areas drawn in by the artist, producing bold and effective images when printed. If this is done successively with several inks a multi-coloured image can be cheaply produced ('chromolithograhy'). The process became widespread from the mid-nineteenth century.

Myth

Stories that explain natural, cosmic and spiritual phenomena, such as floods or the creation of the world, and that are notionally believed to be true. A collection – or mythology – can form the basis of a particular society, but some very similar myths are found in distant and diverse cultures.

Nonsense

Verse or prose that distorts or inverts reality, or employs made-up language, but usually remains within rigid formal structures. It has been used, for comic or satirical effect, for several centuries, but was most influentially adopted for use in children's books by Edward Lear and Lewis Carroll in the mid-nineteenth century.

Penny dreadful

Name given, usually by its critics, to a cheap pamphlet, designed for a mixed-aged audience, containing crime, supernatural or other sensational stories. Often written in parts, and popular in the mid-nineteenth century. See **dime novel**.

Picturebook

A text in which pictures and words are equally significant (so that the pictures do not merely function as illustrations of the text), and in which the interaction between them produces gratification and meaning for readers. Although they pre-date printing, picturebooks in the modern sense became popular only in the early nineteenth century.

Postcolonial literature and criticism

Work both deriving from, and written about, countries and cultures that have formerly been under the control of European colonial powers is called postcolonial. Postcolonial critics may study the many children's texts written about imperialism, Daniel Defoe's *Robinson Crusoe* (1719) or Rudyard Kipling's *Kim* (1901) for instance, as well as looking at more strictly postcolonial work such as Anita Desai's *The Peacock Garden* (1979) or Ken Kalonde's *Smiles Around Africa* (1997).

Primer

Originally a prayer book, usually in Latin, but from the Reformation, used to describe books of simple instruction, in letters, religion or secular subjects.

Problem novel

Fiction designed to represent and offer indirect advice on particular physiological, psychological and social issues, such as obesity, learning disability, divorce or racism. Usually, but not always, for older children and young adults, and common from the 1970s. See **young adult literature**.

Process engraving

A means of transferring a drawing to a printing block photographically, so that the artist's design can be engraved, then printed, precisely as drawn. Before this process was perfected in the late nineteenth century it had been customary for engravers to modify artists' designs.

Puritans

English Protestants who were convinced that the Church of England needed further reform after the Reformation. They believed in the absolute truth of the scriptures and that all carried the stain of

Original Sin, regardless of age. Puritanism, and Puritan children's literature, flourished in England in the later seventeenth century.

Realism

The accurate depiction of real life in a literary work, but also sometimes the portrayal of lower-class life.

Recontextualisation

The **adaptation** of a written text in a new medium, for instance as television programme, film, stage-play or computer game, rather than as another written text. See also **remediation**.

Religious Tract Society (RTS)

Founded in 1799 to produce **Evangelical literature**, and by the 1810s specifically targeting children. During the nineteenth century, its publications became less overtly religious, including *The Boy's Own Paper* and *Girl's Own Paper* from 1879 and 1880 respectively.

Remediation

The representation of one medium in another, as when a website imitates a newspaper. In children's literature, this process often works in reverse, as when a novel attempts to imitate a website or animated film. See also **harlequinade**.

Robinsonnade

A literary descendent of Daniel Defoe's *Robinson Crusoe* (1719) in which the protagonists struggle to survive in an isolated and hostile environment and, in doing so, learn more about themselves.

Romances

Adventure narratives, most often in verse, circulating orally and in written form in the Middle Ages, for instance *Guy of Warwick*.

Always popular with children, they were printed as **abridgements** especially for them, often as **chapbooks**, from the late eighteenth century.

Second golden age

See **Golden Age**.

Secondary world

A term, first used by J. R. R. Tolkien, for the complete alternative realities used in much fantasy fiction. Although travel between these alternative universes and our own may be possible in some fantasy literature, Tolkien held that, if full credibility is to be retained, secondary worlds ought to be an alternative not an addition to our primary universe.

Series fiction

Novels designed from their inception to be part of a potentially infinite series, united by the same characters, narrative patterns or settings, thus not, at least strictly speaking, a limited set, such as J. K. Rowling's *Harry Potter* novels. Derived from the **dime novel** and **penny dreadful**, series fiction has been increasingly common since the early twentieth century.

Society for Promotion of Christian Knowledge (SPCK)

Founded in 1698 to distribute religious publications, it published many books for children in the eighteenth and nineteenth centuries, including fiction and natural history.

Time-slip fantasy

A text in which protagonists find themselves transported to a different time, either accidentally, through their own agency or by the intervention of others, or in which a character from the past or future appears in the main characters' present. In some books, more than one time period is present simultaneously, and characters can wander between them. A frequently used device in children's literature since the early twentieth century.

Urchin verse

Children's poetry that aims to capture the ordinary voice and attitudes of real, usually urban, children, and popular especially in Britain since the 1970s.

Vignette

A small, separate illustration, either pictorial or purely ornamental, used to decorate a book, often found at the start or end of a section.

Wood engraving

A finer-lined and more subtly shaded woodcut, made on the more durable end-grain of wood, not the planed plank, and by tools used for copperplate engraving. The technique was pioneered and perfected by Thomas Bewick in the late eighteenth century, and remained the primary form of children's book illustration for a century.

Woodcut

A picture produced by cutting away parts of a wooden block around the lines to be inked and printed. These blocks could be set along with type to print illustration and letterpress on the same page. Because it was simple and cheap, most pre-nineteenth century children's books were illustrated in this way.

Young adult literature

Texts, mostly fiction, designed to be suitable for teenagers. In print from the 1950s, most 'YA' literature has sought to dramatise real-life events and concerns, especially sex, selfhood, and the quest for autonomy. See problem novel.

GUIDE TO FURTHER READING

This section is intended as a concise guide to the books, websites and journals (but not individual articles) currently available that will help with general aspects of children's literature studies. It should be used in conjunction with the references to more specifically relevant critical material that are to be found in the notes to the main chapters of this book.

Children's literature journals

Canadian Children's Literature/Littérature canadienne pour la jeunesse (University of Winnipeg)
Children's Literature (Modern Language Association Division on Children's Literature and Children's Literature Association, Johns Hopkins University Press)
The Children's Literature Association Quarterly (Children's Literature Association, Johns Hopkins University Press)
Children's Literature in Education (Springer)
Horn Book Magazine (The Horn Book Inc.)
International Research in Children's Literature (Edinburgh University Press)
The Journal of Children's Literature Studies (Pied Piper Publishing)
The Lion and the Unicorn (Johns Hopkins University Press)
The Looking Glass: an Online Children's Literature Journal (www.the-looking-glass.net)
New Review of Children's Literature and Librarianship (Taylor and Francis)

Theory of children's literature

Beckett, Sandra L. (ed.), *Reflections of Change: Children's Literature Since 1945* (Westport, CT: Greenwood, 1997).
Dusinberre, Juliet, *Alice to the Lighthouse: Children's Books and Radical Experiments in Art* (London: Macmillan, 1987).
Hollindale, Peter, *Ideology and the Children's Book* (Stroud: Thimble Press, 1988).

Hollindale, Peter, *Signs of Childness in Children's Books* (Stroud: Thimble Press, 1997).

Hourihan, Margery, *Deconstructing the Hero: Literary Theory and Children's Literature* (London: Routledge, 1997).

Hunt, Peter, *Criticism, Theory and Children's Literature* (Oxford: Blackwell, 1991).

Lesnik-Oberstein, Karín, *Children's Literature: Criticism and the Fictional Child* (Oxford: Clarendon Press, 1994).

Lesnik-Oberstein, Karín, *Children's Literature: New Approaches* (Basingstoke: Palgrave, 2004).

Lurie, Alison, *Not in Front of the Grown-Ups: The Subversive Power of Children's Literature* (London: Bloomsbury, 1990).

McGillis, Rod, *The Nimble Reader: Literary Theory and Children's Literature* (New York: Twayne, 1996).

Nikolajeva, Maria, *Children's Literature Comes of Age: Towards a New Aesthetic* (New York: Garland, 1996).

Nodelman, Perry, *Words About Pictures: The Narrative Art of Picture Books* (Athens, GA: University of Georgia Press, 1988).

Rose, Jacqueline, *The Case Against Peter Pan, or the Impossibility of Children's Literature* (London: Macmillan, 1984).

Stephens, John, *Language and Ideology in Children's Fiction* (London: Longman, 1992).

Early history of children's literature (pre-1860)

Alderson, Brian and Felix De Marez Oyens, *Be Merry and Wise: The Origins of Children's Book Publishing in England, 1650–1850* (New Castle, DE: Oak Knoll Press, 2006).

Darton, F. J. Harvey, *Children's Books in England*, 3rd edn, revised by Brian Alderson (Cambridge: Cambridge University Press, 1982).

Hilton, Mary, Morag Styles and Victor Watson (eds), *Opening the Nursery Door: Reading, Writing and Childhood, 1600–1900* (London: Routledge, 1997).

Immel, Andrea and Michael Witmore (eds), *Childhood and Children's Books in Early Modern Europe, 1550–1800* (New York: Routledge, 2006).

Jackson, Mary J., *Engines of Instruction, Mischief and Magic: Children's Literature in England from its Beginnings to 1839* (Lincoln, NB: University of Nebraska Press, 1989).

McGavran, James (ed.), *Romanticism and Children's Literature in the Nineteenth Century* (Athens, GA: University of Georgia Press, 1991).

Marks, Sylvia Kasey, *Writing for the Rising Generation: British Fiction for Young People, 1672–1839* (Victoria, BC: University of Victoria, 2003).

O'Malley, Andrew, *The Making of the Modern Child: Children's Literature and Childhood in the Late Eighteenth Century* (New York: Routledge, 2003).

Pickering, Samuel F., *John Locke and Children's Books in Eighteenth-Century England* (Knoxville, TN: The University of Tennessee Press, 1981).

Pickering, Samuel F., *Moral Instruction and Fiction for Children, 1749–1820* (Athens, GA: University of Georgia Press, 1993).

Richardson, Alan, *Literature, Education, and Romanticism: Reading as Social Practice, 1780–1832* (Cambridge: Cambridge University Press, 1994).

Vallone, Lynne, *Disciplines of Virtue: Girls' Culture in the Eighteenth and Nineteenth Centuries* (New Haven, CT: Yale University Press, 1995).

Modern and contemporary children's literature (post-1860)

Carpenter, Humphrey, *Secret Gardens: A Study of the Golden Age of Children's Literature* (London: Unwin, 1985).

Clark, Beverley Lyon, *Kiddie Lit: The Cultural Construction of Children's Literature in America* (Baltimore, MD: Johns Hopkins University Press, 2003).

Edwards, Owen Dudley, *British Children's Fiction in the Second World War* (Edinburgh: Edinburgh University Press, 2007).

Foster, Shirley and Judy Simons, *What Katy Read: Feminist Re-Readings of 'Classic' Stories for Girls* (Iowa City, IA: University of Iowa Press, 1995).

Hunt, Peter, and Millicent Lenz, *Alternative Worlds in Fantasy Fiction* (London: Continuum, 2001).

Knoepflmacher, U. C., *Ventures into Childhood: Victorians, Fairy Tales and Femininity* (Chicago, IL: University of Chicago Press, 1998).

Natov, Roni, *The Poetics of Childhood* (New York: Routledge, 2003).

Nelson, Claudia, *Boys Will Be Girls: The Feminine Ethic and British Children's Fiction, 1857–1917* (New Brunswick, NJ: Rutgers University Press, 1991).

Reynolds, Kimberley, *Radical Children's Literature: Future Visions and Aesthetic Transformations in Juvenile Fiction* (Basingstoke: Palgrave, 2007).

Reynolds, Kimberley (ed.), *Modern Children's Literature: An Introduction* (Basingstoke: Palgrave Macmillan, 2005).

Miscellanies and general histories

Avery, Gillian and Julia Briggs (eds), *Children and their Books: A Celebration of the Work of Iona and Peter Opie* (Oxford: Clarendon, 1989).

Clark, Beverley Lyon and Margaret Higgonet (eds), *Girls, Boys, Books, Toys: Gender in Children's Literature and Culture* (Baltimore, MD: Johns Hopkins University Press, 1999).

Egoff, Sheila, Gordon Stubbs, Ralph Ashley and Wendy Sutton (eds), *Only Connect: Readings on Children's Literature*, rev. edn (New York: Oxford University Press, 1996).

Hunt, Peter, *An Introduction to Children's Literature* (Oxford: Oxford University Press, 1994).

Styles, Morag, *From the Garden to the Street: Three Hundred Years of Poetry for Children* (London: Cassell, 1998).

Thacker, Deborah Cogan and Jean Webb, *Introducing Children's Literature: From Romanticism to Postmodernism* (London: Routledge, 2002).

Reference and anthologies

Carpenter, Humphrey and Mari Prichard, *The Oxford Companion to Children's Literature* (Oxford: Oxford University Press, 1984).

Demers, Patricia (ed.), *From Instruction to Delight: An Anthology of Children's Literature to 1815*, 2nd edn (Don Mills, Ontario: Oxford University Press Canada, 2004).

Hunt, Peter (ed.), *International Companion Encyclopedia of Children's Literature* 2nd edn, 2 vols (London: Routledge, 2004).

Hunt, Peter, *Children's Literature* (Oxford: Blackwell Guides to Literature, 2001).

Kline, Daniel, *Medieval Literature for Children* (New York: Routledge, 2003).

Watson, Victor (ed.), *The Cambridge Guide to Children's Books in English* (Cambridge: Cambridge University Press, 2001).

Zipes, Jack (ed.), *The Oxford Encyclopedia of Children's Literature*, 4 vols (New York: Oxford University Press, 2006).

Zipes, Jack, Lissa Paul, Lynne Vallone, Peter Hunt and Gillian Avery (eds), *The Norton Anthology of Children's Literature: The Traditions in English* (New York: Norton, 2005).

Websites

Perry Nodelman's bibliography of children's literature: http://www.uwinnipeg.ca/~nodelman/resources/allbib.htm

Hockliffe Project (British children's books 1700–1840): http://www.cts.dmu.ac.uk/hockliffe

Jane Johnson's manuscript nursery library: http://www.dlib.indiana.edu/collections/janejohnson

Baldwin Collection of Children's Books: http://palmm.fcla.edu/juv/juvAuthorList.html

International Children's Digital Library: http://www.icdlbooks.org/

Seven Stories: the Centre for Children's Books: http://www.sevenstories.org.uk

Index